D0948906

Nationalism &
Self Determination
in the
Horn of Africa

edited by I. M. Lewis

Ithaca Press London 1983

The Publishers gratefully acknowledge the
support of The Anti-Slavery Society in the
production of this book.

ISBN 0 903729 93 8

First published in 1983 by
Ithaca Press, 13 Southwark Street, London SE1

Typeset by Carlton Photosetters, Westcliff-on-Sea, Essex
Printed and bound in Great Britain by
Biddles Ltd, Guildford and King's Lynn

CONTENTS

CONTRIBUTORS

Hussein M. Adam, Chairman of Social Sciences, Lafoole College of Education, Somali National University. Chairman of Editorial Board of *Haglan*, journal of Somali Revolutionary Socialist Party. Has worked extensively on the political and other problems connected with the adoption of a script for the Somali language. Author (with Charles Geshekter) of *The Revolutionary Development of the Somali language*, 1980; editor of *Somalia and the World*, Mogadishu, 1980.

Paul Baxter, Senior Lecturer in Social Anthropology, University of Manchester. Has carried out extensive field research in northern Kenya and Southern Ethiopia among the Oromo peoples. He has also carried out field research in Uganda and in Ghana, and lectured in the University of Ghana for five years.

Patrick Gilkes, Africa Service, BBC, London. Taught at the University of Addis Ababa for several years. Author of *The Dying Lion* (1975) – s study of the events leading to the Ethiopian Revolution, and other works on Ethiopian politics and history.

Sally Healy. Carried out research on self-determination in the Horn of Africa in the Department of International Relations, London School of Economics and Political Science, London University. Has worked for the voluntary relief organization, Action Aid, where she was especially concerned with the refugee problem in the Horn of Africa.

I. M. Lewis, Professor of Social Anthropology, London School of Economics and Political Science, London University; Director of the International African Institute. Has carried out extensive field research in Somalia before and after independence. Author of *A Pastoral Democracy: Pastoralism and Politics among the Northern Somali of the Horn of Africa* (new edition 1982), *A Modern History of Somalia* (1980), *Social Anthropology in Perspective* (1976); edited works include *Islam in Tropical Africa* (new edition 1980).

James Mayall, Senior Lecturer in International Relations, London School of Economics and Political Science, author of *Africa: The Cold War and After* (1971) and many articles on the Organization of African Unity and other aspects of African international politics.

David Pool is Lecturer in Government at Manchester University where he teaches Middle Eastern politics. He taught at the University of Khartoum from 1972 to 1977 and has written on Sudanese, Iraqi, Libyan and Eritrean politics. He is currently completing a study of the Eritrean liberation movement.

Michael Reisman is Professor of Law at the Yale Law School and an editor of the *American Journal of International Law* as well as the *Journal of Conflict Resolution*. His most recent books are *International Law in Contemporary Perspective* (1981) and *International Law Essays* (1981), both with Myres S. McDougal.

A. Triulzi is Associate Professor of Subsaharian African History at the Istituto Universitario Orientale of Naples, Italy. He conducted research in Ethiopia from 1971 to 1973 and co-edited *Oral Sources, Anthropology and History* (Bologna, 1978) and *Storia dell'Africa a sud del Sahara* (Florence, 1979). He is author of *Salt, Gold and Legitimacy – Prelude to the history of Bela Shangul, Wallaga, Ethiopia (1800–1898)*, (1981) and has written numerous articles on Western Ethiopia.

Joseph Tubiana, Director CNRS Laboratoire Peiresc, (East African Research Centre), Valbonne, France is a specialist in the Semitic Languages of Ethiopia, which he taught at the Ecole Nationale des Langues Orientales Vivantes (Paris), and on which he has published extensively. He has carried out prolonged research in Ethiopia, Chad and the Sudan. His recent books include *Modern Ethiopia from the accession of Menilek II to the Present* (1980) which he edited.

Hakan Wiberg is Professor of Sociology at Lund University, Sweden. He was previously Director and Associate Professor at the Department of Peace and Conflict Research, Lund. He is the author of books on conflict theory and peace research, people's images of the future, the Horn of Africa, and armament and security issues.

PREFACE

In keeping with its subject-matter, the putting together of this book has engendered a certain amount of conflict. A full account of this cannot be given here. But the reader is entitled to know the general background which I set down for the record. In the spring of 1979 I was approached by the Chairman of the Anti-Slavery Society and invited to consider convening a small inter-disciplinary workshop on self-determination in the Horn of Africa. Having secured a Ford Foundation grant for research on self-determination as an issue of general concern in the contemporary world (and without reference to particular areas), the Society was reviewing regions where the problem was acute and raised complex issues which might benefit from inter-disciplinary scrutiny. The Horn of Africa was clearly one such region where there were sharply conflicting conceptions of self-determination and national identity. Hence the proposed workshop.

In accepting this task, as a Somali specialist I was, naturally, particularly aware of the necessity of securing effective participation by scholars sympathetic to the Ethiopian 'centralist' position (or positions) as well as by those who were experts on Eritrean and other 'separatist' or 'peripheral' nationalism. From the start, therefore, these considerations and that of obtaining specialists spanning a range of disciplines – including language, social anthropology, history and international relations and law – informed the selection of prospective participants. Bearing these issues in mind, I proposed that the workshop be held at the Laboratoire Peiresc, the East African Research Centre in France specializing in Ethiopian Studies under the direction of the distinguished Ethiopianist and Amharic specialist, Joseph Tubiana. We had now arrived at a preliminary list of participants which included five Ethiopianists (one from Ethiopia and one from eastern Europe), an Eritrean (who, in fact, never materialized) and a Somali political scientist, an Italian historian of Ethiopia, a geographer interested in Oromo ('Galla') history, an Africanist specializing in Pan-Africanism, and myself. Following Joseph Tubiana's kind agreement that the workshop should be held under his roof, preliminary invitations were sent out in late November and early December. These emphasized the academic and non-polemical objectives of the workshop.

The response was dramatic. The Ethiopian Ambassador in London (who had been sent a copy of the letter inviting political scientists from the

University of Addis Ababa) urgently requested meetings with the Chairman of the Anti-Slavery Society and myself. In the course of these, we did our best to explain that the project was a serious academic enterprise, not a publicity exercise, and that we were particularly anxious to give adequate scope to the 'centralist' Ethiopian position. The Ambassador expressed surprise when we drew his attention to the list of Ethiopianists sympathetic to the centralist position (including one Ethiopian scholar) on our list. At the risk of tipping the delicate balance in favour of this Ethiopian centralist view, we invited the Ambassador, in consultation with his government, to propose the names of up to four 'acceptable' scholars. I had already had extensive discussion with Ethiopianist colleagues of 'centralist' sympathies, and it was also now proposed that the workshop should, formally, be jointly organized.

Unfortunately, these negotiations which we hoped would allay the Ethiopian Ambassador's disquiet proved unavailing. A few days later a strongly worded 'follow-up' letter was addressed by the Ambassador to the Anti-Slavery Society Chairman (Appendix I). Making no reference to our offer of increased 'centralist' participation and apparently misunderstanding the unspecific nature of the Ford grant to the Anti-Slavery Society, this letter denounced the workshop as a reactionary American and Somali expansionist exercise, designed not to further scholarly understanding but to discredit the Ethiopian Revolution. The Ambassador's letter concluded with the somewhat menacing announcement that his 'government cannot remain indifferent in the face of imperialist machinations and gross abuse and contempt of scholastic practices.' In his Chairman's absence abroad, the Anti-Slavery Society secretary, Colonel Patrick Montgomery, who had been present at the meeting with the Ambassador, replied denying these allegations and stressed the lengths to which we had gone to try to secure effective participation by Ethiopian academics associated with the present Ethiopian government (Appendix II).

While these exchanges were taking place in London, Ethiopian ambassadors in other parts of Europe were actively engaged in attempting to discourage scholars and students from attending the workshop. Official protests were made to the French government as well as direct representations to the Laboratoire Peiresc, which is government-financed through the Centre National de Recherche Scientifique. In these discouraging circumstances, it became necessary to find a new site, outside France, for the workshop. The meeting was consequently re-routed to Oxford, where it was held without incident from 31 March to 2 April 1980 at St Edmund Hall. In the event, despite continued efforts to stop the meeting taking place and to discredit it, it was attended by a wider range of participants than had originally been envisaged. These included, amongst others, Hakan Wiberg, Ernest Gellner, John Markakis and Kenneth Kirkwood (whose oral contributions are reflected in the introductory chapter) as well as a lively group of students – many from the Horn of Africa ('centralist' and 'non-centralist'). It is perhaps in some ways a reflection of the vigour and comprehensiveness with which Patrick Gilkes presented his view of the Ethiopian government's policies on the nationalities question that it remained, after our meeting, to find parallel contributions on Eritrean and Oromo nationalism to include in this volume. I am therefore particularly grateful to David Pool and Paul Baxter for agreeing to provide papers on these themes at short notice.

 A warm tribute must be paid to Colonel Patrick Montgomery, Secretary of the Anti-Slavery Society, for his staunch support at all times. Also, in trying to organize this difficult meeting and in editing the papers resulting from it, I owe a great deal to Sally Healy, whose good sense and confidence reduced our manifold problems and crises to manageable proportions. Finally, as always, I am especially grateful to the secretaries of the anthropology department, LSE, particularly to Joan Wells and Pat Blair through whose speeding typewriters at one time or another most of this text has passed. The resulting book had developed considerably from its original conception. Whatever its other shortcomings, I hope that it still preserves the open-minded spirit in which it was begun and which pervaded our discussions at Oxford.

I. M. Lewis
London, August 1982

INTRODUCTION

I. M. Lewis

The right to self-determination for 'all peoples' is a basic principle of contemporary international relations and law. The fact that the doctrine enjoys this unique and universal status and that it continues to possess such evocative and provocative force is, of course, connected with its inherent ambiguity. The doctrine leaves basic questions unresolved. What precisely does 'self-determination' mean; what is 'a people' (such that they should qualify for this dispensation); or, since it is usually framed in terms of 'national self-determination', what is a 'nation'? This book examines these issues, and their significance for theories of nationalism, in the context of competing claims for self-determination in the Horn of Africa and from the perspectives of a variety of disciplines, ranging from linguistics to international law and politics. In addition to its current topicality, north-east Africa is especially appropriate for this exercise because it contains both *states* and *autonomist movements* which base their claims to self-determination on mutually contradictory foundations.

The Historical and cultural setting

The Horn of Africa is one of those regions of the world where the present never seems to disentangle itself completely from the past. Through its ancient Judao–Christian[1] and Islamic legacies[2], this region has for centuries provided a unique bridge between sub-saharan Africa and the 'Great Traditions' of the Middle East and Europe. The two main elements in its richly varied ethnic heritage are the numerically dominant, Cushitic-speaking peoples, traditionally scattered as pastoralists on the foothills and lowlands, and the politically dominant, Semitic-speaking peoples of the highlands who derive from a fusion of Cushitic and South Arabian immigrant stock which is generally traced to the first millenium BC. The Semitic-speaking Tigreans and Amharas who have dominated Ethiopia's political history since its foundation at Axum and whose rulers adopted Christianity in the 4th century comprise a loose tripartite hierarchy of military aristocrats, clergy and lay peasantry. The last, whose surplus production sustained their masters, live in loosely aggregated parishes, cultivating cereals (including the indigenous *teff*) with an ox-drawn plough. They also rear cattle. The Tigreans (numbering two million) occupy the northern highlands of Tigre and Eritrea, sharing part of the plains with Cushitic-speaking and mainly Muslim Beja, Saho and Afar. The rights, conferred or confirmed by the monarchy, enjoyed by the clergy and provincial and national aristocracy to extract tribute and labour from this Semitic-speaking highland peasantry were balanced by the latter's, in principle, inalienable right to work the land it traditionally occupied.[3] Such title to usufruct was protected by and shrouded in the idiom of kinship which bridged the gap between commoner and aristocrat in a hierarchical system where there was considerable scope for social mobility.

As the Christian-ruled state has expanded over the centuries, its capital has moved further and further south away from Tigre into the central highlands occupied by the Amharas (five million) who have monopolized power for the last five hundred years. The hierarchical Amhara conquest state, whose kings traced descent from the legendary son of Solomon and Sheba, contrasts sharply with the egalitatian institutions of the nomadic and semi-nomadic Cushitic pastoralists. Traditionally leadership among the Oromo (or 'Galla') and their many divisions (in total population some ten million) was widely decentralized and changed hands every eight years as a new generation assumed control (see Baxter, below, pp 132). The Muslim Somalis (3–4 million) were organized in a segmentary system of lineages and led by assemblies of elders rather than formally appointed 'chiefs' (see Lewis, below, pp 71).

Superimposed upon the earlier Judaic tradition (which survives among the Falasha or 'Black Jews', an exotic ethnic minority), the distinction between the Christianity of the Amhara core-culture and Islam, reinforces but also partly transcends the ethnic divisions between Semite and Cushite. In the middle ages, the Christian kingdom then surrounded by a ring of hostile Muslim and partly Cushitic states, almost collapsed under the onslaught of the Islamic conqueror, Ahmad Gran 'the left-handed' (1506–1543), to whose shortlived victories Somali soldiery are recorded as contributing significantly. On Gran's defeat in 1542, the embattled Abyssinians found themselves confronting a new threat – shared with the Muslim adversaries – in the form of the massive influx of Oromo pastoralists pouring northwards in seemingly endless and irresistible numbers from their earlier grazing grounds in the south. Over a period of several centuries, sustained invasion by what the Christian Amharas saw as barbarian hordes established the Oromo in their present distribution as the demographic backbone of Ethiopia, stretching from Bale and Sidamo in the south, where they mingle with Somali pastoralists and tend to adopt Islam, to as far north as Wollo province, north of Addis Ababa. Many of those who settled in the well-watered highlands turned to cultivation in the style of the local Amhara, often also adopting Christianity and the Amharic language. This process of Amharaization was facilitated by the open-textured bilateral Amhara kinship system which places almost equal emphasis on maternal and paternal ties. In succeeding centuries Amharaized Oromo and other assimilated elements contributed to the re-establishment of Amhara ascendancy and the expansion of the frontiers of the empire to the south and east. Under the forceful rule of Emperor Menelik (1889–1911), this process of Amhara conquest and expansion reached its zenith.

The Imperial partition

It was no accident that this coincided with the period of serious European intervention in the Horn which had a reactive 'demonstration effect' and also provided Ethiopia with new military resources and other technical equipment. In the closing decades of the nineteenth century, Britain and France were the two rival 'super-powers' vying with each other for control of the Nile. Their 'Cubans' were respectively the Italian and Russians[4] each seeking to secure 'protectorate' status in Ethiopia. Like the French, they thus poured arms (and some military advisers) into Ethiopia, each believing that it would acquire a corresponding measure of local leverage. This influx of military equipment was adroitly employed by Menelik to extend Ethiopian conquest on an unprecedented scale at the expense, first of the ancient Islamic city state of Harar (1887) and then of the surrounding Somali and southern Oromo peoples. The Italians, thrusting inland from the colony they were building up in Eritrea, received a rude shock when their forces were defeated at the epic battle of Adowa in 1896. It was now evident to these European imperialists that there was a 'local super-power' with which they would have to negotiate if they wished to pursue their interests in the area. Russia effectively withdrew from the game (to resume it again in the 1970s) leaving the other powers to treat with Menelik. In a series of treaties, Britain, France and Italy all secured trading rights and Menelik's recognition for their various spheres of interest on the coastal periphery in return for legitimating his new conquests. Thus Eritrea and three parts of the Somali nation remained in European hands, while a fourth part (the Ogaden), Harar, and the southern Oromo areas were assigned to the Ethiopian sphere. Bearing the proud motto 'Conquering lion of Judah' and the same name as the original founder of the legendary Solomonic dynasty, Menelik was as emphatic as his European counterparts in emphasizing his sacred civilizing mission to impart the benefits of Christian rule to his heathen subjects. What actually happened in practice has an equally familiar ring. In contrast to the pattern in the northern and central highlands where, as we have seen, peasant landrights were protected by kinship and shared ethnicity, the recently conquered peoples of the south lost most of their traditional land to the new Amhara rulers, being frequently reduced to the status of tenants on their own land (see below pp 115-116, 134-135).

As a Black Christian state which had not only retained its independence during the European scramble for Africa but had also astutely profited from it, Ethiopia clearly occupied a unique position. This formidable legacy was enhanced rather than diminished when Mussolini's armies ruthlessly quelled the resistance of the local Ethiopian 'patriots' and established the short lived Italian East African Empire (1935-1940). Subsequent events are well-known.

De-colonization

After the Italian defeat, Haile Selassie was restored as Emperor of Ethiopia by the Allied Powers and, after much dispute first among the 'Big Four' (Britain, France, Russia and the US) and then at the United Nations, Eritrea was in 1952 federated to Ethiopia as a locally autonomous state (and in 1962 fully incorporated (see below, p 183). As Michael Reisman recounts below (p 153), acknowledging past betrayals and mistreatment, Britain's Foreign Secretary, Ernest Bevin, originally proposed the re-unification of the Somalilands (including the Ogaden) in a UN trust territory. This proposal did not gain international assent, and the Ogaden was relinquished to Ethiopia, and Somalia made a UN trusteeship under Italian administration for a ten-year-period of preparation for self-government (1950-1960).

This represented a signal victory for centralist Amhara nationalism – or at least for the Shoan élite led by Haile Selassie. Not only had the monarchy been restored in all its glory (with modifications and modernizations), but Ethiopia had also been generously compensated for the pusillanimous fashion in which, prior to the Second World War, Britain, France and other countries had connived at the Fascist conquest. By being given *both* Eritrea and the Ogaden, Ethiopia, it might be argued, had been over-compensated – as usual at the expense of the peripheral peoples. The subsequent career, remarkable by any standards, of Haile Selassie, Ethiopia's last and most famous emperor, Africa's leading statesman, inevitably further consolidated and magnified this brilliant legacy. However discriminatory and harsh the Amhara hegemony might be in its treatment of subject populations inside the country, to the outside world and especially the under-privileged of the third world, Ethiopia offered a resplendent symbol of Black Power.

The clearest evidence of this is the Ras Tafari movement[5] which has such a wide following today in Carribean communities within and outside the West Indies. This messianic cult developed in the early 1930s from the evangelical teaching of the Jamaican Black Power pioneer, Marcus Garvey

(1881–1940) who founded the United Negro Improvement Association in 1918, advocating the mass migration of American Negroes to Africa as a return to the biblical Ethiopian homeland. This rapidly spreading movement now sometimes regarded as a syncretic religion, takes its name from 'Ras Tafari', the title which Haile Selassie held as governor of Harar (where his father was installed by Menelik as the first Amhara governor after the conquest) before his coronation as emperor. For Rastafarians, Haile Selassie is the Black Messiah, and Ethiopia heaven on earth. The old emperor's deposition in September 1974 and death in captivity a few months later have done nothing to weaken the appeal of this cult which, with the music of such famous pop stars as Bob Marley, is today an extremely potent vehicle for Black identity, especially for the younger generation in the Caribbean and Black immigrant committees in Britain and elsewhere.

The Ethiopian Revolution

Although various assessments have been offered, we can hardly yet expect to find a definitive analysis of the Ethiopian Revolution of 1974.[6] Nevertheless, a few salient points need to be made here about the revolution which, at least in some African circles, regularized Ethiopia's position by transforming an anachronistic 'traditional' African monarchy into a 'modern' republic. Conflict between the centre (or centres) and the periphery (or peripheries) is deeply engrained in Ethiopia's long history. But the sudden vast southwards expansion under Emperor Menelik at the end of the 19th century exacerbated the cleavage between the (largely Semitic) north and the (largely Cushitic) south, creating conditions which encouraged profound social and political transformations. Further fundamental changes in the structure of the empire resulted from the impact on internal forces of western capitalism. Haile Selassie vigorously pursued a policy of modernization, with small-scale industrialization, encouraging western education to create a powerful new Amhara (or Amharaized) bureaucracy whose leaders were his personal proteges and could be depended on as he sought to entrench power at the centre.[6] Relying on personal patronage and the traditional formula of divide and rule, the emperor encouraged land tenure and land tax reforms, which would undermine the traditional power of the northern aristocrats. He thus depended increasingly on the new 'bureaucratic–military bourgeoisie' (Markakis) (predominantly recruited from his own province of Shoa) to which, lacking local roots and allegiance, the Amhara and Amharaized settlers in the south also looked for support. This process of bureaucratic centralization associated with a core administrative culture which Hinsley[8] and Gellner[9] see as intrinsic to modern nationalism, thus alienated the traditional provincial northern aristocrats whose peasantry were also sensitive to 'reforms' which appeared to jeopardize their traditionsal kinship-sanctioned land right. At the same time, the expansion in the 1960s of capitalist commercial agriculture in the south and on the periphery, directly threatened the already precarious position of the disenfranchized indigenous subject population. In the towns, foreign capital investment (and usually ownership) in manufacturing industries created a poorly paid proletariat, mainly of rural origin. Trade union activity was only permitted after 1962 and was closely controlled by the government. Increasingly capital-intensive methods of production were accompanied by growing public and private sector unemployment.

By the early 1970s, these and other economic pressures were also affecting white-collar public employees (junior civil servants, teachers etc) and self-employed traders who were still largely Muslim and subject to discriminatory treatment by the Christian establishment – which despised petty commerce. Although a parliament had existed since 1931 and universal suffrage since 1957, Haile Selassie's 'palace government' (as Clapham calls it) did not permit political parties or organized political activity of any kind. The clandestine radical movement which was to provide the revolutionary spark to ignite this promising tinder developed among the student body at home and overseas whose members were increasingly of petty bourgeois affiliation. Junior officer ranks in the military were held for the most part by people of this social class and from a similar range of ethnic backgrounds.

This petty bourgeois class which played such a prominent role in Eritrean nationalism from its inception in the 1950s and which elsewhere in Africa had by the late 1960s assumed prominence, in Ethiopia increasingly found its ambitions blocked by the earlier, higher status bourgeois–military elite which formed the cornerstone of Haile Selassie's 'ancien regime'. The regime's inhuman mismanagement of the appalling Wollo famine of 1972 followed by the economic crisis caused by inflation and widespread unemployment in 1973/74 produced a general paralysis, by no means restricted only to major towns, causing the anachronistic edifice to begin to crumble as power ebbed slowly away from the aged emperor's grasp. A series of strikes in January and February 1974 involving some military units, school-teachers and taxi drivers (after a 50% petrol price rise) led Haile Selassie to grant wage increases and other demands, including a purge of the top-ranking military hierarchy. A quickly changing series of governments, the last bastions of Haile Selassie's old guard, desperately sought to find compromises for the increasingly insistant demands for general reform presented by the Council (or Dergue) which was gradually emerging amongst the armed forces to articulate their requests and those of their civilian allies. For years radical university teachers and students had been appealing to their friends in the armed forces (often former classmates) to support their progressive aims instead of allowing themselves to be used to repress all opposition to Haile Selassie's rule. This protracted campaign had at last borne fruit and the military hierarchy was collapsing as low ranking officers and non-commissioned ranks began to assume control in the numerous branches of the byzantine military machine created by Haile Selassie with American support. The mass of ordinary soldiers were of peasant origin, and included many southern Oromo who, in the short run at least, would regain control of their traditional lands through the application of the principle of 'land to the tiller'. With the nationalist slogan 'Ethiopia First' (*Ethiopia tikdem* – soon a popular motto on T-shirts), the Dergue, which consisted of elected unit representatives of all ranks, gradually but relentlessly eroded Haile Selassie's power base, arresting most of the prominent members of the old order until virtually only the emperor remained. Finally, after a carefully orchestrated campaign to discredit his integrity and expose him as a corrupt exploiter of his impoverished subjects, on 12 September Haile Selassie was himself taken captive and the military revolution officially proclaimed as tanks garlanded with bouquets of flowers patrolled the streets of Addis Ababa. Exchanging the traditional Solomonic myth of political legitimacy for that of revolutionary socialism, an extremely bloody power struggle then ensued within the Dergue. It was not long before the present head of state, Colonel Mengıstu (a former major in the 3rd Division stationed in the Ogaden), emerged as unquestioned leader. His political advisers included members of MEISON, one of the two fratricidally opposed radical political groups (see below pp 195–6) which briefly flourished in the early days of the revolution.

In the process of this 'creeping revolution' (as it was known in Ethiopia) which unfolded like a slow motion film it was easy to see the remarkable coincidence of interests and solidarity amongst urban workers, southern peasantry, soldiers and petty bourgoisie which, guided and inspired by the radical intelligentsia, succeeded in finally toppling Haile Selassie's effete regime when it was already weakened by the alienation of the northern provincial aristocrats. Whether as Ayele and Markakis contend (1978, p. 73) this concurrence of interests was not fortuitous, the alliance did not long survive the transformation it had brought about from imperial rule to soldiers' socialism. In this respect despite the obvious parallels between imperial Ethiopia and Tsarist Russia and their respective revolutions, there was a significant difference which, since replacing the Americans as super-power patron, the Russians have been endeavouring (so far without much success) to remedy by encouraging the establishment of a civilian regime.

Analogies with both the Russian and Hapsburg empires suggest the main lines of conflict which have confronted Ethiopia's new military rulers as the alliance of class and ethnic interest which brought them to power acrimoniously fell apart. The ensuing explosion of regional and national autonomist movements has been strongly influenced by the two contrasting pre-existing prototypes: multi-national (pluralist) Eritrea and mono-cultural Somali nationalism enshrined in the Somali Republic. In the fierce struggle between these movements and revolutionary Ethiopia, the new regime while encouraging discussion of the nationalities problem, appears in practice to be at least as firmly committed as Haile Selassie to centralist rule (see Gilkes below, p 200). Confronted by what it perceives as subversive Eritrean and Somali secessionist aims which inevitably encourage similar aspirations in other traditionally disadvantaged 'nation-alities', Mengistu's regime has adopted what his opponents regard as an extreme form of Amhara chauvinist nationalism.[10] In Gellner's and Hinsley's terms, this might perhaps be viewed as a further response to a new wave of modernization and state integration through the medium of the traditional centralist Amharic culture by a regime whose traditional base and legitimacy is less secure than Haile Selassie's. Of partly non-Amhara origin and having been brought up in the home of one of Haile Selassie's closest advisers, Mengistu's tendency to focus state ceremonies in Addis Ababa on the statue of Emperor Menelik can hardly be accidental, suggesting as it does an equivalence between the present military strongman and his illustrious predecessor, the founder of the expanded Ethiopian empire. While the regime does not lack Amhara opponents, for those non-Amhara who still feel excluded and under-privileged the new Ethiopean regime appears essentially as an expression, however disguised, of aggressive Amhara nationalism. In line with Gellner's and Hinsley's and to some extent Kedourie's[11] emphasis on the formative role of deprivation and disaffection, this in turn promotes the generation of other reactive ethnic and regional nationalisms which, from the perspectives of our different disciplines, we analyse in the following pages.

Language and nationalism

In examining the various components which can be employed to generate such shared national identity we begin with the most obvious, and because it is basic to social interaction, the at first sight most fundamental factor: language.

Samuel Johnston declared languages to be 'the pedigree of nations' and this sentiment is echoed by those political scientists and others who, in the final analysis, define a nation as those 'who speak the same language' (although they do not always mean this to be taken entirely literally).

Joseph Tubiana, with whose subtle reflections on language and identity we open, readily concedes that language is indeed the simplest and most obvious criterion of national identity and exclusiveness. He also emphasizes its totalizing, political character, noting that it is rare for aspirations for self-determination to develop in the absence of a common language. The linguistic component in the growth of nationalist aspirations is very often stimulated when the language of government is not one's own mother-tongue. The writing of an oral language – such as Cushitic Oromo in Ethiopia – in the script of the politically dominant language (Amharic) may also be seen as a form of imperialism and so fuel local (Oromo) nationalist aspirations.

Equally, however, the introduction of literacy may, as in the case of Somali discussed by Hussein Adam, increase sentiments of linguistic self-confidence and national pride. Here we might usefully distinguish between Somali nationalism 'mark I and mark II'. As I have argued elsewhere,[12] unlike so many other cases, Somali cultural nationalism is a centuries old phenomenon and not something which has been recently drummed up to given credence to political claims. It is the source rather than the product of nationalist aspirations. It is not, however, a static, inert force and we can discern at least two phases in its modern political expression. In the late 1940s and early 1950s, the first modern Somali nationalists *politicized* their traditional cultural heritage, seeking national self-determination for a people balkanized by the imperial partition but also traditionally divided into mutually hostile clans. Although culture, language and the pastoral mode of production transcend them, these divisions are those of traditional political allegiance. Consequently, Somali nationalism 'Mark I' is based on what in Durkheim's terminology would be 'mechanical' rather than 'organic' solidarity. Attempts to transform this qualitatively, led civilian nationalist politicians in the 1960s to attempt to suppress and overcome traditional clan cleavages by officially relegating them to past history, using the conveniently distancing prefix 'ex' in place of 'clan'. This, however, soon became a pseudonym for continuing clan identity.

As Hussein Adam explains in the context of recent language policy in Somalia, the revolutionary military regime which came to power in October 1969 applied more radical and energetic nationalist measures than its civilian predecessors. The use of such clan sophistries as 'ex' was outlawed, clan identity was publicly abolished (and behaviour based on clan loyalty made an offence), and literacy was seen as a crucial force in promoting the attainment of a new populist nationalism, based on organic rather than mechanical solidarity. As this state-directed 'cultural revolution' proceeded, elements of 'traditional culture' were revamped in the guise of 'folklore' for the entertainment of visiting dignitaries and as a demonstration of the progress which had been achieved in transcending the past. In the same progressive spirit 'comrade' was officially introduced to replace 'cousin' as the standard term of polite address. Significantly, a primer for adult education in the new Somali script defined 'friends' ('comrades') in the same way that many political scientists define nationalists as 'those who understand each other's speech'. As Hussein Adam graphically reports, this 'instant literacy' palpably sharpened linguistic self-consciousness and so fuelled nationalist feeling both inside the Somali Republic and in the adjacent Ogaden. Indeed, it is tempting to suggest that this 'Mark II' nationalism, of the type associated with modernity and literacy by Ernest Gellner,[13] was a contributory factor in the outbreak of the Ogaden war of 1977/78. The resurgence of traditional clan ties, after the subsequent reversal of Somali fortunes in the Ogaden, suggests that literacy cannot, in itself, achieve or sustain the radical transformation of nationalism from the 'mechanical' to the 'organic' mode. Written or unwritten language is after all a means of expression, not an end in itself.

As Tubiana concludes, linguistic identity is secondary to other more profound differences – political, religious, historical – in shaping the group consciousness which language expresses. Thus, from the linguistic point of view, it is hard to seize the distinction between 'nation' and 'nationality' on which so much hinges in the Soviet Union and by extension in Marxist Ethiopia. According to the Marxist canons discussed by Wiberg, Healy, Gilkes, Triulzi and others, 'nations' qualify, or under appropriate conditions, may qualify for full self-government (a separate state) whereas 'nationalities' are only entitled to a limited degree of regional autonomy – including, possibly, the according of official status locally to their language.

Nation and State

This fine distinction serves to remind us of the importance of distinguishing clearly between 'nation' as a group sharing common culture (including language) and 'state' meaning autonomous political group – not necessarily based on uniform culture. That we tend to confound the two notions and speak losely of states ('nation-states') as nations, when they are not strictly so, reflects, of course, much of the ambiguity which is present in the concept of national self-determination and the universal tendency, already mentioned, to anchor cultural divisions in ostensibly natural distinctions. As Hakan Wiberg shows in his wide-ranging appraisal of the fate of national self-determination as a principle for state-formation, if we take the exclusive possession of a common language as the criterion, only a tenth of the world's contemporary states are actually 'nation–states' in the strict sense. (A quarter are nation–states in this sense if we include those with languages (such as English or Arabic) shared by several nation–states.)

The most culturally homogeneous states tend to be in Europe, the least in Africa, Asia and the Americas. In their modern European forms, concepts of nation–state and national self-determination are of course, as Wiberg, reminds us, products of the Enlightenment and Romanticism, widely disseminated in the wake of the French Revolution. Thus the 'Herder Programme' of, in effect, one people (or nation) one state has been much less extensively implemented than the ubiquitous association between 'state' and 'nation' would suggest.

This touches on the complex interplay between subjective and objective criteria in defining the boundaries of group identity – attempting to answer the question: what is a people or a nation? Or, more concretely: when does the nation begin and end? A basic problem here is that the only criteria that really matter, however ostensibly objectivized, acquire their evocative force through their subjective appeal: as Weber saw, what is crucial is 'the belief in common ethnicity'. Group adhesion is most emphatically not in the eye of the beholder. People who speak the same language may after all not wish to stand shoulder to shoulder. Linguistic discriminations are in any case often arbitrary: what for one linguist is merely two dialects of the same language is for another two separate languages. Tubiana was right to warn that language is not a sufficient criterion. As Wiberg amply demonstrates, the more international legal experts try to rigorously define what constitutes a people qualified to enjoy self-determination, the more ambiguous, vague and tautological the definition becomes.

At first sight, Marxist concepts seem to hold out the promise of a sharper approach to the problem. Criteria relating to mode of production, derived ultimately from the evolutionary frame-work of Maine and Morgan are here utilized to distinguish different levels of collectivity. In this schema 'clan' and 'tribe' precede the development of class-organized 'nationalities' and 'nations'. The 'clan' is based on communal ownership, while the 'tribe' includes a division between clan and tribal property. 'The nation', on the other hand, is 'the form of human community corresponding to the capitalist mode of production'.[14] 'Tribes' in the view of Stalin are merely 'ethnographic categories' whereas 'nations' are 'historical' and belong to 'the epoch of rising capitalism'. These criteria (which receive a wider and more interesting sociological base in Hinsley's and Gellner's theories of nationalism) are employed by the Ethiopian geographer Mesfin Wolde-Mariam, in a spirited polemic dimissing Somali claims to constitute a nation.[15] On the Marxist side there is, however, by no means general agreement on the universal applicability of these ostensibly diacritical distinctions between, in effect, genuine and pseudo-nationalism. A recent Soviet contributor to the debate on the nationalities question in the Horn of Africa, Georgi Galperin[16] observes that 'in the Soviet solution for the nationalities question . . . entire nations inhabiting vast expanses skipped the capitalist phase of development, while some northern, far eastern and Siberian peoples even bypassed this pre-capitalist phase of development.' If such bold evolutionary leaps can be extended to peoples and nations of the Soviet Union an avowedly 'multi-national state' with 'much in common' with Ethiopia, it is a little puzzling to understand why they do not also apply to peoples like the Somali. For Marxists the solution to the dilemma is to distinguish between 'broad', 'progressive' and so acceptable nationalism, and 'narrow' unacceptable nationalism. But it is difficult to see how to make these distinctions without introducing arbitrary criteria whose objective status is, inevitably, controversial.

As Wiberg (in common with Triulzi, Healy and Gilkes) notes, there are thus limits to the utility of the orthodox Marxist approach in distinguishing between those entities which, according to the doctrine, should be treated as fully-fledged nations qualifying for self-determination. These limitations are reinforced when we consider the additional criteria which Marxist–Leninism – and following the second World War the international community generally – require to justify a secessionist struggle seeking full self-determination. What is at stake here is, in effect, the right to wage a 'legitimate' nationalist rebellion – or revolution – against (imperialist) oppression. The general acceptance of the 'salt-water' theory of extra-metropolitan colonialism rather than the rival 'Belgian thesis' admitting the possibility of internal, local colonialism, offered a more decisive means of distinguishing between justified and unjustified anti-colonial nationalist movements. Ethiopia, which having defeated the Italians at the battle of Adowa in 1896, and from 1923 a member of the League of Nations, treated with the British, Italian and French colonial powers virtually as an equal, is an interesting test case here. As Triulzi indicates, there are some who maintain that under Emperor Haile Selassie Ethiopia was not really capable of imperialism, on the grounds that it had not reached the stage of monopoly capitalism. The more general view, apparently espoused by Soviet theoreticians, is that if under Haile Selassie, Ethiopia was imperialist, as soon as the Socialist Revolution became firmly established, all traces of colonialism withered away. For other Marxists who are not necessarily so committed to the present Ethiopian regime, the problem is to decide between the competing claims to revolutionary legitimacy of the Ethiopian centralists on the one hand, and the Eritreans, Ogaden Somalis, Oromo, and other 'peripheralist' nationalists on the other. As Gilkes, Pool, Reisman, Triulzi and other contributors who discuss this issue illustrate, the question invites arbitrary judgements.

National self-determination in Africa
The issue of national self-determination which Wiberg delineates in its

international and historical dimensions can be posed in relation to political autonomy in another way. If, in the 'international state system' there is a general presumption that states should be nations, the corollary that nations should be states is, as we have seen, more problematic, especially, as James Mayall and Sally Healy emphasize, in the wake of European decolonization.

The rise and international legitimation of the *principle* of nationalism and its anticipated realization in true (culturally homogeous) nation–states, has in practice led to the creation of multi-national, culturally heterogeneous or pluralist states. As Wiberg points out, the majority of the most recent of these derive directly from the *colonial* legacy in America, Asia and Africa, and there are only twelve true nation states. Thus the colonial map has not been redrawn; on the contrary, its demarcations have been underlined in the decolonization process.

As far as Africa (or more accurately, sub-Saharan) Africa is concerned, as I attempt to show below (p 67), the process of colonization and decolonization has upset the traditional balance between ethnically homogeneous and ethnically heterogeneous political formations. Prior to European partition, Africa's political units, whether centralized or uncentralized, included both multi-national (pluralist) and mono-ethnic (homogeneous) political units. Moreover, viewed historically, trends in both directions were apparent. Some ethnically heterogeneous polities were engaged in what today would be called 'nation-building', while in others an elite power group actively sought to differentiate itself culturally from those it ruled. Colonization and decolonization has the unintended effect of establishing the multi-national, pluralist state as the dominant strain on the continent. Thus the majority of Africa's new states (misleadingly referred to as new 'nations') are fortuitously, cast in the mould of Ethiopia. Like that traditional African conquest state, they consist of a loose assemblage of different ethnic groups and 'tribes' (which I equate with 'nations'). Hence de-colonization has led to what might be called the 'Ethiopianization' of Africa.

At the same time, the application by the international community of the principle of national self-determination to *part* of the Somali nation (the former British and Italian Somali territories) has produced a situation in the Horn of Africa where a traditionally expansive multi-national state, Ethiopia, confronts an incomplete, and therefore also expansive, nation-state – the Somali Republic. The bone of mutual contention arises from the demand for self (ie Somali) determination on the part of the Somali population of eastern Ethiopia (ethnically western Somaliland) – who, as Reisman describes, were allocated to Ethiopia – mainly by Britain and in defiance of prior Anglo–Somali treaties of 'protection'. Since with the exception of Lesotho, Botswana and perhaps Burundi, the rest of Africa (including pluralist South Africa) now resembles the multi-ethnic Ethiopia, it would indeed be surprising if the Somali case had much appeal for other African governments. By the same token, it might be expected that the Eritrean nationalist case which, as David Pool recounts, involves an ethnically heterogeneous population welded together by Italian colonization, should strike a chord of sympathy elsewhere in Africa. Perhaps the most significant factor militating against this is the unique prestige which, as we have indicated, Ethiopia possesses as the one traditional African state to survive European partition – not merely unscathed but with its territory actually enlarged.

More generally, as James Mayall argues, as Africa has become progressively de-colonized so there has been a marked shift in African circles in the interpretation of the 'explosive' (Reisman) principle of self-determination. In the interests of international order and self-preservation, the OAU has gravitated towards a strong emphasis on the conservative anti-colonial interpretation of self-determination as applying only to communities under *European* colonial rule. This, in effect, racist understanding is of course encouraged by the continued existence of white supremacy in 'pluralist' South Africa. Pan-Africanism which looked idealistically towards a continent-wide African unity has, as Mayall aptly puts it, been 'domesticated' in the interests of preserving the post-colonial status-quo. A crucial aspect of this is the OAU doctrine on the sanctity of the frontiers which each state has inherited from the former colonial powers. This 'frontier fetishism', as I call it, is indeed a marked feature of post-colonial Africa and relates, I think, to the fact that these new states (sometimes called 'state–nations') possess few other distinguishing features in terms of which to assert their identity and exclusiveness. It is thus not surprising that in addition to accusing the Somalis of tribalism, most African states outside the Horn of Africa should also construe the Ethiopian–Somali problem as a routine 'boundary dispute'. But as Reisman points out, this can hardly be the case when there are no legally defined boundaries to dispute. On a broader front, Mayall contrasts the restrictive 'anti-colonial' view of self-determination maintained by the OAU with the more flexible attitude of Arab states prepared, when it suits them, to aid co-religionist nationalists in the Horn of Africa and elsewhere. This seems consistent with the embracive potential of Arab nationalism which, despite its perennially shifting divisions, unites Muslim communities across state boundaries.

Towards a re-definition of self-determination

In step with this increasingly rigid commitment on the part of African states to territorial sovereignty and the curtailment of self-determination other than for ex-European colonies, there has, as Sally Healy demonstrates, been a corresponding shift of emphasis in the presentation of the case for self-determination by nationalist groups. As she says, the crucial question has switched from: 'What is a nation?' to 'What is a colony?' As the chapters by Baxter, Reisman and Triulzi indicate, Ethiopia's historical role as an expansionist empire–state make this particularly appropriate in the context of the Horn of Africa. Thus, more emphatically than before, the Eritrean, Western Somali and Oromo nationalists all now couch their claims to self-determination in terms of the 'colonization' by 'chauvinist' Amhara imperialists. This has led to an ideological debate of special interest for students of Marxism. Here, as was noted earlier, some Ethiopian centralists attempt to rebut these charges on the grounds that Emperor Haile Selassie's state wasn't *exactly* an empire because, they assert, it did not export surplus capital. Soviet Marxists who rightly stress the obvious parallels between pre-revolutionary Russian and Ethiopia, lacking this Ethiopian ethnocentricity, do not seem to find it necessary to resort to such elaborate sophistries. And here, at least, they share common ground with Marxist Eritrean, Oromo and other nationalists. They differ, of course, on the issue of whether the present regime in Ethiopia is, or is not, truly 'progressive'. Despite this shift of emphasis from a 'nation' to a 'colonized nation' in assessing the authenticity of nationalist claims, it is interesting, as Sally Healy notes, that the defenders of the Ethiopian centralist position should still devote time and energy to arguing – not without some justice that, because of its mixed ethnic character, Eritrea is not a 'nation'.

In his detailed examination of the debate among the Ethiopian left-wing radicals, one camp envisaging full independence for the ethnic 'minorities' (often actually majorities), the other 'regional autonomy', Alessandro Triulzi explores the close relationship between the 'national question' and feudalism'. These issues, he proposes, can more usefully be subsumed under the rubric of centre-periphery relations in a multi-ethnic centralized conquest state and are inextricably bound up with national oppression. In common with the radical Ethiopian writer Addis Hiwet, Triulzi emphasizes the distinction discussed above between the oppressive colonial character of Amhara domination in the southern, largely Cushitic-speaking areas, and the situation among the northern, Semitic-speaking peasantry.

It is often argued that, historically, domination of the Amhara as an ethnic elite was mitigated by their implicit 'melting-pot' philosophy and readiness to absorb upwardly mobile non-Amhara subjects as long as they adopted the Amharic language and their Christian religion. In Triulzi's view, the mixed origins of the Amhara leadership (Haile Selassie was partly of Oromo origin) begs the question of what it means to be an 'Amhara' in the Ethiopian context and what its meaning is for the non-Amhara peoples. This cannot be satisfactorily analysed solely in class or ethnic terms. In southern Ethiopia, 'Amhara' is synonymous with *naftaanya* – the usurping soldiery employed by Menelik to colonize the south. The conquerors literally lived off the land and its indigenous population – frequently as absentee *naftaanya* landlords.

As Triulzi notes, the brilliant Italian orientalist, Enrico Cerulli, who visited these *naftaanya* colonies in southern Ethiopia in 1927, delineated the process of Amhara expansion and incorporation with prophetic insight. The aim of the Amhara military settlers was to establish local roots so that in time their children by local women, maintained by locally extorted tithes, would gradually become a uniquely privileged local aristocracy, claiming foreign origins and tracing their ancestry to the first Amhara conquerors of the area. With this history of conquest and forced incorporation it is not surprising that people who suddenly became 'Greater Ethiopians' (in D. Levine's[17] phrase) in the late 1880s, should today be involved in liberation movements fighting their Amhara *naftaanya* colonizers for self-determination.

Oromo and Somali nationalism

Paul Baxter provides us with a vivid account of the subjective aspects of this colonial experience in the context of the situation among the Oromo of Arusi province on the eve of the Revolution. Like Triulzi, he finds the label 'feudal' mystifying rather than illuminating in relation to pre-revolutionary Ethiopia. In his view, the Oromo are just as much colonial subjects as Black South Africans, and their liberation movements part of the continental drive towards de-colonization. Perhaps because it is at a much earlier stage in its development than the older Eritrean and Somali movements, Oromo nationalists today stress those shared traditional institutions – such as the *gada* generation system and the myth of common descent – which bind them together and distinguish them from other peoples in the area. (This indeed is the kind of nationalism-in-the-making envisaged by most theories of nationalism.)

Apart from those who through the adoption of the Amharic language and Christianity have become Amharas, the other most distinctive group are the Muslim Oromo of Arussi and Bale provinces, many of whom have made common cause with the Western Somali freedom fighters under the leadership of the veteran Oromo guerrilla, Wako Guto, in the so-called 'Somali Abo Liberation Front'. (This takes its name from the Oromo term *abo* meaning 'you!' used to attract someone's attention in the same way as the Somali expression '*wariya*'.) There are close ethnic as well as religious ties between these Muslim Oromo and the Somali of southern Ethiopia and Northern Kenya where many groups are bilingual in Oromo and Somali.[18] The Somali–Abo Liberation Front is thus a mixed Oromo–Somali alliance loosely associated with the Western Somali Liberation Front based on the Ogaden Somalis in eastern Ethiopia. Like the latter, it has received moral and other support from the government of the Somali Republic. Naturally, SALF is seen by some non-Muslim Oromo as an expression of Somali chauvinism and this, with the repressive policies of the Ethiopian central government, encourages the reactive Oromo Liberation Front. Moreover, although their most outspoken nationalists insist that the Oromo must first secure independence from Amhara colonization and *then* decide on their future relationship, it is obvious that simply in terms of their overwhelming size and distribution, no other ethnic group has a greater demographic stake in the Ethiopian state.

From this perspective, as Baxter observes, Eritrea and the Western Somalis are peripheral. The marginal historical and civil status of the latter and Ethiopia's claims to rule this segment of the Somali nation and the land they live on, are examined in terms of international law by Michael Reisman. Reisman argues the case for Western Somali independence stressing the illegality of the Anglo-Ethiopian treaty of 1897, made by Britain in defiance of prior Anglo-Somali treaties and in effect transferring to a third party precisely what the Anglo-Somali treaties of 1884–6 purported to be designed to affirm: the independence of the Somali signatories. He also contends that, prior to the authority now granted to the principle of self-determination in international law, the Ethiopians did not create any effective title to the Ogaden on the basis of occupation, since they did not exercise effective or continuous control over it.

Today in international law the primary authority in a disposition of territory is the principle of self-determination. Since, evidently, this principle must sometimes, as here, explosively challenge the structure of an existing state, which principle then prevails? Reisman maintains that the International Court judgement in the case of Western Sahara confirms the primacy of the principle of self-determination, that it is potentially available to all subjugated peoples, and that subjugation can be inferred from such features as geographical, ethnic or cultural distinctiveness. The Namibia judgement is cited to the same effect, Reisman arguing that, in international law, the 1963 OAU resolution on African boundaries cannot be understood to abridge this right to self-determination. As we have seen, however, in practice in order not to upset the status quo, the OAU in general here tends to operate a double standard – only giving unqualified approval for self-determination from *white* colonial rule. Reisman concludes by suggesting various ways in which the principle of self-determination might be applied to the Western Somali population.

Eritrea: an unliberated colony?

The Somalis and the Eritreans have been described, not entirely inappropriately, as allies in adversity. Their situation at first sight is certainly very different. The irony of the Somali position is that they have been subject to two opposed dispensations. On the one hand, an independent African state – the Somali Democratic Republic – has been created on the basis of the ethnic identity of two segments of the nation; other segments have achieved independence with neighbouring peoples in Kenya and more recently (1975) in the Republic of Djibouti under a Somali President. On the other hand, a final large segment of the nation remains, as Somalis see it, under colonial rule in Ethiopia where the 1974 Revolution has not liberated them.

Eritrea's case is very different, as David Pool's analysis of the rise of Eritrean nationalism indicates. Here we are not concerned with a single nation, like the Somali, dismembered in the colonial partition. On the contrary Eritrea, like Ethiopia, is multi-ethnic in composition, and like other new African states owes most of its identity (transcending its Christian and Muslim divisions) to its colonial experience. The colony of Eritrea was established and ruled by the Italians from 1884 until 1941. Between 1941 and 1952 British military administration created a framework for the rise of modern Eritrean nationalism which Eritrea's federation to Ethiopia in 1952 and annexation in 1962, inadvertently strengthened. In 1961 the militant Eritrean Liberation Front was founded, whose activist core was drawn initially from the Muslim Bani Amir tribe, an important section of the Cushitic-speaking Beja people who extend into the Sudan. The ELF, Pool argues, functioned primarily as a pastoralist military organization, lacking the capacity to satisfactorily accommodate substantial numbers of the Christian and partly Semitic-speaking peasantry. As the ELF expanded in size and popularity with the escalation of the nationalist war against the Ethiopians, inevitable internal strains developed between Muslims and Christians and pastoralists and peasants. A further complicating factor was the advantage to be gained in attracting external support from sympathetic Arab states, by stressing the Front's Islamic credentials. Ultimately the main breakaway group consisted of Tigrinya-speaking Christian dissidents who played a leading role in the formation of the more radical Marxist Eritrean Peoples Liberation Front in 1970. It is, of course, this populist movement appealing to Muslims as well as Christians, which, with its emphasis on peasant and urban proletariat mobilization, on land reform and political education, and its remarkable military success, has captured most of the limelight in the recent phases of the Eritrean nationalist struggle.

Prior to the Ethiopian Revolution in 1974, as former subjects of a colonial power struggling for independence from a western-supported imperial regime, the Eritrean nationalists attracted sympathetic if usually covert support from sources as politically disparate as conservative Arab states on the one hand and Cuba and East European satellites on the other. As Pool indicates, and as Patrick Gilkes corroborates from the opposing centralist perspective, the situation has become much more complex – for the Ethiopians and their Soviet allies – since the official adoption of Scientific Socialism in Addis Ababa. This is, no doubt, partly reflected in Soviet-sponsored attempts at mediation between the parties which seem much more vigorously pursued than in the case of the Somali Ethiopian conflict, where the direct intervention of Cuban forces as well as equipment enabled Ethiopia to reconquer the Ogaden.

The Centralist stance on the 'nationalities problem'

Of course, a solution to both these 'separatist movements' as Ethiopian centralists perceive them, might be found in some form of local autonomy. It is this vital question of finding a recipe to accommodate the 'nationalities problem' in a manner acceptable to the Ethiopian Provisional Military Administrative Council (the Dergue) that Patrick Gilkes explores at length in our final chapter. He examines the impact on the military of the debate amongst the left-wing Ethiopian intelligentsia discussed by Triulzi. The two civilian Marxist movements which, before one (EPRP)* was virtually eliminated and elements of the other (MEISON)** assimilated, sought to influence the policy of the new military leaders in the Dergue were, as we have seen, divided on the issue of national self-determination. The EPRP supported the Eritrean independence struggle. MEISON objected, rejecting the Eritrean claims to constitute an authentic liberation movement. This is the line which has been generally adopted by the Provisional Military Administrative Council (PMAC) whose policies have naturally been influenced by both the Eritrean and Somali conflicts, the latter reaching a climax in 1977/78. The Eritrean peace-plan announced in May 1976 made reference to conceding 'regional autonomy' in the form of the 'right to free self-government implemented with all democratic procedures'. The subsequent upsurge of conflict has obscured whatever substantive content this negotiating declaration might have contained.

The PMAC claims to be a progressive, revolutionary regime, and cites its land-reform programme and peasant and urban associations (*kebeles*) in evidence. All local nationalist movements opposing the government – including those in Eritrea and the Ogaden – become, therefore, by

*The Ethiopian Peoples Revolutionary Party – EPRP
**All Ethiopia Socialist Movement – MEISON

definition anti-democratic, imperialist forms of 'narrow nationalism' to be suppressed rather than encouraged. The Eritrean EPLF may even, Gilkes suggests, be felt by members of the PMAC to have betrayed them since it spurns their 'progressive' socialist policies.

It may not be without significance, that the PMAC's favourite candidate for the possible implementation of 'local autonomy' seems to be the Kunama who, with a population of some 20,000, must be one of the smallest of the 86 or 85 officially recognized 'nationalities' in the state. Preyed on traditionally by Beja pastoralists and more recently by the Eritrean ELF, the Kunama have loyally supported the Dergue (PMAC) and could hardly pose a serious threat. However, any further progress in implementing any of the various degrees and forms of possible local autonomy canvassed must wait the establishment of a properly constituted Ethiopian Workers Party, with 'progressive' regional cadres to protect the interests of the masses in the regions. Whatever measures of decentralization may then be applied, Ethiopia will retain its territorial integrity. In the meantime, Gilkes concludes that the inevitable effect of such widespread discussion of this vital issue, accompanied by ruthless applications of military force, has been to tantalizingly raise the expectations of the nationalities without, as yet, much tangible outcome.

Pan-African implications?

All this, I think, has important implications beyond the confines of the Horn of Africa. By referring to its traditional tribal divisions as 'nationalities' if not nations, Ethiopia's new ideologues have created a new legitimacy for parallel divisions in other African states. This gives added validity to mono-ethnic movements elsewhere and is likely to have further implications for the interpretation and implementation (or disregard) of the principle of national self-determination. If, as I argue, the boundary fetishism of the new ex-colonial African states adds weight to Ethiopia's understandable desire to conserve its territorial integrity, Ethiopia's official recognition of the 'nationalities problem' adds potential fuel to those forces which, in their quest for autonomy, do not necessarily recognize existing state frontiers. If as James Mayall contends, the OAU, whose headquarters are in Addis Ababa, has over the last decade 'domesticated' the principle of national self-determination, this new development may encourage a reversal to the feral state.

The Horn and theories of Nationalism

This is not without significance since, as Anthony Smith[19] concludes in a recent assessment of contemporary trends, everything suggests that nationalism (which in its modern form like Hinsley and Gellner he associates with modernity) is growing rather than declining in significance throughout the world. While Kedourie[20] is no doubt right to stress the special characteristics of modern European nationalism and to emphasize the infectious diffusion of the doctrine elsewhere, its pervasive appeal can hardly be satisfactorily accounted for in such terms alone. Nor can this be explained by the present status of the doctrine of national self-determination as the prevailing legitimating concept in the modern international state system. For, as we have seen, although this is the formal 'norm' it is in fact an ideal to which only a minority of contemporary states (nation–states) actually conform. This disparity between ideal (nation-state) and practice (state) in the modern world might at first sight appear to challenge such theories as those of Hinsley[21] (with reference to Europe) and Gellner[22] (more generally) which present nationalism as the necessary cultural base for effective industrial (or post-traditional) bureaucracy. However, this can obviously be reconciled as long as the general modernizing trend – either at the existing state level (where it appears as 'nation-building') or at subsidiary intra-state levels ('regional nationalism') – continues to be in this direction. Here, for Gellner, the decisive modern bureaucratic dynamic disassociates (it is tempting to say 'uproots') nationalism from other, older forms of group loyalty which involve a bridging hierarchy, or chain, of intermediate sub-loyalties. As I have suggested above (p 10) with reference to Somali nationalism this distinction has analogies with Durkheim's[23] contrast between mechanical and organic solidarity (and with Maine's between Status and Contract).

This interpretation certainly convincingly elucidates cardinal features of modern nationalism, linking them to an evolutionary schema reminiscent of Marxism. It seems, however, that somewhat paradoxically it risks presenting an absolutist (and centralist) view of nationalism which decontextualizes the phenomenon, in the sense of disregarding or de-emphasizing its relativist character as *one* rather than *the only possible*, loyalty possessed by the individual (Gellner's notion of immediacy). In order to understand its seemingly ubiquitous character and pan-human appeal, we need, I think, to realign nationalism with the broader family of types and levels of group identity which, of course, are always relative in the sense that my identity is a function of the situation in which I am called upon to act on or declare it (a Scotsman vers an Englishman, a Glaswegian vers a citizen of Edinburgh etc).

It is in this wider context that we can best understand the pervasive appeal of an ideology which seeks to make culturally constructed (sometimes off the peg, sometimes tailor-made) and reconstructed identity appear to be a natural, biologically grounded and hence unassailable and indisputable given. All this is present in the etymological sense of the word 'nation'. In exactly this tradition ordinary English usage refers to the incorporation process (an enculturation) by which foreigners acquire citizenship as 'naturalization'. What nationalism above all provides is an ostensibly biological basis for patriotism and group interest. One cannot act otherwise, it proclaims, because one's allegiance is in the blood. This is hardly a modern idea.

Notes

1. Edward Ullendorff, *Ethiopia and the Bible*, London, 1968.
2. J. S. Trimingham, *Islam in Ethiopia*, London, 1952
3. A. Hoben, *Land Tenure among the Amhara of Ethiopia*, Chicago, 1973
4. C. Jesman, *The Russians in Ethiopia: an essay in futility*, London, 1958
5. L. E. Barrett, *The Rastafarians*, London, 1977
6. See eg P. Gilkes, *The Dying Lion*, London 1975; J. Markakis and N. Ayele, *Class and Revolution in Ethiopia*, Nottingham 1978; Raul Valdes Vivo, *Ethiopia's Revolution*, New York, 1978
7. See C. Clapham,. *Haile-Selassie's Government*, London, 1969; J. Markakis, Ethiopia: *Anatomy of a Traditional Polity*, London, 1975
8. F. Hinsley, *Nationalism and the International Political System*, London 1973
9. E. Gellner, *Thought and Change*, London, 1964, and 'Scale and Nation', *Philosophy of the Social Sciences*, 3, 1973
10. Contrast, however, the interpretation offered by H. Erlich, 'The Horn of Africa and the Middle East: Politicization of Islam in the Horn and depoliticization of Ethiopian Christianity' in J. Tubiana (ed) *Modern Ethiopia: from the accession of Menelik II to the Present*, Rotterdam, 1980, pp. 399–408
11. E. Kedourie (ed. and intro.) *Nationalism in Asia and Africa*,London, 1970
12. I. M. Lewis, *A Modern History of Somalia*, London, 1980.
13. E. Gellner, *Thought and Change*, London, 1965
14. R. Daglish (trs) *The Fundamentals of Marxist-Leninist Philosophy*, Moscow, 1974, p 394
15. Mesfin Wolde-Mariam, *Somalia: the problem child of Africa*, Addis Ababa, 1977
16. G. Galperin, 'Ethiopia: some aspects of the nationalities question', *Asia and Africa today*, No 6, 1979
17. D. Levine, *Greater Ethiopia: the evolution of a multi-ethnic society*, Chicago, 1974
18. See I. M. Lewis, 'The Western Somali Liberation Front (WSLF) and the legacy of Sheikh Hussein of Bale' in J. Tubiana (ed.), *Modern Ethiopia*, Rotterdam, 1980, pp 409–416
19. A. D. Smith, *Theories of Nationalism*, London, 1971, p. 23
20. E. Kedourie, *op cit* and *Nationalism*, London, 1966
21. F. Hinsley, *op cit.*
22. E. Gellner, *Thought and Change*, chapter 7
23. E. Durkheim, *The Division of Labour in Society*, New York, 1947 (French original, 1893)
24. H. Maine, Ancient Law, London, 1861

THE LINGUISTIC APPROACH TO SELF DETERMINATION

Joseph Tubiana

To begin with we shall consider terminology. In everyday French we prefer to talk about the 'droit des peuples à disposer d'eux mêmes'* rather than self-determination; or more precisely self-determination describes the way in which the right of peoples to self-government can be expressed. There has therefore been much discussion about 'the right to self-determination', particularly with regard to Algeria.

One finds that when a people claim their right to self-determination (one is immediately led to say: 'the right to determine themselves') they always seek to break away from the state structure in which they consider they are wrongly confined against their wishes. Hence the term 'separatists' applied by their adversaries to the proponents of self-determination for the people concerned (be they Algerians, Quebecois or the inhabitants of the Bernese Jura in Switzerland), and the tendency to substitute the negative term 'separatism' for the positive term 'self-determination'. General de Gaulle did much to popularize the terms 'separatism' and 'separatist' at the time of the Algerian war. Likewise 'secession' and 'secessionist' . . .

While it is undeniable that the claim to self-determination expresses the desire to separate, the extent of the separation envisaged can vary, as is shown in the examples of the extreme cases of Algeria and Bernese Jura. Above all it is necessary to acknowledge the fact that the desire for separation always springs from the recognition that a certain socio-economic and cultural community is badly governed by the state to which it belongs; this engenders the hope that the community itself, being better qualified to do so, would govern the patrimony for the good of the people. Language is part of this patrimony.

Language and the State

Languages are conventional systems which use vocal signs to convey information. These systems tend towards coherence, they combine the finite number of vocal signs at their disposal into an articulated language.

*English equivalent: the right of peoples to self-government

They are susceptible to change, particularly when in contact with other languages.

The information conveyed encompasses the totality of the material culture of the community which speaks the language, and beyond that the totality of the entire culture: patterns of behaviour, moral values, beliefs, as well as the sum total of the history of the community.

It will later be shown that common language, common culture and common history are the criteria for belonging to a particular national community. Language differences, sometimes linked with religious differences, are a determining factor in the formation of a desire for self-determination, as much in the case of Algeria as in that of Quebec or the Bernese Jura. It is rare to find a case where the wish for self-determination evolves in the absence of a common language.

It is of little consequence whether the language is written or not. For the linguist a non-written language is in no way inferior to a written one, and besides all languages can be written. What distinguishes a non-written language from a written one is that in the former the archives are non-existent, or nearly so: the history of the language remains largely unknown. Writing is in effect the oldest and most economical means of preserving a language: the written message persists indefinitely through time.

Writing furnishes a convenient and unlimited method of recording culture through the accumulation of chronological strata. It facilitates conservation and records change. All that is lost in oral languages would be preserved in a written one. However, writing is a false and misleading means of fixing behaviour, values, beliefs and historical events because after a certain lapse of time language is no longer understood in the same way as it was at the time of writing: it is no longer understood as it ought to be.

In another connection the written word has become a formidable means of governing people which is more and more intrusive, especially in our times: it is the weapon which renders the bureaucracy of the state all powerful, but which sometimes, fortunately, then becomes checked by its own proliferation.

If the written word is a means of administering individuals, the spoken word remains, above all others, the means of influencing their minds. The modern state makes use of both to maintain its authority. In every case, all the relations between the individual and the state are mediated through a single language which conveys information from the state to the individual and vice versa. This is so regardless of whether there is an extremely elaborate state machinery or more rudimentary forms such as those described by historians or observed by anthropologists. The choice of this language is entirely the decision of the state and the choice is based purely on the convenience, needs and interests of the continuity of the state. The impartial observer would note that the individual who challenges the choice of official language has automatically challenged the structure of the state, and has sought to change this in seeking to change the choice of language – and, if he is not successful, it is often the case that he will want to break away.

Even unitary states, which only recognize one official language, have come to authorize the use both on radio and television of other languages which are spoken in the country (but it is important to note here that this does not apply to the press). This exception to the rule is explained by the refusal of the state to deny itself an effective means of influencing the people; for it is recognized at the same time that without this the people concerned would remain by and large inaccessible. This recognition of their identity, besides its immediate positive uses, helps to defuse the resentment of a community which feels itself to be ignored – and hence persecuted – inasmuch as the instruments of the state are supposed to personify the nation of which they are a part.

The citizen who is constantly addressed by his radio or television set in a language which he does not understand would feel attacked, or at least excluded and rejected by the official national community. Even for those who understand this language although it is not their own, the feeling would be of exclusion or at least of unjust discrimination. This ridicules the idea of the social contract in which the state has an obligation to treat individuals equally.

Of course no one is forced to make use of a radio or television set, but in practice these tools of culture have assumed a primary and indispensable character. Neither the individual nor the state can pretend that they do not exist.

However, situations arise daily in which – whether one likes it or not – one cannot in any way avoid the official language. These are the obligatory contacts with the public services: law, police, customs, education, municipal services etc . . .

The person who finds himself completely unable to use his language in the social relations which are imposed from outside finds himself in a critical position here and now, both in the particular moment and more lastingly at the level of his identification and his place in the society.[1] The linguistic claims which ensue take, therefore, one or other of two aspects. If the language in question is an unwritten one – an insurmountable obstacle to its administrative use – one would first want it to be written; ingenious minds will find a solution, even if it requires one or several scripts.[2] If it is a written language or could be made so by enterprising people, one would ask that it be recognized alongside the official language as is the case, for example, with Tigrinya, or Kabyle, or even Breton.

The refusal to accede to these demands, which would be felt as a rejection by the dominant community, aggravates the identity crisis. Such a refusal, in addition to others in other spheres could lead the affected people to believe that, in view of all these incompatabilities, there is no longer any possibilty of living as part of that community. As a result, they would expressly demand to form their own national community in a more or less autonomous state. The examples one finds are very varied: the populations of Southern Sudan, or Eritrea, the Kabyles, the Kurds etc.

Language and Identity

It is well known that for both individuals as well as groups, identity is affirmed in relation to others. The person who must communicate with the authorities of his country through an intervening interpreter feels himself to be excluded from the dominant group which controls and to some extent appropriates the state. The same is true for someone who must conduct his dealings in a language which he has had to make an effort to learn and which he only more or less masters.

His cultural identity casts him in a subservient position. Thus there develops a feeling of group consciousness. I have often been able to observe in various places the expression of unacknowledged superiority, sometimes expressed in anger, sometimes with disdain. The exclusive 'we' as opposed to 'them' or 'you' . . . We do . . . you do . . . we think . . . you think . . . we say . . . you say . . . our fathers came from . . . your fathers came from . . . our home . . . your home . . . etc . . .

Yet one could not say that the process of identification (I would even say of self-identification) begins with the conflict of languages. Other more profound cultural factors of separation must already have existed relating to history, religion, political organization, education, law . . . In fact, the existence of a common language is only one of the criteria of belonging to a national group; language as such figures amongst other criteria certain of which we have already touched upon; origins and history, religion and beliefs, moral values and patterns of behaviour, the territory inhabited and, on a more subtle level, the feeling of belonging which results in the desire to form a state. Contrary to what one might say, I do not believe that of all these criteria language is the prime or most decisive factor. But it is the simplest to define and the easiest to grasp.

When languages are mutually incomprehensible the distinction is hardly noticed. But when mutual comprehension is possible, we know how much people notice the differences of vocabulary and grammatical form. The difference are even more frequently marked when – mutual comprehension being almost perfect – they are on the plane of phonetics and rest upon pronunciation. All this has been known for a long time.

It can happen that, under constant pressure from the state, reinforced by the diffuse social pressures of the dominant group, a people may be tempted to abandon or change its language. All that is needed – as I have witnessed in several places – is that the parents stop using their language when they talk to their children and use the official language instead. In the space of one generation the original language is no more than a relic in the mouths of the old people.

Yet the attachment of a minority community in a state to their own language is such that one could say that the abandonment of the language is the beginning of a cultural suicide. A state which does not recognize the cultural identity of its people, which represses the use of their own language, is engaged in a process of cultural genocide.[3] In effect language is one of the elements constituting a culture yet at the same time it embodies the entire culture. It is also a new situation: all that threatens the language threatens the culture as a whole.

When the state prohibits the use of a language in education, even in independent schools outside the state system, when it prohibits the study of a language and research into it, when it does not allow the existence of a press in a language, it is attacking the very culture of the community which uses it. In limiting the spread of a language, in threatening its preservation, it is undertaking a course of action of which the legitimacy may be contested by the community which is threatened. Such a community generally grants the unlimited right of the state to control political information and accepts censorship as a matter of course, but it resents as an attack on its vital interests any restriction on what is considered to be the free sector of information which does not need to be under state control, that is to say cultural information in the spheres which we have already listed.

Language use in the Horn

What is the situation in the Horn of Africa? If one excludes the foreign languages: Arabic, English, French, Italian, one finds two languages which rank as official languages, Amharic for the Ethiopian state and Somali for the Somali state. One language which has an ill-defined status as an official regional language in the Ethiopian province of Eritrea is Tigrinya, a Semitic language related to Amharic, although they are not mutually comprehensible. Under the Imperial regime the policy with regard to this use of Tigrinya fluctuated, sometimes tolerant, sometimes restrictive in Eritrea, totally restrictive in the province of Tigre. Tigrinya was treated as a cultural language, written in the traditional script, but with limited potential for development and expansion.

Other Semitic languages spoken by the major communities living in Ethiopia, namely Tigré (or Khasi) and Gurage, which could easily be written in the Ethiopian script, have no official status, even in their regions. A final Semitic language, Harari, albeit of limited importance quantitively, could also be accorded official status as a regional cultural language for which there is no problem of writing either.

With regard to the Cushitic languages of the region, the Somali Republic has adopted an official script for Somali, in Latin characters, which seems to have been largely accepted, and this is also true even in the Republic of Djibuti where neither Somali nor Afar have any well defined status. In Ethiopia, Oromo has been and is written in Ethiopian and Latin scripts; we need to know which of the two systems is more effective for education and general usage. Under the Imperial regime the use of written Oromo, even in the Ethiopian script, was hardly permitted. For a long time the introduction of an Oromo version of the Bible was prohibited. Later there was an embryonic press in Oromo and it was kept on for an alphabetization campaign, but I do not think that its status has been officially defined; its development does not seem to be very encouraging. Wolaytsa or Walamo is another Cushitic language retained in Ethiopia for an alphabetization campaign. It does not seem that the situation is any different from that of Oromo, whose importance in terms of population strength is superior. One could also see a language like Afar attaining the rank of a cultural regional language, inasmuch as a certain number of literate Afars use the official Somali alphabet to write their language.

There are other Cushitic languages in the Horn of Africa such as the Agaw languages, written in the Ethiopian scripts by missionaries . . . One could say that they are fully accepted insofar as they have not left the level of everyday speech, and recognition of them as a cultural language of a major community is not sought. In contrast to other languages cited, Agaw is not used for television or radio.

Language, nation and nationality
Are the communities which speak the languages which we have just listed 'nations' or 'nationalities'? The latter term, as used in the Soviet Union, fuels the debate over language in the inner circles of the revolutionary élites in the Horn of Africa. For some people it seems to designate a 'nation' which is not qualified to seek expression as a state. But if one excludes the political aspects, the roots of the controversy appear rather obscure.[4]

The political implications of the linguistic problem are beyond the scope of this discussion. However, politicians should consider more practically the status of living languages and pay more attention to the linguistic approach to the problem of nationalities. I was surprised to find, for example, that the word language does not appear once in the entry in a very simple dictionary[5] which I quote by way of conclusion.

'*Principle of nationalities*', the right to independence of any social group with a common origin, history, way of life and outlook, from the time that they occupy a defined territory.

The *principle of nationalities*, which is the origin of the theory of the rights of peoples to self government, was proclaimed, in fact, by the French Revolution, and spread by the Imperial Revolutionary army throughout Europe. It played a very important role after 1815, favouring in Europe the independence of Greece (1882-1830), and Belgium (1830-1831), and the unification of Italy (1864-1870), and of Germany (1864-1870). The emancipation of the Balkan peoples between 1870 and 1924, Wilson's Fourteen Points (1918) and the Treaty of Versailles (1919) only served to give full expression in Europe to the principle of nationalities.

Unfortunately this contributed to the downfall of the Double Monarchy which created a dangerous vacuum in South Eastern Europe at a time when the aroused nationalities turned it (partially) from its basic goal; the principle then became a means to justify territorial aims, such as the claims of Hitler on Austria, the Sudetan etc . . . Since then, and especially since the end of World War II, the attainment of independence and the admission to the United Nations of the previously colonized peoples, had marked the official triumph, universally, of the principle of nationalities and the right of peoples to self-government.'

NOTES

1. As early as 1838 the French traveller Arnauld d'Abbadie, when visiting Adowa in Tigre, made the following observation: 'Dedjesmach Wube, who came from Simien, West of Takkaze, where they speak only Amharic, came to extend his rule over an important portion of Tigre, and it was a major cause of annoyance to the Tigreans that they were obliged to use Amharic in their dealings with the authorities, or else speak through an interpreter.' Arnauld d'Abbadie, *Douze ans de sejour dans la Haute-Ethiopie (Abyssinia)*, t.I, p. 31.
2. This was what happened in about 1920 or 1925 in what was then Italian Somalia, when Osman Yusuf Kenadid invented a completely original alphabet for writing the vowels and consonants of the Somali language. Afterwards there were several imitators who tried to perfect his alphabet or proposed alternatives based on the same principles. Details of this can be found in a special number of the periodical *Somaliya* (7-8 June, 1969) published by the Ministry of Education of the Republic of Somalia, entitled, 'Il problema della lingua somala'. Here can be found, in particular, the report of the Unesco group of experts on the writing of Somali (p. 215-234) and the memorandum

which Muuse Galaal presented to this group (p. 190–201). See also Enrico Cerulli, 'Tentativo indigeno per formare un alfabet somalo' *Oriente Moderno*, 4 April, 1932; M. Maino, 'L'alfabeto "osmania" in Somalia' *Rassenga di Studi Ectiopici*, X, 1951, p. 108–121; L. Ricci, 'corrispondenza epistolare in osmania' *Rassegna di Studi Ectiopici*, XIV, 1959, p. 108–150)

3. This was the case in France under the centralized monarchy, whose policies were perpetuated by the Jacobin Revolution. The oppressive policies of Haile Selassie I in language matters were directly inspired by the model formulated by the French state through various exponents.

4. A particularly sharp echo of this can be found in Dr Hagos Gebre Yesus' communication to the Fifth International Congress of Ethiopian Studies ('The Bankruptcy of the Ethiopian "Left": Meison – EPRP etc . . .' in *Modern Ethiopia from the Acession of Menilek II to the present*, Balkema, Rotterdam, 1980, pp. 447–457). Amongst others: 'The ideological cover for this programme of national self-hatred of these nihilistic groups is the alleged claim that Ethiopia is full of dozens of full-fledged nations, *not* nationalities. Starting from this false assertion, they proclaim their anarchist position according to which the so-called fullfledged nations must separate. This politics of separatism is then dressed up as the principle of self-determination . . .' (p. 456).

LANGUAGE, NATIONAL CONSCIOUSNESS AND IDENTITY — THE SOMALI EXPERIENCE

Hussein M. Adam

This paper offers some brief reflections on national consciousness and identity focusing on the writing and modernization of the Somali language. The Somali language has played and continues to play a crucial role in the formulation of Somali identity, in the struggle for Somali self-determination, independence and unification. There is much to suggest that the use of written Somali since 1972 has indeed strengthened the content of Somali national consciousness.

The bases of national consciousness

The term 'nation' is generally used to denote a unit of population, having a common language, being associated with a certain territory, and possessing a common culture, history and traditions. Somalis manifest these general characteristics used to categorize 'nations'. They inhabit a certain fairly-defined geographical territory, share a common history and traditions. The practice of the same religion, Islam, provides an important ingredient of their common culture.

The Somali language constitutes a crucial element in Somali identity. Somalis speaking different dialects generally comprehend one another.[1] Linguists place the Somali language within the Afro-asiatic family, a member of the Cushitic sub-family or rather, the eastern branch of Cushitic which includes, among others, Aweera (Boni), Rendille, Afar, Saho, and Oromo (Galla).[2]

National consciousness generally implies a feeling of solidarity, an awareness of one's own identity, a 'we' versus 'them' attitude. As the Somali language developed as a separate language from a common ancestor it may have shared with Rendille and Aweera (Boni), we can assume that a people who referred to themselves as 'we', (Somali speakers) began to distinguish themselves from 'them', namely the Rendille, Aweera and others. Speaking Somali provided its speakers with a basis for an identity that separated them from the other inhabitants of the Horn who speak related eastern Cushitic languages. The linguistic factor is an important aspect of the process of national differentiation among the peoples of the Horn – especially since they tend to share common physical characteristics and, to some extent, traditions and customs.

The linguistic factor is also important in the historical assessment of the Arabic impact on Somali culture and society.[3] Islam, the Arabic language and culture have had a profound impact on the development of the Somali identity and nation. Nevertheless, historical evidence on Somali and related languages shows that the Somalis had already constituted themselves as a distinct people with a common language and traditions before assimilating Islam and the Arabic impact. Linguistic and other evidence suggests for example, that camel-keeping must have played an important role in the economy of Somali and related peoples for roughly 2,000 years; accordingly it was introduced much earlier than Islam.[4]

The Somali language, in short, helps to give the Somalis a sense of identity and national consciousness that sets them apart from other related peoples of the Horn as well as from the Arab peoples of the peninsula who have, through Islam, contributed much to the development of the Somali nation.

As already indicated, national consciousness was essentially the Somalis' feeling of solidarity, an awareness of their own identity, a 'we' versus 'them' attitude. Somalis, like other peoples, developed this sense of national consciousness as a result of struggles against 'others'. In the past, these struggles took the form of jihads against the Christian rulers of the Abyssinian Highlands who were periodically sending raiding parties to the coastal Islamic city-states of the Horn. These struggles were particularly intensive during the sixteenth century.

As is well-known, Britain, France, Italy and Ethiopia participated in the dismemberment of Somali territory, the division of its people and the imposition of colonial domination and boundaries in the last half of the nineteenth and the early part of this century. Every action has a reaction. The partition and colonization of Somali territory and people led to vigorous anti-colonial struggles which facilitated the further development of Somali national consciousness. This early form of Somali resistance to colonialism was led by Sayyid Muhammad Abdilleh Hassan (the so-called 'Mad Mullah') who fought the British, the Italians and the Abyssinians for twenty years.

The religious and proto-nationalist movement led by Sayyid was followed by the secular nationalist movement in the form of political parties after World War II. These parties helped to develop and expand the Somali language through political speech-making, mobilization and organization, slogans and the literature of protest. The nationalist parties raised the question of providiing Somali with a script. Certain elements within the main nationalist party, the Somali Youth League, (SYL), showed an interest in the 'Osmaniya' script (invented by Osman Yusaf Kenadid in 1920). Later on, others campaigned for the Arabic scripts and others for a modified version of the Latin script.[5] The problem was not resolved until 1972.

A nation is not merely a group of people who have certain characteristics in common. A nation is also a group of people who form a society, communicating with one another. The state of communications within society thus provides a useful indicator of whether national integration is taking place or whether it is possible at all. The Somali language traditionally provided Somalis with an effective means of oral communication. Oral poetry has historically been highly developed and esteemed. Some of this poetry reflected poetic combats conducted by antagonistic lineages.[6] Clan and lineage antagonisms do not preclude a will to unite or a feeling of common destiny, especially with regard to the common foe. Somali (tribal) genealogies serve both to distinguish clan-families and clans and, at the same time, to remind them all of common ancestry.

Nomadic movements, a long tradition of urban connections and the existence of Somali sailors and travellers strengthened the extent of oral communication among the Somalis.[7] The introduction of the radio and Somali broadcasters (in Somalia and abroad) played a crucial role in expanding oral communication. Even before the advent of written Somali, Somali broadcasters pioneered the expression of new concepts and ideas while avoiding foreign borrowings as far as possible.[8]

In 1960 the former Italian and British Somalilands attained independence and joined to form the Somali Republic. In spite of oral communication strengthened by radio broadcasting, the lack of a script for Somali created obstacles to efficient administration. The inability to adopt a script for Somali plagued the various regimes that ruled Somalia between 1960 and 1969. This is one of the factors that prompted the military coup and coming to power of the Supreme Revolutionary Council (SRC) on 21 October, 1969. On 21 October, 1972, the SRC fulfilled one of its major pledges by adopting a modified version of the Latin script. The implementation of written Somali in various spheres of public life gave greater content to the rudimentary notion of Somali consciousness, namely the simple feeling of solidarity, the awareness of identity, strengthening the 'we' versus 'them' attitude.

From oral to written Somali

Three months after the adoption of a script, written Somali officially replaced English and Italian which, until then, had been the administrative languages of the country. The decisive implementation of written Somali in state administration also challenged the language to develop a suitable vocabulary and style to cover all aspects of life: politics, law, education, economics, sociology, culture, science and technology. In the creation of a new Somali vocabulary to meet modern needs, various methods have been applied. One utilizes the wide range and subtle distinctions potentially existing in everyday speech. Another draws upon traditional and archaic vocabulary to provide words and expressions to meet the new demands of modern economic, social and political change. Yet another technique employs, often in a combined form, old roots from both the general everyday speech and the more specialized vocabulary, to form new words. In addition borrowed words from Arabic, Italian and English are also adopted. Typical examples (kindly supplied by B. W. Andrzejewski) are:

agaasime 'manager' (a noun derived from the verb *agaasin* 'arrange', 'look after', usually applied to the care of flocks in the pastoral interior)

akadeemiye 'academy' (Italian *accedemia*)

aydiyoolojiyad 'ideology' (from English, but with a Somali nominal suffix)

bulsho 'society' (originally 'a group of young men living in a nomadic outer camp and looking after cattle or horses'; such groups were marked by a high degree of solidarity and egalitarianism in the sharing of both tasks and food)

culaysatam 'atomic weight' (*culays* 'heaviness', 'weight' and *atam* 'atom')

danab hayaan 'electric current' (originally *danab* 'thunderbolt' and *hayaan* 'migratory journey of a pastoralist nomadic village')

dhaqan 'culture' (originally 'a way of gaining livelihood and conducting the life of the community', 'a way of living')

goonigoosi 'monopoly' (*gooni* 'separateness' and *goosi* 'cutting something out or off for one's own use')

haydarojiin 'hydrogen' (English)

isle'eg saabley ah 'quadratic equation' (*isle'eg* 'equality', 'equation' and *saabley ah* 'one which has *saab*; *saab* is a basket frame for transporting water-vessels on camels, and its contours are of a parbolic shape like the graph of quadratic equations)

jalle 'comrade', 'citizen' (an egalitarian term of address, applied to both sexes, introduced since the Revolution; it is an archaic word which survived mainly in children's games, where it means 'team-mate')

kacaan 'revolution' (a new word formed from the root *kac* 'rise', 'wake up', which suggests both progress and awakening)

kulmis 'focus' [of a parabola] (in ordinary language 'meeting point')

manhaj 'educational curriculum' (Arabic)

madhxiye 'capacitor' (a new word formed from the verb *madhxi* 'store for future use')

qabaal 'ellipse' (in ordinary language 'wooden watering-trough', which is usually of elliptical shape when viewed from above)

suugaan 'literature' (an archaic word preserved only in proverbs and poems meaning 'a discursive or ornamental way of talking')

taxane 'matrix' (a new word derived from the verb *tax* 'arrange in a sequence')

tolayn 'nationalization' (a new word derived from *tol* 'bond of kinship solidarity' and the applicative suffix -ayn)

xeer ilaaliye 'attorney general' (*xeer* 'law', originally 'customary law' and *ilaaliye* 'he who guards', 'he who looks after')

At first officials tried to write letters, memos, reports and notices in a style that was purely imitative of English or Italian. This produced written material that sounded crude, often unintelligible. A natural reaction against this trend developed. A proper Somali administrative language began to develop; letters, officials reports and memos began to sound precise and pleasing. The 'oralism' of everyday Somali had to be eschewed, as well as the crude tone of foreign imitative styles. The need to save paper and ensure other practicalities, such as the efficient storage and retrieval of administrative records, obliges administrative languages to be as precise and to the point as possible. Such a conceptual exercise is not only beneficial in administrative spheres; it tends to bring positive influences in other fields of language use as well.

The modernized Somali language reaches its peak of succinctness and precision in the field of science and mathematics. Let us take as an example the following statement in a textbook of physics for secondary schools concerning the application of Ohm's law:

Danab hayaanka maraya mareegta dhan ee ay ka mid tahay isha danabku wuxu saamigal qumman ku yahay xoog danab wadaha isha danabka, wuxuna saamigal isweydaar ah ku yahay caabbiga mareegta dhan.

(*Fisigiska*, Dugsiga sare III, p. 143)

'The electric current which passes through the whole circuit, including the source of current, is in direct proportion to the electromotive force of that source, but in inverse proportion to the resistance of the whole circuit.'

In a similar vein is the following statement found in a handbook of mathematics:

Taxane waa teed laydi oo ka kooban m dhinactax iyo n joogtax oo tirooyin maangal ah. Taxane waxaa aalaaba lagu muujiya tibixda m X n; m waxay u taagantahay inta dinactax ee taxanuhu leeyahay, n inta joogtax ee taxanuhu leeyahay. Haddii m = n, taxanaha waxa la yiraahdaa Taxana Labajibbaarane ah. Taxane waxa lagu dhex laba bilood ama laba sakal.

(*Xisaab*, Dugsiga Sare III, p. 327)

'A matrix is a rectangular array composed of the column m and the row n, which consist of rational numbers. Usually a matrix is represented by the expression m X n; m stands for the number [of figures] in the column and n stands for the number [of figures] in the row. If m = n the matrix is called a Square Matrix. A matrix is enclosed between two parentheses or two brackets.'

The examples given above are typical and could be multiplied *ad infinitum*.

National Language and political participation

Written Somali has proved efficient in communication both within and between ministries and agencies. It has also helped to reduce the former gap between the State and the public. Ordinary Somalis are now able to read and understand government regulations, legal documents, and financial transactions that affect their lives. They are able to participate in court procedures without the bothersome mediation of interpreters. Somali is now used not only in administrative communications, but also in the running of various training courses for public officials.[9] Lower level training programmes utilize Somali to a considerable extent. Middle level training programmes often use Somali lectures and also training material in foreign languages (English or Italian). In higher level training programmes (as well as in university education) foreign languages are still used, sometimes with interpretation into Somali depending on the background of the students involved.

Measures have been taken to ensure relatively greater public participation in the decision-making process, especially at local levels. The decentralization law (1974) increased the number of regions from eight to sixteen and the number of districts from 47 to 81. Representatives of workers, women and youth began to participate in local commissions to oversee various state functions – justice, security, health and sanitation, social and educational matters and economic matters such as the fair allocation and distribution of commodities that had become scarce as a result of the current international economic crisis. In the distribution of sugar for example, the system of popular self-management has shown itself to be fairly effective in spite of serious deficiencies in transportation and accounting. There is an effective system of popular juries all over the Republic. Worker committees were established in 1973 to participate in production affairs as well as labour disputes.

All this would have been an empty and futile exercise without the use of written Somali. The oral use of Somali is not sufficient to assure the meaningful process described. Written Somali is necessary in recording minutes of meetings, in matters involving correspondence, filling up forms, recording financial transactions, and drafting legal and other proposals. There is, therefore, an objective process facilitating the radical development of the Somali language, Somali identity and national consciousness. A recent example is provided by the process followed in the adoption of the new national constitution, with provision for a national assembly and related local representative bodies. Prior to the national referendum on the constitution meetings were held throughout the Republic during which the participants read aloud in Somali and discussed each article of the new constitution. This was, to a large extent, a remarkable exerise in mass education involving constitutional terms and concepts such as sovereignty, equality of citizens, fundamental rights and duties of citizens, the organs of state power etc. This contrasts sharply with the previous exercise involved in adopting the 1961 independence constitution. The final provision of that constitution stated: 'Until the proclamation of the results of the referendum, the text of the constitution shall be posted at town halls and at the offices of the District Commissioners of the Republic so that every citizen may become acquainted with it.'[10] Obviously not many citizens could possibly become acquainted with such limited copies in English and Italian. Yet they were urged to vote for a document whose contents were completely alien.

Further progress in securing popular participation naturally depends on raising the general cultural, technical and political awareness of the Somali people. This task requires a planned long-range educational and cultural revolution involving wide-scale literacy campaigns. This would permit educational socialization in the national language thereby strengthening Somali identity and national consciousness.

On 8 March, 1973, a National Literacy Campaign was launched. This campaign focused on the urban areas, operating on the basis of the self-help principle. The Ministry of Education reports that as a result of this urban campaign 400,000 persons were taught the new alphabet. On 1 August, 1974 a major Rural Development campaign was launched. The importance attached to the campaign was underlined by the fact that schools were closed for one academic year to permit the full-scale mobilization of teachers and students in the campaign. On the whole, 1,757,779 persons of whom 597,665 were women, participated in the urban and rural literacy campaigns. Somalia claims today a literacy rate of over 60%.

The struggle now is to prevent the relapse into illiteracy by organizing functional education programmes for adults on a permanent basis. It is also important to insure wider distribution of newspapers and other publications as a necessary supplement. The Ministery of Information prints a daily paper, *Xiddigta Oktoobar* (The October Star) as well as various books and pamphlets. The Somali Revolutionary Socialist Party (SRSP, established since 1976) puts out a monthly organ *Halgan* (3,500 copies in Somali and 1,500 in English). Various educational institutions, local bodies, social organizations, ministries and agencies issue books, pamphlets and various occasional publications.

In the large new settlements that were established for the victims of the 1974 drought, it is possible to continue the literacy campaign on a more permanent basis. By 1976, these settlements had rudimentary schools and other cultural facilities. The National Adult Education Center had printed functional literacy booklets geared to the needs of nomadic livestock herders, farmers, fishermen and craftsmen.

Language Literature and education

In most societies, formal schooling is an important institution for transmitting knowledge and culture from generation to generation and for developing traits that contribute to national identity, social stability, economic output and the production of new knowledge. The adoption of written Somali has permitted a vast expansion of schools. 55,000 students were enrolled in all schools during the year 1969–1970. By 1976, school enrolment jumped to 240,500. In 1980 school enrolment reached over half a million.

Utilizing Somali in primary, intermediate and secondary schools, has necessitated the preparation and printing of Somali books covering various school subjects: arithmetic, algebra, geometry, chemistry, biology, physics, history, geography, language, literature and technical, vocational subjects. By 1976, 135 textbooks had been produced for various school subjects. By 1976 over six million copies of Somali books had been printed for schools and the general public.

As we had mentioned above, Somali literature had developed advanced oral forms. New literary forms such as novels, short stories, written drama and poetry have emerged as a result of the introduction of a written form for Somali.[11] The emergence of written Somali has also given Somali art – especially poster art – a needed boost. Between 1969–1972, political art appeared but the slogans accompanying the art had to be in English or Italian. The use of written Somali slogans has facilitated the creation of posters which are often amusing, striking and informative. The Somali slogans accompanying them are very useful for thousands of people who are just beginning to read and write and to enjoy their mother tongue proudly displayed in written form. Characteristic examples are as follows:

Fartaada ha qorin waa filkaaga ka har.
'Not using one's own system of writing means being left behind by one's peers'.

Haddaad taqaan bar, haddaanad aqoon baro.
'If you know [how to read and write] – teach it, if you don't – learn it'.

Qof wax aqoon waa qof kala dhiman, qof wax yaqaanna waa qof dhan.
'A person who is ignorant is an incomplete person, a person who has knowledge is complete'.

Dadweynaha wax yaqaan uun baa dantiisa garan kara daba-deedna gaari kara.
'Only a community which has knowledge can understand its interests and can succeed in securing them'.

Aqoon uun baa hantiwadaag kuu geysa.
'Only knowledge can lead you to socialism'.

To a great extent, however, literary efforts are being devoted to the task of writing down already existing oral poems, narratives, proverbs and other aspects of oral folklore. Efforts have also been given to the task of translating foreign literary works into Somali. Works already translated include:
Ein gute Mensch von Sezuan by Bertolt Brecht, *Robinson Crusoe* by Daniel Defoe and *The cat of Bubastes* by G. A. Henty.

Among the institutions involved in the task of modernizing Somali we may cite the Ministry of Higher Education and Culture which includes the Somali National University and the Somali Academy of Sciences and Arts. The College of Education of the National University has a Department of Somali Studies. The Academy has obtained numerous Somali manuscripts and has published over 30 books including two Somali language dictionaries. The Ministry of Education has the Curriculum Department charged with the task of preparing textbooks. It also supervises the National Adult Education Center which is charged with the task of organizing functional literacy programmes on a more continuing basis. The

Ministry of Information publishes newspapers, books, pamphlets and generally disseminates the Somali language and culture through the mass media and the cultural troupes it sponsors. The Ideological Bureau of the Party issues various publications as well as supervising the Party School whose curriculum requires the preparation of Somali language materials in the social sciences, and the translation of scientific socialist literature. Certain external institutions, such as the BBC and the School of African and Oriental Studies London must be mentioned as assisting, at least indirectly, in the task of modernizing and propagating Somali.

As we pointed out before, a nation is not merely a group of people who possess certain characteristics in common. The writing and modernizing of Somali has made the Somalis a people who constitute a society with rapidly developing means of communication. It has also assisted in narrowing the gaps between Somali dialects by providing one main 'Standard Dialect' in all mass media (radio and press) and in books and publications for the schools and for literacy campaigns. This represents the attainment of one of the long-frustrated objectives of the self-determination struggle.

The wider consequences of Somali literacy

Generally, Somalis living outside the Republic have viewed with pride the writing of their native language. The Western Somali Liberation Front has utilized written Somali in its campaigns (poster slogans etc) and its organizational and logistical efforts. To a limited extent, on account of the military situation, it has manifested its intention to promote mass literacy.

In Jibuti, the question of national languages has been shelved for the time being in order to defuse the previously antagonistic atmosphere between Somalis and Afars. Jibuti has opted, for the time being, for an official language policy including Arabic and French. Informally, a number of Somalis are learning to write and read their mother-tongue in Jibuti as well as in many parts of the Somali diaspora.[12]

Certain elements among the Afars have been impressed by the process of implementing written Somali and have manifested the desire to create a viable written form for their language. The developing drive for self-determination among the Oromos has similarly seen remarkable efforts aimed at writing and disseminating Oromo language publications. The self-determination struggles in the Horn involve actions in favour of the revival, resurgence, and propagation of national languages. The emergence of an African polity (Somalia) which relies extensively on its indigenous linguistic resources serves as a model for the Horn and Africa as a whole. The forms and practical aspects of applying such measures within other African contexts will naturally vary according to the circumstances.

It is, perhaps, valid to speculate that the consequences of writing and modernizing Somali have more immediate relevance to the Horn of Africa, an area of other Eastern Cushitic language and where we witness intensive struggles for national self-determination. The rendering of Somali in written form, the way the words, phrases and sentences are written in Somali, the preparation of mathematics and science books, the method of creation of new Somali vocabulary to meet modern needs – these are but some examples of immediate relevance to the other Eastern Cushitic languages. It has been argued that Somali linguistics has contributed to a general theory of human linguisitic capabilities.[13] Others have taken advantage of written Somali to decipher the linguistic structure of Somali poetry.[14] Again, perhaps these and other concrete, detailed consequences of writing Somali may prove of more direct relevance to the study, revival and propagation of the other Eastern Cushitic languages.

Meanwhile, the task of modernizing Somali continues. A great deal remains to be done. The quality of the textbooks prepared so far, for example, still leaves much to be desired. School textbooks of better quality and diversity have yet to be prepared. Printed books, pamphlets and newspapers have to be better distributed throughout the country and abroad. A more consistent foreign language policy with regard to the University, higher education, training and advanced research, has to be formulated and implemented in a planned, systematic manner. Printing facilities have to be improved and expanded etc.

Nevertheless, the writing and modernizing of the language has facilitated national integration, and it has strengthened Somali identity while giving a more meaningful content to national consciousness. These achievements serve as an inspiration for others struggling for self-determination and the modernization of their national languages.

Notes

1. The most differentiated traditional dialect is that spoken in the Baidoa region of southern Somalia.
2. Bernd Heine, 'The Sa Languages: A History of Rendille, Boni and Somali' *Afroasiatic Linguistics* 6, 2 (1978); H. S. Lewis 'The Origins of the Galla and Somali', *Journal of African History* 7 (1966); See also Harold C. Fleming, 'Baiso and Rendille: Somali Outliers', *Rassegna di Studi Etiopici* 20 (1964)
3. Bernd Hein, 'Linguistic Evidence on the Early History of the Somali People', in *Somalia and the World : Proceedings of the International Symposium Held in Mogadishu, October 15-21, 1979*, ed. Hussein M. Adam, (Mogadishu: Halgan Editorial Board, 1980) 23-33. See also Ali Abdarahman Hersi, *The Arab Factor in Somali History* UCLA PhD 1977.
4. Bernd Heine, *Ibid.*, pp. 30-31.

5. Hussein M. Adam, *A Nation in Search of a Script* (MA Thesis, Makerere University College, Kampala, Uganda 1968). See also David D. Laitin, *Politics, Language and Thoughht - The Somali Experience*, Chicago: University of Chicago Press, 1977.
6. B. W. Andrzejewski and Muuse H. I. Galaal, 'A Somali Poetic Combat', *Journal of African Languages*, ii, (1963) part 1, pp. 15–28, part 2, pp. 93–196, part 3, pp. 190–205.
7. B. W. Andrzejewski, 'The Art of the Verbal Message in Somali Society'. Pages 29–39 in J. Lucas (ed) *Neue-Afrikanistische Studien*, Hamburg: Deutsches Institut fur Afrika-Forschung, 1966.
8. B. W. Andrzejewski, 'The Role of Broadcasting in the Adaptation of the Somali Language to Modern Needs'. Pages 263–273 in W. H. Whiteley (Ed) *Language Use in Social Change: Problems of Multilingualism with special reference to Eastern Africa* London: Oxford University Press, 1971.
9. Hussein M. Adam, 'The Revolutionary Development of the Somali Language' in H. M. Adam (Ed) *Somalia: Revolutionary Transformations* (Mogadishu: First Halgan Publication, 1979). Republished and expanded as Hussein M. Adam and Charles L. Geshekter, *The Revolutionary Development of the Somali Language*, Occasional Paper No 20 (Los Angeles: African Studies Centre, University of California, 1980) pp. 33.
10. *The Constitution of the Somali Republic* (Mogadishu: State Printing Press, 1963)
11. B. W. Andrzejewski, 'The rise of Written Somali Literature', *African Research and Documentation* No 8/9, 1975.
12. Mohamed Hassan, 'Consequences of the Modernization of Somali for the People of Jibuti', paper presented at the International Symposium on Somalia. (1979)
13. Joseph Pia, 'Contribution of Somali Linguistics to a General Theory of Human Linguistic Capabilities', paper presented at the International Symposium on Somalia.
14. Mohamed Haashi Dhamac (Gaarife), Abdullahi Dirie, John Johnson and Francesco Antinucci. See Abdullahi Dirie. 'The Scansion of Somali Poetry' in *Somalia and the World: Proceedings of the International Symposium Held in Mogadishu, October 15–21, 1979*, ed. Hussein M. Adam, (Mogadishu: Halgan Editorial Board, 1980) pp. 132–140; John Johnson, 'Recent Contributions by Somalis and Somalists to the Study of Oral Literature', *Ibid*, pp. 117–131; and F. Antinucci 'Notes on the Linguistic Structure of Somali Poetry', *Ibid*, pp. 141–153.

SELF-DETERMINATION AS AN INTERNATIONAL ISSUE

Hakan Wiberg

The Norm

'All peoples have the right to self-determination; by virtue of that right they freely determine their political status and freely pursue their economic, social and cultural development'[1]

This norm today enjoys international consensus, being recognized as a legal norm and no state having officially made any explicit objections to it. As in so many other cases, this consensus is largely due to a considerable degree of ambiguity. This chapter is devoted to the history, theory and practice of the norm.

Self-determination in History

If we define nationality by language, the contemporary world contains very approximately 1,500 nations, 150 states, and 15 nation states, in a restricted interpretation of the latter phrase.[2] Even with a less restrictive definition, the nation state is a rather local and rather recent phenomenon. To illustrate the first fact, let us take as an index of ethnic homogeneity of a state the probability that two randomly chosen citizens have the same mother tongue. The distribution of homogenous states over continents is given in Table One.[3]

Table 1. *Ethnic homogeneity by continent: percentages of nations.*

Quartile	Homogeneity: Index range	Europe	Africa	Asia+ Oceania	America	World
First	.90 and over	52	9	16	31	25
Second	.60 – .89	27	12	39	38	27
Third	.30 – .59	17	30	29	27	26
Fourth	under .30	3	49	16	4	22
Sum		99	100	100	100	100
(Number of states)		(29)	(43)	(31)	(26)	(129)

By whatever measure we choose, the most homogeneous states (on this dimension of ethnicity) are found in Europe, the average homogeneity being lower in the Americas, still lower in Asia and Oceania and very low in Africa. To see the historial recency of the nation state, let us concentrate on the first quartile of the table, containing 32 states (ie a quarter of all states). When we exclude those whose majority language is also an official language of some other state with at least a million inhabitants, we are left with exactly a dozen: Poland, Norway, Italy, Burundi, Iceland, Denmark, Madagascar, Sweden, Somalia, Malta, Albania, Hungary and Greece. *Not a single one of these existed in its present shape as a sovereign state around 1800 AD.*[4] In addition, only a small minority of the remaining homogeneous states in the quartile existed as such at that time either.

The political idea of the nation state and of national self-determination is also largely a child of the nineteenth century, its parents being the emancipatory and democratic ideas of the Enlightenment and the metaphysical conception of nationhood prevailing in Romanticism.[5] To interpret older historical developments in the light of that idea is rather misleading: if one may see a red line of struggle for self-determination in milennia of history, it has to be kept in mind that the self-determination involved was typically that of rulers, rather than peoples, legitimized in dynastic or religious or other ideological terms, not in democratic or modern nationalist ones.[6]

Even so, it might be tempting to see the last two centuries or so as a march of triumph for the idea of national self-determination; but that, too, would be so schematic as to be close to meaningless, and the reservations are obvious. The revolutions in the Americas were mainly carried out by settlers from the metropoles rebelled against, who were at the same time engaged in colonizing indigenous peoples. During the century after the liberation of Latin America, Western colonialism swallowed Africa and Asia almost entirely. And even in Europe, after the unification of Italy and Germany and a contraction of the Ottoman empire around the middle of the century, it is only in the second decade of the twentieth century that the 'Herder programme' of a state for each people had any new successes; the ideological banner here being waved by Woodrow Wilson with much misgivings from the British and the French, who managed to stop the idea of national self-determination from being explicitly established as a legal principle in the Covenant of the League of Nations.[7] These misgivings proved prophetically correct – half a century later, only isolated remnants remained of the Western empires, national self-determination had made great advances, and finally been given legal status by the United Nations. At the same time, the spread of the idea had gone beyond emancipation from traditional colonialism to peoples inside existing states in many countries in all continents claiming more rights.

To avoid a lengthy philosophical treatise, let us just submit that there are two naïve mistakes to make in analysing the relationships between political idea and actual changes: to see the ideas as *causes* of the changes, and to see them as entirely epiphenomenal to changes taking place anyhow through other causes. Ideas are important factors among others, whose relative weight must be assessed in specific cases or groups of cases, rather than in blanket terms. To go beyond this somewhat bland statement, let us indicate two different ways in which the idea of national self-determination has been destructive to Western colonialism. First, it has spread rapidly, mixed and merged with ideas from other cultures to contribute to idealogies of liberation all over the world.[8] Second, it has made legitimation of colonialism more and more difficult, being in manifest contradiction to it, so that *ad hoc* justifications had to be produced, in terms of 'backwardness', 'political immaturity', etc, carrying decreasing conviction and eventually getting abandoned, too, as the idea of self-determination became more entrenched by achieving legal status. Since both international law and political ideas are today in a flux, we may expect that the legal formulations of the idea will rapidly lose their political relevance, the political content moving in directions that will ultimately call for new legal considerations. Before discussing this, let us attempt to delimit the legal status today of the principle of national self-determination.

Self-determination: Legal Aspects

We have already mentioned that it is only after World War II that the norm of national self-determination is laid down as a legal principle. In addition to the formulation cited above, we find several very similar ones in resolutions from the General Assembly or the Security Council of the United Nations.[9] One of the variations is that instead of 'peoples' we sometimes find 'peoples and nations'. In addition, we find a great number of resolutions from the General Assembly, where the right to self-determination has been reaffirmed in concrete terms, as well as similar resolutions from the security council concerning, eg, former Southern Rhodesia, Namibia, the Republic of South Africa and territories formerly under Portuguese administration.[10]

What, then, does all this mean? And what does it mean to ask what it means? To take the second, and more fundamental, question first, how we are to interpret the key terms in the norm quoted very much depends on what we are going to use the answer for: a treatise in social science, a political polemic, a legal discourse, etc – and there is no reason to assume that the same answers are meaningful in the different contexts. Even if we limit ourselves to a legal discourse, this may ramify in two different directions, depending on whether we take a more positivist or a more rationalist stand, or crudely put, whether we investigate how different organs *actually* interpret the norm or how, according to some logic or standard of interpretation, it ought to be interpreted. Let us therefore tackle the pertinent issues one by one.

3.1. What is a people?

Let us start by presenting the three main candidates for definitions of 'people' or 'nation'. One of them, perhaps the most traditional one, makes the very concept superfluous: 'the totality of persons born or naturalized in a country and living under a single government'[11]. With this definition, the set of 'peoples' or 'nations' in the world will coincide with the set of states (at least when colonialism is completely abolished). If, instead, we make the relationship with states an open empirical question, there remain two main types of definitions, one subjective and one objective. The latter may be exemplified by saying that by a people is meant a population that constitutes a nation by some combination of such objective but personal criteria as common language, common culture, common race, common religion, etc. One main problem with this type of definition is that it does not appear possible to lay down any single criterion or any single combination of criteria which appears relevant everywhere, if 'relevant' is defined in terms of, *inter alia*, subjective collective identifications. In some cases, state loyalties override differences in several dimensions, in other cases they do not. In some parts of the world, differences in religion make two different peoples of a group with the same language, in others differences in language make people of the same religion identify themselves as different nations.

Nor are the criteria as 'objective' as they may appear. In areas where 'race' is defined as important, the line may be drawn between the 'lilywhite' and the rest, as in the traditional south of USA, or between the 'coal black' and the rest, as in parts of the Caribbean. When we deal with languages of the same family, it may often appear arbitrary what pairs of tongues are counted as different dialects of the same language, and what are counted as two different languages; and 'arbitrary' here means that the lines are often drawn on political rather than linguistic grounds, hence not 'objectively' in the intended sense.

Furthermore, unless we make habitat one of the objective criteria, we may well find situations where a 'people', as defined by some combination of objective criteria does not form the majority of the population in any connected geographical area, or even in any area at all.

If objective definitions entail some problems, this is also the case for a more subjective definition, say, eg, that a people is a group of persons that identify themselves as a people distinct from other peoples, on whatever basis they do it. As in the case of various objective definitions, this leaves us with categories whose size of dispersion appears to exclude independent statehood, or even other forms of forming a political unit.

If we set ourselves the task of interpreting the norm of self-determination, that imposes limits on what definitions are relevant and what are not. It appears, however, that no legal document lays down any generally accepted definition of 'people'. One of the most recent major treatises on national self-determination[12], states that:

'(i)   The term 'people' denotes a social entity possessing a clear identity and its own characteristics

(ii)   It implies a relationship with a territory, even if the people in question has been wrongfully expelled from it and artificially replaced by another population

(iii) A people should not be confused with ethnic, religious or linguistic minorities, whose existence and rights are recognized in article 27 of the International Covenant on Civil and Political Rights.'

These statements, taken together, hardly constitute a definition in any sense of that word which would satisfy a logician. It may rather be said that it lays down some criteria of adequacy that any legal definition must satisfy, and it then becomes interesting what it does and what it does not exclude. Thus, it appears that defining the citizens of any state as a people is perfectly consistent with all three conditions, apart from the ambiguity of 'identity'. In fact, the question is whether any other definition is entirely consistent with the three criteria taken together. For even if a group is clearly identitified and in addition equally clearly territorial, condition (iii) might be used to relegate it from being a 'people' to being a 'minority', having no valid claims to self-determination. This depends on where we draw the line between 'people' and 'minority', on which the cited paragraph 27 does not enlighten us; nor does any other legally binding definition appear to exist. In practice, however, the 'state' connotation of 'people' seems rather strong in legal thinking, at least when manifested in verdicts and resolutions. One indication of this is the clause that tends to follow formulations of the right to national self-determination in many contexts, stating that nothing in that principle

'shall be construed as authorizing or encouraging any action which would dismember or impair, totally or in part, the territorial integrity or political unity of sovereign and independent States conducting themselves in compliance with the principle of equal rights and self-determination of peoples as described above and thus possessed of a government representing the whole people belonging to the territory without distinction as to race, creed and colour. Every State shall refrain from any action aimed at the partial or total disruption of the national unity and territorial integrity of any other State or country.'[13]

It would, however, be too strong an interpretation to say that 'state' and 'people' are treated as synonymous. The quotation indicates that in some circumstances, inhabitants in a sovereign state may be regarded as forming more than one people, and this had also been explicity affirmed in cases with, eg, openly racist restrictions in enfranchisement.

Another way of formulating the question is by means of the term 'non-self-governing territory', which subsumes, *inter alia*, colonies, mandates and trust territories. Some clarification is provided in the Annex of Resolution (1541) (XV) of the General Assembly, which indicates that *prima facie* evidence of that status of a territory exists if it 'is geographically separate and is distinct ethnically and/or culturally from the country administering it' (principle IV), and adds that once this is established other elements may be brought into consideration, which may be 'inter alia, of an administrative, political, juridical, economic or historical nature', where the crucial issue is whether 'they affect the relationship between the metropolitan State and the territory concerned in a manner which arbitrarily places the latter in a position or status of subordination' (Principle V).

There has been considerable controversy after World War II as to how to make the definitions called for. At one end of the spectrum, we find the early position of the colonial powers, sometimes referred to as the 'Belgian thesis', to the effect that there are many cases of 'internal colonization' of peoples inside a state boundary, and at the other pole the position, also called the 'salt water theory of colonialism', according to which only overseas possessions count.[14] In the United Nations, where the 'Belgian thesis' – with considerable justification – was seen as an attempt to obstruct the struggle against colonialism, the latter interpretation has prevailed, both in the important general resolutions (eg 1514 (XV)), and in specific applications. One may see the case of Bangladesh as an indication of this. It appears difficult to find interpretations of the crucial phrases, in which it would not be seen as geographically separate and ethnically distinct from West Pakistan, in addition to which several authors have argued the existence of internal colonialism[15] – and yet no UN support was forthcoming for its self-determination; in fact, it had to wait for years for membership after *de facto* independence. From a political point of view, this is what to expect. A considerable majority of the members of the UN have a vested interest in not allowing interpretations according to which the relations between nationalities inside a state boundary would be open to international criticism in legal or other 'official' forms.

On the other hand, if the principle of self-determination has undergone changes in the past, we should also expect that changes will continue to emerge. For one thing, with a few more changes in political geography in the world, including achievement of self-determination in Southern Africa, Palestine, and a few remnants of European colonialism, at least one major argument against the 'Belgian thesis' would become obsolete, and it might be more possible for the United Nations to deal with other forms of national subjugation. Also, the fact that the vast majority of wars since 1945 have been fought inside the territory of one single country[16] might bring the United Nations to seek increasing competance in dealing with at least some types of – in this sense – internal conflicts, given that – in another sense – they are *not* internal: most of them involve some form of armed foreign intervention, with or without legal pretext.

3.2. When and how does this right to national self-determination apply?

If we go by an interpretation of international law in terms of how it has been applied, it appears that the only body that can have the right to self-determination is a Non-self-governing Territory; and that in this category it is only possible to be included either by being under some form of formal colonial rule, or by being subjected to explicit and legal racism or similar forms of political discrimination, or by being under military occupation. Several resolutions concerning remaining European and United States colonies and dependencies illustrate the first point, those concerning different parts of Southern Africa the second point, and some resolutions concerning Palestine appear relevant to both the second and third points. In no single case do we find resolutions from the United Nations about concrete cases of any other type than these three.

Normally, the entire population of the territory classified as Non-self-governing is taken to be the subject of self-determination, so that smaller parts of the population are not seen as having such a right. The will of the entire population is to be found out, by investigations, by elections or by referendum. Administrative changes that have been made by colonial powers are usually not accepted, if they can be construed as aiming at 'balkanization'.[17] There have been some exceptions here: Ruanda-Urundi, British Cameroons, and to some extent British Togoland – but in all these cases existing administrative boundaries were taken into account. It should be added that the population entitled to self-determination does not necessarily consist precisely of the population living in the territory. It may also incluse people attached to the territory who have been evicted from it and presently live as refugees, the most notable example being the Palestinians.[18]

When does right apply? The legal answer appears to be 'once and for all'. Once the right has been exercised by a Non-self-governing territory, whatever the decision arrived at, it cannot be resuscitated as such, but is transformed into 'equal rights of nations' (which in this context clearly means 'states'). It should be noted that this does not mean that implemented mechanisms for such decisions are always recognized. Thus the United Nations, having taken upon itself the competence to decide what is and what is not a Non-self-governing Territory, on several occasions refused to recognize referenda (Gibraltar and Djibouti) or elections (Namibia and Zimbabwe) as proofs that the right to self-determination had been exercised. Nor have the Bantustans in South Africa been recognized as independent states.[19]

There are three ways, or have so far been three ways, of exercising the right to self-determination. The most common by far is the transformation of the Non-self-governing Territory into an independent and sovereign state. The second possibility, integration with an already existing state, is exemplified by a few cases of enclaves in Africa and India,[20] by Sabah and Sarawak joining Malaysia, by British Togoland and Cameroons, and a few other cases. The third way, finally, association with an existing state, is mainly exemplified in some cases of previous colonies, mainly in the early postwar period. Whereas, theoretically, the right to self-determination would include the possibility to revise such associations, there has so far been no case of the issue being reopened, even if attempts have been made, eg in the case of Puerto Rico.[21]

Summing this section up, we are bound to arrive at a 'pessimistic'[22] conclusion in so far as we judge the position of international law by the record of the United Nations.[23] It has little support to offer populations living inside the territories of recognized sovereign states, when they strive for independence or autonomy. We have already referred to the fate of Bangladesh, which is also the only postwar case of post facto recognition of a successful rebellion against anything else than a colonial power (in the traditional sense). Temporarily successful rebellions have never been recognized in any form, with the possible exception of some resolutions on Tibet,[24] and they have on occasions been actively counteracted by the United Nations, most notably in Katanga.

But then, it is questionable whether the UN action in Congo can be taken as any indication of what is the position of international law, especially since both France and the Soviet Union refused to contribute to the Congo operation, arguing that it was not legal. Generally speaking, rebellion, whether civilian or armed, falls outside the scope of international law, thus being in itself neither forbidden nor permitted, unless specific circumstances obtain. Thus, whereas rebellion is neither legal nor illegal, certain types of aid to rebels by foreign powers is illegal. Furthermore, the United Nations have long recognized the right of peoples under colonial rule to use force in their struggle for liberation, and thereby also the right of third party states to assist such liberation movements, without this being considered interference in the domestic affairs of the colonial power.[25] Hence, the second principle overrides the first one in colonial cases. It is less clear what the situation is in other cases of domination. Thus, Resolution 2649 (XXV) of the General Assembly in Article 1 'affirms the legitimacy of the struggle of peoples under colonial and alien domination recognized as being entitled to the right of self-determination to restore to themselves that right by any means at their disposal'.[26] There is, however, no general definition of the concept of alien domination; but it has been applied to Rhodesia, Namibia, South Africa and Palestine, that is, cases which come fairly close to colonial situations in the traditional sense.

As we have already indicated, it seems unlikely that the United Nations will go beyond this class of cases, until these cases have ceased to exist as such. Whether such a hypothetical situation would lead to a change in legal positions must be left as an open question, even if most extrapolations from the present situation appear to point to a No.

Marxism, Leninism and Self-determination

Apart from international law, there are other bodies of thought which have been invoked in discussions about national self-determination. We have already cursorily referred to some trends in 'Western' thinking. In this section, we will deal with the Marxist tradition, especially in its Marxist–Leninist ramifications.

There are, of course, several reasons to devote particular attention to Marxism and Marxism–Leninism here. The issue of national self-determination is one of long standing in this tradition, being hotly debated already at the beginning of the century. Some of the states where Marxism–Leninism is the dominant body of thought, at least in political terms, have for a long time appeared as champions of the struggle against colonialism and imperialism, usually allying themselves in the United Nations with the 'Third World' on these issues. Still, critics of Soviet as well as of Chinese foreign policy have often pointed out that there appears to be some distance between theory and practice. Likewise, the positions of

Communist parties in imperial powers, eg France, have sometimes left colonized peoples, like those in Algeria and in Indochina, bitterly disappointed.

The understanding of Marxism–Leninism becomes particularly interesting in the case of the Horn of Africa, where several of the actors profess to be guided by it: the USSR, the Ethiopian and Somalian governments, and the two major Eritrean movements. The Soviet Union, which once voted in the United Nations for Eritrean independence, is today supporting the Ethiopian government against the Eritrean movements – after supporting at least the ELF against Addis Ababa until a few years ago. Much of the polemics between the Ethiopian government and the ELF and the EPLF is couched in Marxist–Leninist terms, as well as some of the criticism that the Eritrean movements direct at the Soviet Union.

What, then, is the stand of Marxism–Leninism on national self-determination? To what extent does there exist some systematic and permanent position, leading to different conclusions when applied to different situations, and to what extent do we find mere opportunism?

Before pronouncing any judgments on this, we have to underline that the issue has always been a secondary one for the classics in the Marxist–Leninist tradition as well as for their modern successors – at least in the sense that it is never given priority over the class struggle, nor seen as possible to isolate from it.[27] Hence, the issues concerning national self-determination are seen to depend on several other things, such as the position and strategy of the class struggle, the character of the state, and economic and other ties between the imperial metropolis and other areas. In concrete issues, we find some of the classics – Engels, Lenin, Stalin – changing their minds over time. We also find considerable divergencies of opinion in the early Marxist debate in the period around World War I. Furthermore, we have to keep in mind that much of this classical debate concerned specific situations, where there was a strong need for making rapid decisions with wide-ranging political implications. The summary that follows therefore makes no pretence of doing justice to all the stands and arguments in that long and complicated debate, but mainly depicts Lenin's later positions, since it is these that have come to form the theoretical core of latter-day Marxism–Leninism.

To put it very crudely, Lenin is for the *right* to separation, and asserts it concretely in the cases of Poland, Finland, Armenia, etc. This does not mean that he is for *separation*. More concretely, he argues that the correct line for the *Russian* party to take is to underline and support the right for other parts of the empire to self-determination, including secession. At the same time, the correct line for the Polish and other parties to take was to aim at the unity of the oppressed classes in all countries, and in particular in all parts of the Russian empire.

To make this less paradoxical, we have to add one hidden premise and one tactical concern. The premise is that once the revolution has succeeded in the Russian empire, it is not expected that the proletariat will opt for secession, since nationalism is seen as a bourgeois ideology. The tactical concern is to avoid making the Russian party vulnerable to accusations of supporting the chauvinism of Tsarist Russia. Hence it makes sense to support the right to secession, hoping that it will not be made use of. This hope, however, turned out to be in vain.[28]

There is a strong centralist and 'statist' line in Lenin's thinking, and even more so in later Marxism–Leninism. Only nationalities with a clear territorial base and a certain size are recognized as possible candidates for self-determination, including secession. The much-debated notion of 'cultural autonomy' is rejected as weakening the – socialist – state. The stand taken on federation is also a pragmatic one. When there already exist cleavages between different nationalities, federation is seen as a possible way of bridging the cleavages, and hence as an advantageous alternative to defining the situation as a choice between unity and dissolution. In other cases, schemes of federation should be avoided, since they carry risks for the strength of the socialist state.

Let us now specifically return to the issue whether the policy of the USSR in the Horn of Africa has been opportunist or not. The answer must be that this very much depends on how we define the terms. If we look for a stand on, eg, Eritrean independence, that is not affected by changing political developments in the area, including changing relationships to the Soviet Union, then the verdict must obviously be one of opportunism. But then this is a way of asking the question that in a sense contains the answer. To state this, we do not have to accept the almost ecclesiastical self-image of coherence and permanence of the doctrine projected by the Soviet leadership. It is quite enough to point out that according to the doctrine, national issues *must* be seen in relationship to the class struggle, the character of the state and economic realities.

Hence, Soviet behaviour must be related to Soviet perceptions of various facts and tendencies. What actors represent what classes? What is the class character of what state or movement in the area? What will be the objective consequences of what actions? But then, this may be putting the cart before the horse, since there are at least two possibilities to account for the seeming fact that these perceptions very rarely clash with official Soviet foreign policy. We may, of course, choose to believe that this policy is 'scientific' in the sense of being guided by specific information in addition to general tenets, which would be rather misleading to term 'opportunism'. The alternative is to assume that officially held perceptions are changed so as to fit with changes in the policy, so that there is a 'primacy of foreign policy' – and the perceptions opportunistic, as it were. As a key to understanding motives and strategies of the behaviour of the USSR in this area and elsewhere, the latter alternative appears more fruitful.

The Extreme Case: Emergence and Loss of Statehood

Attempts of a people or a group of peoples at controlling their own destiny may take many different forms, where the setting up of an independent state is an extreme case only. The creation of a new state can have many different backgrounds, popular struggle for national self-determination being merely one type. Thus, going through the creation – and occasional dissolution – of new states since 1815 can only give information on some aspects of national self-determination. Nevertheless, it appears worth while to see what generalizations can be made for a systematic data base.[29]

To start with, there are difficult definitional problems to solve when we attempt an analysis over such a great span of space and time. The notion of 'independent state' appears fairly clear-cut and easy to operationalize, when we deal with, eg, Europe today, but is very difficult to give a well-defined meaning when we study, say, Africa at the beginning of the nineteenth century. We have therefore taken over the notion of 'autonomous geopolitical unit' from our data base, which gives the definition that such a unit is one that satisfies the following three criteria:[30]

'a) its government maintains an autonomous military organization. A military organization shall be considered autonomous if it satisfies the following three conditions:

1) it is not subject to any authority acting as the representative of any other political unit

2) either it is not integrated into the command structure of any other military organization, or else its governments retains the legal right to withdraw its forces at its own discretion

b) its government maintains control over some portion, however small, of the territory which it claims as its metropolitan territory

c) if the geopolitical unit in question was formerly subordinate to another political unit, either its autonomy has been formally acknowledged by that other unit, or else it is able to maintain an autonomous military organization for six months without engaging in hostilities with that other unit'.

We omit discussing in detail the definition, as well as the uncertainty of some of the early data. The essential point here is that in the world of today, this concept becomes roughly coterminous with 'independent state', whereas in earlier periods it is a more inclusive concept than legal statehood, and therefore empirically more interesting in some respects.

The phenomenon that interests us here is the creation of new 'states': to be more precise, the event under study is the creation of a new autonomous geopolitical unit in any other way than a merger of previous autonomous geopolitical units. In the time period 1815–1980, we find at least 209 such events. Let us start by summarizing them in a few tables.

Table Two. Creation of New Autonomous Geopolitical Units, 1815–1980

	1815–1899	*1900–1980*	*Sum*
Africa	31	48	79
Asia	14	38	52
The Americas	20	13	32
Oceania	0	11	11
Europe	12	22	34
Sum	77	132	209

Our first question is, How were they brought about? We have used four categories. The first, *Decolonization*, includes all cases where overseas possessions of European powers or USA have acquired independence. *Dissolution of empires* contains the cases where independence has been achieved by what was previously a part of a contiguous empire. *Other dissolution* comprises those cases where previous states ceased to exist, or only minor parts were left of them. *Simple secession*, as the last category, takes the cases where one part of a surviving unit seceded. Obviously, it is meaningless to attempt to draw any sharp line between the second and third and fourth categories; but since they all contain rather well-defined cores, we have kept them apart.

Table Three. How did the New Units Emerge?

	1815–1899							*1900–1980*								
	Afr.	As.	Oc.	Am.	Eur.	Sum	%	Afr.	As.	Oc.	Am.	Eur.	Sum	%	Sum	%
Decolonization	3	2	0	7	1	13	17	48	24	11	12	2	97	75	110	53
Dissol of empire	19	3	0	0	7	29	38	0	10	0	0	13	23	18	52	25
Other dissol	2	4	0	5	0	11	14	0	0	0	0	2	2	2	13	6
Secession	7	5	0	8	4	24	31	0	4	0	1	5	9	7	33	16
Sum	31	14	0	20	12	77	100	48	38	11	13	22	131	102	209	100

By far the most common way of creating new units is decolonization, with its two main waves in the early nineteenth century and the post-war period, and very little in between. By definition, this mechanism is now nearly exhausted, there being very little left to colonize. The role of violence varies widely: from protracted wars costing about 10% of the lives of the colony, over local battles, terrorism, massive campaigns of civilian resistance, to constitutional conferences preceded by no overt use of violence. No simple generalizations appear possible, although we would hypothesize that much of the peaceful dissolution of British and French colonialism was aided by the early prices paid in, eg, Kenya and Algeria. Dissolution of empires mainly means some African cases in the nineteenth century, the Turkish and Chinese empires in both centuries and the Hapsburg, Russian and Japanese ones in the twentieth. Almost without exception they were brought about by wars, whether costly local ones or lost world wars. Other cases of dissolution are rare (we have excluded 'wartime only' cases that were reforged at the end of the war, such as Yugoslavia and Czechoslovakia). The Asian cases in the nineteenth century all refer to the dismemberment of Afghanistan in 1819, and the American cases to the collapse of the United States of Central America in 1839. In the twentieth century we have placed the creation of the two post-war Germanies here.

The absolute and relative frequency of secession as a means of creating new units has also been decreasing. The bulk of the nineteenth century cases consists of African, Malay and Latin American examples: the European ones are Belgium, Luxembourg, Monaco and Saxe-Altenburg, whereas our century adds Norway, Iceland, Vatican City, Ireland and postwar Austria. The other cases are Panama, where the United States encouraged rebellion against Colombia to build the Canal, and in Asia Nejd, Singapore, Bangladesh and Gilan. In both centuries, violence and war have played a role in most cases which makes those the more interesting that took place without either in our century: the Vatican City was created by the Concordat with the Italian state in 1929, thus restoring some territorial position, the Papal States, having been swallowed up in the Italian reunification in 1870. Iceland was under allied occupation in 1944, when severing the personal union under the Danish Crown that remained after virtual independence in 1918. Singapore had only been a part of Malaysia for two years, when in 1965 disunity had increased to the extent that Tunku Abdul Rahman of Malaysia in a letter suggested that Singapore leave the state, which it agreed to do in a reply stating how sad it was to have to leave. In the Scandinavian case, finally, Norway already had a very large degree of autonomy in the personal union under the Swedish crown, and pronounced a UDI when refused separate consular representation by the Swedes. Elements in the Swedish conservative government that wanted to drive the issue to war were in a minority and, in addition, the liberal and socialist parties were loudly against this course. At Swedish request, a referendum was held in Norway, which confirmed the secession by 368,208 votes against 184.

The main conclusion to draw from the data seems to be that it usually takes violence, often much of it, and often foreign intervention as well to bring about successful secession, but that this is no natural law: under specific circumstances both secession and even dissolution can be brought about peacefully.

Let us now go through our 209 cases from another perspective: what happened to them after their emergence. The following categories have been used: (1) survival as independent states since then; (2) survival, except for some period of wartime occupation; (3) return to the state they left; (4) colonization; (5) joining some other state; (6) merger with some other unit to form a new state; (7) dissolution. Again, some borderlines may be hard to draw, but each category contains clear cases. The result of this calculation is presented in Table Four.

Table Four. Fates of New Autonomous Geopolitical Units

| Eventual Fate | Created 1815-1899 | | | | | | | Created 1900-1980 | | | | | | |
	Afr.	As.	Oc.	Am.	Eur.	Sum	%	Afr.	As.	Oc.	Am.	Eur.	Sum	%
1) Independence	1	0	0	13	0	14	18	44	23	11	12	9	99	75
2) Indep (temp,mil,occ)	0	0	0	3	5	8	10	1	1	0	1	5	8	6
3) Return to origin	2	8	0	2	0	12	16	0	5	0	0	7	12	9
4) Colonization	25	1	0	0	0	26	34	0	0	0	0	0	0	0
5) Joined other state	3	2	0	1	3	9	12	0	3	0	0	1	4	3
6) Merged with other	0	3	0	0	4	7	9	3	5	0	0	0	8	6
7) Dissolution	0	0	0	1	0	1	1	0	1	0	0	0	1	1
Sum	31	14	0	20	12	77	100	48	38	11	13	22	132	100

Here, as in the previous cases, the nineteenth century figures for Asia and Africa are likely to be fairly uncertain, but the rest more reliable. To start with the general tendencies, survivability of new units has increased remarkably. Much of the explanation of this may lie in the simple statistical fact that the early states have had it tested for a much longer time period than the most recent ones, but probably not all. For example, colonization has ceased, and the tendency to swallow up neighbours diminished; and in both cases, this may be the result of such phenomena having become explicity illegal.

At closer inspection, 'return to origin' is a heterogeneous category. In the nineteenth century, it comprises the British recapture of Natal and Transvaal and the Dutch of two Malay states; the short-lived republics of Yucatan and Buenos Aires; the reforging of Afghanistan; and the recapture of some fugitive Chinese provinces. In our century, all cases but one (the short secession of Gilan from Iran) are accounted for by most of the Russian and Chinese empires eventually getting recaptured.

Practically all the cases in the last three categories have been rather short-lived. The three African cases in (5) were quickly swallowed up by Ibadan before it was colonized itself; the American case is Texas; the Ionian Islands and Crete rapidly join Greece, and, Saxe-Altenburg Germany. Three of the Asian cases are part of the incorporation of neighbours by Nejd, eventually resulting in Saudi Arabia, and in addition to that one of the splinters from Afghanistan is taken by Lahore before colonization, and the Republic of Hatay gets independence from France in 1938, to be sacrificed to Turkey in 1939 to keep her away from Hitler, who also appropriated the young republic of Austria.

The mergers of old states consist of three Malay states eventually becoming parts of Malaysia, and some cases of 'debalkanization': just after independence, Bulgaria and Rumelia formed a bigger Bulgaria, and Romania was created from Moldavia and Wallachia. (To this category, we might also have added the creation of Yugoslavia from Serbia, Montenegro and part of two collapsed empires). The twentieth century also offers the creation of Tanzania, the very short-lived United Arab Republic, the reforging of Vietnam and the history of Malaysia. The two cases of dissolution, finally, are the United States of Central America in the nineteenth century, and Pakistan in the twentieth.

Let us now make some attempts at drawing provisional conclusions. The over-arching one seems to be that the state, or state apparatus, is an utterly conservative phenomenon: it resists *any* changes, division as well as merger, with great tenacity, and with few exceptions it takes enormous amounts of political energy, mostly in violent forms, to overcome this resistance. We use the phrase, 'state, or state apparatus', rather than 'national state', the latter being, as mentioned, rather an exception in the international system, and the resistance not being specific to this form of states. Furthermore, the expression 'apparatus' alludes to the phenomenon that the resistance is by no means tied to independent states. For example, the map of Latin America today agrees fairly well with the administrative division from the Spanish era, and most attempts at creating greater units rapidly fell apart. The decolonization of Africa and Asia also offers a long list of examples of how administrative divisions, even when unrelated to ethnic boundaries, economic links, etc, in a sense started living their own life. To some extent, this is probably a result of the gradually emerging norm in the UN system against changing administrative boundaries in a way that would prejudge eventual independence;[31] but the phenomenon seems much older than the norm, as witnessed by Latin America. After World War II, the only so far successful post-independence mergers have been Tanzania and Vietnam (to which you might add Somalia), and the only completed secessions have been those of Bangladesh and Singapore, both of which left ethnically heterogeneous states which had been created by recent decolonization.

In neither case has this been for lack of trying. 'Arab unity' has been a password for decades, and a number of schemes for mergers have been announced: between the two Yemens; between Libya and its neighbours; between Syria and Iraq; and a few others. The only one that was actually created, between Egypt and Syria (and, with looser links, the then Kingdom of Yemen) fell apart after three years. African leaders had grandiose plans for redrawing the map of Africa in meetings in the fifties, but nothing came out of them after independence, nor have the few discussions and attempts at local mergers after independence had any success. The British colonial administration made a number of attempts at mergers before, on the eve of independence, but hardly one worked according to plan: the Central African Federation fell apart; Brunei did not join, and Singapore seceded from, Malaysia; the federation attempts in the Caribbean failed; those in South Arabia resulted, or at least contributed to a revolution that created a state of a quite different character from that intended; and the United Arab Emirates fell far short of the original plans, both Kuwait, Bahrein and Qatar staying out.

The list of failed, or not yet successful, attempts at secession, whether to form an independent state or to join a neighbour could also be made very long, even if we limit ourselves to the cases where violence has been used. To indicate that success is very much an exception, the following examples may suffice: the Moros in the Philippines; the Karen and Shan peoples in Burma; Hyderabad, Nagaland and Mizoland in India; Tibet in China; Baluchis and Pathans in Pakistan; the Kurds in Iraq (and Iran and Turkey); the Lebanese situation; Southern Sudan; several peoples in Ethiopia; the Somalis in Kenya; Biafra and Katanga; Northern Ireland and South Tirolia; and many more.

This is, indeed, a heterogeneous collection in many respects. Some of them are poorer than the metropolis, and some are richer – and both have been used as arguments for seceding. In some cases it appears obvious that the demand for independence is backed by a very heavy majority, in other cases, the ethnic group that wants to secede is only a minority in the territory proposed to leave the state – and the demand for independence is a minority opinion èven in that ethnic group. The state may be recently created or have a history of centuries; and the ethnic conflict underlying the demand may have become manifest very recently or have been acted out for generations.[32]

One conclusion from this is that it is hardly meaningful to attempt making generalizations from existing data, whether by marginal analysis, correlational analysis, or more sophisticated statistical methods. In order for data to give meaningful answers, there must be asked meaningful questions by means of a more developed theoretical framework. In particular, it would be very difficult to extrapolate probable futures from knowledge of past history. For example, Western Europe is the area whose history is probably best known – but experience there will hardly be repeated in the newly created states of today, which emerge under very different conditions.[33] In addition, even in Western Europe, ethnic revival has taken forms that might have been difficult to predict.[34]

Hence, we need both a methodology and a theoretical framework – and they have to be linked. As for methodology, we would assume that a compromise has to be struck between the pure cases of nomothetic and idiographic analysis, so as to avoid the shortcomings of both.[35] This would mean identifying one or a few typical cases of each major type of conflict, identifying crucial dimensions and possible relationships to be investigated, making in-depth studies of the cases in these respects, so as to get some comparability more or less assured, and then making the comparisons and drawing tentative conclusions, which can be used as points of departure for deeper case studies as well as for systematic data collection and statistical analysis of a wider range of cases.

Such a methodological approach obviously presupposes more of a theoretical framework than is now available.[36] Let us therefore at least try to formulate some questions to be taken into account.

Some Theoretical Issues

What, then, are the key dimensions and the most important paths of analysis in a social science investigation of national self-determination? All the preceding sections of this chapter, or at least the topics taken up in them, may contribute to answering this pretentious question – and all of them have too serious limitations to be made *the* perspective. The history of ideas of the notion of 'nation' and of 'self-determination' is useful for indicating the ambiguities – and at the same time, the potential richness – of these concepts, but does not take us very far towards systematic analysis. Apart from its inherent interest and its moral implications, the position of international law on 'national self-determination' tells us something important about the external conditions of related conflicts – but there are no reasons to assume that the concept as defined in international law is a useful one for social science analysis, and some grounds for assuming the opposite. The peoples struggling for forms of national self-determination are by no means limited to those that – at least according to our 'positivist' interpretation – can validly claim it. On the contrary, less and less of these peoples live in what are defined as Non-Self-Governing Territories. Furthermore, the forms taken up by international law only deal with the creation of, association with, or integration into states, whereas political claims for self-determination often concern other matters and hence are irrelevant to international law, and often also to its stipulations concerning the protection of minorities. Different branches of the Marxist tradition have shed important light on aspects of ethnical questions with the aid of such concepts as 'class' and 'imperialism'. They do, however, not have a monopoly on them. Furthermore, our general impression is that much of Marxist analysis has over-simplified things by attempting to reduce ethnic conflict to these terms, thereby both reducing their theoretical understanding and, for that matter, often handicapping the strategic skill of political actors guided by Marxism even to suicidal effect.[37] And the kind of empirical analysis we attempted must be limited to reporting some very general tendencies, unless guided by a more adequate theoretical and methodological framework.

Space does not permit any systematic exposition of such a framework, and we will therefore limit ourselves to suggestions in different directions. First, we would propose the key concepts to be those of *state*, *class* and *ethnicity*, maintaining that while pairwise combinations of these may provide important parts of analysis, any fuller understanding of the forces behind claims for national self-determination will have to take all three into account, also keeping in mind that all of them have 'objective' and 'subjective' sides that have to be related to each other.

Second, we have to formulate a set of good questions by means of these concepts, and possibly others. Let us give a few examples.

We have already referred to the traditional disagreement between those who see the state as more fundamental, arguing that sufficiently long coexistence in a state will eventually create a common sense of nationhood, and those who see the – somehow ethnically defined – nation as primordial, maintaining that nations will eventually seek a statehood of their own. This issue is too crudely formulated to allow generalizable answers, and we therefore have to specify it in various ways. For example, how is it affected by the degree of 'stateness' of the state?[38] A strong state apparatus may have more means for forging a common 'nationhood' – but the process of penetration in building it up is likely to meet with resistance, which may become defined in ethnical terms. In particular, the horns of this dilemma may provide arguments both for centralist and federalist forms of state-building. To assess these arguments would require a careful empirical study of the viability of states of different types, and of the effects of moving in one direction or the other. It is often assumed that identity or loyalty is a 'zero sum game': the more identification with one's ethnic group, the less with one's state. This is not self-evident, and there appears to be some empirical counter-evidence.[39] Hence, we have to reformulate the question to ask under what circumstances – eg, in terms of inter-ethnic equality, character of the state, existence of neighbour irredentism, criteria of ethnicity – will such loyalties reinforce each other or counteract each other.

It appears to be a fairly generalizable rule that if two different types of conflict coexist on a manifest level, then the ethnic conflict takes the upper hand over the class conflict, in the sense of being the one along which people identify themselves primarily, polarize and fight. On the surface, this looks like a refutation of the Marxist insistence on the primacy of the class struggle (from which the standard escape is to refer to ethnic identity as 'false consciousness'). At the very least, it calls for further theorizing about the relationship between 'class consciousness' and 'ethnic consciousness'. In particular, it appears that the carriers of ethnic consciousness are often middle class groups – but under what circumstances does it spread beyond these? Furthermore, the rule above does *not* state that ethnic differences are *always* defining conflicts or overruling class conflicts – only that when both *are* manifest, then the ethnic one tends to 'win'; and this calls for one more way of defining the question when these types of conflict tend to overrule each other, support each other – or even cancel each other.[40]

Reasonable armchair arguments can be given both for expecting positive and negative correlations between internal and external conflict – and empirical studies tend to result in zero correlations.[41] This calls for further specification: under what circumstances do what kinds of external conflict – eg, common anticolonial struggle – increase or decrease internal ethnic cohesion? Another set of very important questions concerns the *dynamics* of conflict. Neither loyalties nor some aspects of identification are static factors, but have in some cases been known to shift rapidly. The same thing applies to the goals and demands of parties or movements representing ethnic groups, which may rapidly escalate from some cultural rights to regional political rights, forms of autonomy and even secession or irredentism. Apart from the initial relationships between the parties and characteristics of the situation, the development of conflict behaviour seems to be important here, eg, the extent to which violence is used by either party. Nor is the relationship a simple one: students of social mobilization have pointed out that mobilization tends to be high when the amount of repression from the state apparatus is high, and lower when it is either low or extremely high.[42] Hence, we can get a spiral upwards when mobilization and repression mutually stimulate each other – but we may also get an explosion when very strong repression is decreased. Again, further empirical study is needed to find out what causal chains obtain under what circumstances. In particular, it would be important to identify 'points of no return', where demands for forms of regional or ethnic autonomy – which in many cases have been negotiable – get transformed to an all-out struggle for secession, which is hardly ever negotiable and very rarely successful.

In developing a framework for the study of national self-determination, there are several neighbouring areas from which to draw resources. For some of the questions indicated above, we may go to the traditions of peace research and general theory of conflict for methods and even some answers; in other cases the more specific traditions in studying ethnic conflicts and boundary conflicts, respectively, will be of importance; we will have to draw on the study of social mobilization and collective behaviour; the tradition of investigations of nation-building has decisive contributions to offer; and so on. In addition, there are the traditions that we have already cursorily reviewed.

It is indeed too early to predict what synthesis will emerge from this. Two things appear clear however. On the one hand, the existence of all these neighbouring territories is likely to give the systematic comparative study on issues concerning national self-determination a better start than many others. On the other hand, considering the apparent increase of older and newer forms of ethnic conflict in several parts of the world, the urgency of such a study seems convincing.

Notes

1. Here cited from Article 1 para 1 of the International Covenants of Human Rights.
2. Restricted in the sense that we count only those states where everybody except a few per cent speak a language the great majority of whose speakers reside in precisely that country.
3. The data are calculated on the basis of figures from *Atlas Naradov Mira* (Moscow, 1964) as processed in C. L. Taylor and M. C. Hudson: *World Handbook of Political and Social Indicators* (New Haven and London, 1972, 2nd ed), Table 4.15.
4. At that time, Poland was divided between three empires, Denmark, Norway and Iceland were joined under the same crown, as were Sweden and Finland. Greece and Albania were parts of the Ottoman Empire, Hungary and parts of Italy under the Hapsburgs, Malta went from French to British occupation, and the rest of Italy split in many political units, as were the Somali areas and Madagascar. To be on the safe side, let us note Burundi as a possible exception, out of ignorance.

5. We have limited ourselves to European ideas here. A more thorough analysis of other cultures might reveal other sources elsewhere, even if we have the impression that the early upsurge of modern nationalism was largely Western.

6. There are, of course, exceptions, such as the history of Haiti, and the later development of the Mexican revolution (Benito Juarez).

7. For a thorough historical overview, see A. Cobban: *National states and national self-determination* (London, 1969).

8. We have to repeat a warning against Eurocentrism here, by hinting at concepts like *Swaraj,* cUruba, *fukoku kyohei,* etc.

9. For example, resolution 183 (1963) of the Security Council; 1514(XV), 2200(XXXI) and 2625(XXV) of the General Assembly.

10. The General Assembly has also passed resolutions on different occasions on Antigua, the Bahamas, Falkland Islands, French Somaliland, Gibraltar, Ifni and Spanish Sahara, Papua, New Guinea, Palestine, Nieu and the Tokelau Islands, the Seychelles, Guam, Gilbert and Ellice Islands, Bermuda, Brunei, the Comoro Archipelago, the Solomon Islands, Belize, American Samoa, Montserrat, the New Hebrides and Timor. Several of these are sovereign states today, others have been given a status ostensibly acceptable to all parties, others still remain objects of conflict (Gibraltar, Belize, etc) or armed struggle (Sahara, Palestine, Timor).

11. Dictionary of the *Academie francaise*, 1878; here cited after Rigo Sureda, p 23.

12. A. Christescu: *The historical and current development of the right to self-determination on the basis of the Charter of the United Nations and other instruments adoped by United Nations organs, with particular reference to the promotion and protection of human rights and fundamental freedoms*, study prepared for the Economic and Social Council of the United Nations, E/CN 4/Sub2/404 (Vol I), p 141f.

13. Here cited after Christescu, p 142.

14. See Rigo Sureda, pp 103ff.

15. Eg, K. P. Misra: 'Inter-State Imperialism: Pakistan', *Journal of Peace Research*, 1972, No 1, pp 27ff.

16. See I. Kendex's articles, 'Twenty-five years of local wars' and 'Wars of ten years, 1967–1976', in *Journal of Peace Research*, 1971, No 1, pp 5ff, and 1978, No 3, pp 227ff, respectively.

17. Rigo Sureda, esp pp 220–221.

18. Eg, in several resolutions condemning displacement and deportation.

19. Nor, for that matter, have the attempts by some colonial powers to define colonies as 'overseas territories' been generally successful in avoiding having them defined as Non-Self-Governing Territories.

20. In fact, the General Assembly has gradually taken the stand that, under certain circumstances, the surrounding state has a right to retrocession of enclaves. See Rigo Sureda, p 176.

21. See S. Marrero, 'Puerto Rico's Status Debate', in W. Phillips Davidson and L. Gordenker (eds): *Resolving National Conflicts: The Role of Public Opinion Research*, New York: Praiger, 1980.

22. The term has been put in quotation marks, so as to avoid value connotations. In our opinion, value judgments on these issues have to be made case by case, hardly being generalizable.

23. It should be kept in mind that we have limited ourselves to one, 'positivist', way of interpretation, which, of course, is not the only one possible.

24. This matter is further complicated by there being divergent opinions as to whether Tibet was an independent state.

25. See, eg, A. Eide: 'International law, dominance and the use of force', *Journal of Peace Research*, 1974, No 1, pp 1ff.

26. See also Resolution 2787(XXVI) from 1971.
27. The following paragraphs rely heavily on K. Gerner: *Bolsjevikerna och Polen* (The Bolsheviks and Poland), mimeo, Lund 1972.
28. In fact, most non-Russian parts of the empire opted for independence. In a couple of them, the Bolsheviks won, and they soon joined the Soviet Union. In Georgia, the Mensheviks got the upper hand, and was plainly invaded. Attempts of revolution in the Baltic states failed, not having much workers' support. In the war with Poland in 1920, those of the Bolsheviks that had counted on support from Polish workers were disappointed. Other parts of the old empire were annexed by force in World War II, eventually leaving only Poland and Finland.
29. We have taken the date from R. W. Bennett and J. Zitomersky: *The Delimitation of International Diplomatic Systems, 1716–1950*, adding to their original list for 1815–1970 a few supplementary cases for that period and in addition to the cases we have found from 1971 through 1980.
30. Bennett and Zitomersky, p 26.
31. See Rigo Sureda, p 200.
32. For some examples, see E. Krippendorff: 'Minorities, Violence and Peace Research', *Journal of Peace Research*, 1979, No 1, pp 27ff. The volatility of public opinion is illustrated in some chapters in Phillips Davidson and Gordenker.
33. This is argued in the introductory chapter, pp 81ff, in C. Tilly (ed): *The Formation of National States in Western Europe*, Princeton University Press, 1975.
34. See E. Allardt: *Implications of the Ethnic Revival in Modern, Industrialized Society*, Helsinki: Societas Scientiarum Fennica, 1979; and also P. F. Sugar (ed): *Ethnic Diversity and Conflict in Eastern Europe*, Oxford: Clio Press, 1980.
35. For a more detailed argument about this, see S. Tagil et al: *Studying Boundary Conflicts: A Theoretical Framework*, Lund: Scandinavian University Books, 1977.
36. For examples from adjacent theoretical territories, see Tagil and the chapter by S. Rokkan in Tilly.
37. It can even be argued that in practically all cases where Marxist-oriented movements have been victorious, one condition for this has been that they have been seen as more representative of national traditions than the incumbent government.
38. The term is borrowed from P. Nettl.
39. Allardt demonstrates this.
40. A classical analysis of criss-crossing conflict is L. Coser: *The Functions of Social Conflict*, Glencoe: Free Press, 1956.
41. For theoretical arguments, see Coser. The preponderance of zero correlations is demonstrated in R. R. Rummel: *Dimensions of Nations*, Berkeley: Sage, 1972. For an argument that the zero correlations may be spurious, see A. Mack: 'Why Big Nations Lose Small Wars', *World Politics*, 1975, No 1.
42. C. L. and R. Tilly: *The Rebellious Century*, New York, 1975.

PRE- AND POST-COLONIAL FORMS OF POLITY IN AFRICA

I. M. Lewis

Nations and Tribes

As is well-known, especially in relation to the Third World, the terms 'nation' and 'tribe' regularly convey a political judgment, the first usually positive, the second usually negative. Of course there are qualifications, ambiguities, ambivalences to which we refer in due course but, in general usage, these terms tend to be opposed in this fashion. 'Nation' is associated with civilization, literacy, progress and development generally: 'tribe', in contrast, has the reverse associations, being intimately linked with parochialism, backwardness and primitiveness.

This is an interesting transformation of the original etymological sense of these two terms. Historically and etymologically, *natio* was often used to designate distant barbarian ethnic groups, possessing cultural and territorial identity. If nation has thus subsequently gone up in the world, tribe has come down. Originally, the Latin *tribus* referred to the three (possibly legendary) founding tribes (Titii, Ramnes and Luceres) whose members were collectively citizens of the Roman city-state. Notwithstanding these impeccable origins and the cachet associated with such expressions as the 'Twelve Tribes of Israel', in the 18th century and 19th century colonizing Europeans applied the word 'tribe' indiscriminately to describe the supposedly 'uncivilized' archaic communities into which the indigenous peoples of Africa, America and parts of Asia were divided before the imperial partition.[1] The term was thus applied to distinctive cultural entities, whose members spoke the same language or dialect, generally occupied a common territory, and might or might not acknowledge the authority of a single chief or political leader and so form a more or less clearly demarcated *political* as well as *social* unit.

Little use was made by colonizing Europeans of the more complimentary term 'nation' in their demarcation and delimitation of the peoples of the Third World, although there are some interesting regional variations. Some of the larger North American Indian groups, for instance the Iroquois – studied by L. H. Morgan – and the Algonkian were sometimes referred to as 'nations', but in the latter part of the 19th century the usage 'tribe' was becoming pervasive.[2] Lewis Henry Morgan appropriated the term to designate an elementary kinship-based level of social grouping in his schema of evolutionary stages, running from the 'family' to the civilized 'state'. This evolutionary framework, with social forms relating to technology and differentiated in terms of increasingly sophisticated political organization, was adopted (with modifications) by Engels and Marx and elaborated by later generations of evolutionary cultural anthropologists such as E. R. Service[3] and M. Sahlins.[4]

While 19th century Europeans rarely dignified the people of the 'Dark Continent' with the title 'nation', it is interesting to note that this, as it were suppressed term, should have reappeared in the religious vocabulary of Voodoo[5] and other similar sycretic Latin American religions where the various gods and spirits, transported with slavery to the new world, are grouped in 'nations'. So, those whom Europeans disparaged as primitive tribes were resurrected as 'nations' (Hausa, Ibo, Guinea, Dahomey, etc) in this syncretic cosmology. Outside Africa and America, India provides a revealing test of imperial European nomenclature since it was generally regarded as a kind of halfway house to western civilization (via the Indo-European languages and 'Great' tradition of Hinduism). There, while not enjoying the ultimate privilege of being Europeans, the majority of people nevertheless lived in *castes* which represented a distinct advance in the evolutionary scale – especially, perhaps, for class-obsessed Englishmen. Outside the pervasive caste-system, peripheral to the great literate tradition on the very margins of the Indian states, lived the unruly 'tribesmen'. Unlike Africa, India was a continent of (relatively civilized) castes *and* tribes.

The concept 'tribe' which the first European administrators employed in Africa, was used to designate a range of traditional socio-political units varying enormously in culture, constitution and size. While individual administrators, especially if they were British, might admire independent-spirited pastoralists and wild nomadic warriors without kings or chiefs, it was usually found easier to recognize and rule centralized states such as BuGanda, Ashanti and the like – even if they had first to be conquered or 'pacified'. Hierarchical political institutions were familiar to the imperial mind and, particularly in the system of 'indirect rule' invented by the British proconsul, Lord Lugard, could be conveniently accommodated within the over-arching imperial superstructure. This grafting on to traditional institutions had the additional benefit of economizing the scarce resources of expatriate administrative personnel. The general assumption of hierarchical government encouraged expatriate European officials to recognize and appoint 'traditional' leaders, even sometimes where they did not actually previously exist. Such innovations, often unreognized and unintended, had the effect of social engineering, leading to the re-grouping or even creation of entirely novel political units. Thus British colonial rule particularly, often rigidified traditional tribal divisions as well as introducing new ones, although this was not always a direct or deliberate policy. Under the *pax colonica*, whole new ethnic groups sometimes formed, modelling themselves on 'traditional tribes'. The case of the Nubis, powerbase of the notorious Field Marshal Amin, is instructive here. Taking its name from the Nuba area of the Sudan, and claiming to speak a distinct language 'Ki-Nubi', this Muslim military caste in Uganda, developed out of a largely Nilotic diaspora (Shilluk, Dinka, Bari and Kakwa etc) of soldiery left behind in the area when the Turko-Egyptian regime in the Sudan collapsed.[6] British administration in Uganda required a local militia and the Nubis were gradually able to monopolize this crucial role and turn it to their advantage. They were not exactly created ex-nihilo by the European administration for this purpose: rather they saw their opportunity and produced a synthetic ethnic identity to safeguard it. As P. H. Gulliver[7] justly observes: 'Critics have often accused the colonial governments of a deliberate policy of "divide and rule", and of suppressing wider African loyalties and individual group development. That this was commonly the effect of colonial rule is evident, but there is limited evidence to demonstrate that such policy was deliberate throughout and put into practise. The process was more subtle and complex than that. But probably most administrators, of both high and low rank, merely took it for granted that the tribe was a readily identifiable, time-honoured unit, indigenous to African perceptions and activities'.

Anthropologists have been aware of this for a long time. As the doyen American cultural anthropologist, A. L. Kroeber[8] recorded over 25 years ago in relation to the American Indians: 'tribe could be a white man's creation of convenience for talking about Indians, negotiating with them, administering them'. So anthropologists, who have sometimes been accused of being tribalists (promoting their subjects of study), have not failed to analyse the delicate interplay between European administrators' stereotypes of tribal identity and the reality of the colonial power structure in which tribes and tribalism flourished. To recognize this does not, of course, entail endorsing M. Godelier's[9] sweeping assertion that 'tribal conflicts are explainable primarily by reference to colonial domination'. The extremely well-informed Soviet Africanist R. N. Ismagilova[10] provides a more realistic assessment: 'The specific features of African society in our day are often explained simply as the effect of colonialism. That view had led to both foreign political scientists and African politicians having an attitude to the traditional structures and surviving institutions of tribal–clan society that is not always correct. Yet many of these phenomena are strong and exert considerable influence on the social development of African peoples'.

Pre-colonial nations and states

Although it was recognized that different African tribes had different customs and different forms of political organization, few colonial administrators (there were, of course, exceptions) had the time or specialist training to study systematically the range of types of African polity. It was consequently in the main left to the first generation of modern social anthropologists conducting intensive field-research in the 1930s and 1940s to attempt to chart the spectrum of indigenous African political formations. If there is some truth, and it is certainly limited in the charge that these anthropologists sometimes failed to emphasize the impact of the colonial superstructure, this was largely because they sought as far as possible to recover the authentic African traditional structures – untainted by Western influence. Hierarchically organized states such as those of the Zulu, Lozi, Bemba, Ganda, Nupe, etc were displayed in all their complex intricacy. More enigmatic were those uncentralized political formations without chiefs which, at first sight, lacked government in the conventional sense and had no specific political institutions to organize their affairs. Acephalous pastoralists like the Nuer of the southern Sudan – studied by Evans-Pritchard[11] challenged the anthropologist to discover how anarchy was averted in such cultures whose constituent political units were so much larger than the small, familistic 'bands' characteristic of hunting and gathering peoples. Evans-Pritchard was able to demonstrate convincingly how amongst the Nuer, in the absence of any chiefly or bureaucratic administrative hierarchy, a minimum degree of order could be effectively maintained through the mobilization of loyalties based on a combination of kinship and neighbourhood. The key lay in the intimate entwining of ties of descent and of locality. In a circle radiating outwards from the level of the village, each local community was identitifed with a corresponding lineage segment. Hence genealogies were political charters, describing how people came together in unity or divided in hostility according to their closeness in kinship on the model of the Arab proverb (describing political loyalties in a similar segmentary system): 'Myself against my brother; my brother and I against my cousin; my cousin and I against the outsider'. Political cohesion was expressed in the idiom of kinship, the 'segmentary lineage system' of balanced kinship divisions, corresponding to that of territorial divisions on the ground – villages and groups of villages.

Within this segmentary structure, political divisions were made democratically in general assemblies of all the adult men of the community involved, this group expanding and contracting along kinship (and neighbourhood) lines according to the political context. So, in such segmentary lineage societies, closely related local groups would temporarily unite against a distant enemy, and dissolve in mutual antagonism when this common threat disappeared. In the absence of chiefs or other official political figures, the strength and limits of such elastic and fluctuating political cohesion could, Evans-Pritchard argued, be measured by examining the procedures followed in ventilating and resolving disputes at the various levels of grouping. As might be expected, the closer the bonds of kinship and political solidarity the greater the constraints on conflict and the more compelling the obligation to find a peaceful solution through the good offices of ritual mediators with, if necessary, the transfer of appropriate compensation. There was in fact a fixed tariff of indemnities corresponding to different injuries and reflecting the closeness or remoteness of the parties. The point at which the moral duty to resolve conflicts by peaceful mediation became completely attenuated marked the limits of the political community. This division of the Nuer people or nation, united internally by the ideal of peace and harmony and externally by war, Evans-Pritchard identified as the 'tribe'. Such acephalous territorially based communities with populations of up to 50,000 were the largest political units. Nuer society thus consisted of a series of independent and mutually hostile political division ('tribes'), loosely inter-connected by culture, language, mode of production and diffuse potential sentiment of Pan-Nuer identity. This emphasis on the regulation of conflict, in the absence of formal political offices, highlighted the crucial role of the 'leopard-skin priests' as mediators in this bellicose culture. Although these were strictly ritual figures, totally lacking political power, it is obvious that without them, conflict could not be controlled or tribal cohesions achieved.

In the wake of Evans-Pritchard's pioneering discovery other anthro-pologists soon found that this system of 'minimal government' based on segmentary lineage organizations was not unique to the Nuer but played a crucial political role in many other traditional African societies as well as elsewhere. Indeed in some cases, notably those such as the Tiv[12] of West Africa and Somali[13] of the Horn, the segmentary lineage system extended beyond the internal divisions called 'tribes' by Evans-Pritchard to embrace the whole people who, at the same time, also recognized a common obligation to settle conflicts and possessed a common 'national' tariff of compensation for injuries and death. This wider recognition of the general currency of what has passed into political science in the terminology of W. J. M. MacKenzie[14] as the 'non-state' encouraged anthropologists to devise ever more elaborate and comprehensive political typologies. Political anthropology thus became preoccupied, some would say obsessed, with the presence or absence of formal political institutions and hierarchy and with isolating variables associated with the transition from 'non-states' to states and vice versa.

This concentration on the presence or absence (qualitatively and quantitatively) of centralized authority (chiefs and kings) deflected attention from the intriguing question of the relationship between political cohesion and cultural identity. Indeed, writing in 1954 Edmund Leach[15], not entirely accurately, accused earlier political anthropologists (mostly Africanists) of assuming that cultural and social boundaries necessarily coincided. This, as we have seen was hardly the case for Evans-Pritchard's analysis of the Nuer. But the most obvious exception to Leach's generalization is the famous 'conquest' theory of state-formation according to which states arise from the collision of peoples of different culture, one group gaining political ascendancy over the other and developing a centralized state organization to maintain control in the face of cultural differences. In endorsing this ancient theory, the founders of modern political anthropology, Evans-Pritchard and Fortes in their *African Political Systems* (1940) also suggested the corollary, that cultural homogeneity was likely to be associated with uncentralized, segmentary political systems such as that found among the Nuer. Other anthropologists contributed splendidly detailed analyses of the power structure of complex, culturally heterogeneous traditional states – such for instance as Schapera's work on the Tswana,[16] Nadel's on Nupe[17] and Cunnison's on the Lunda[18] to name only a few. It is, however, only relatively recently and largely due to M. G. Smith's[19] applications of the concept of 'plural society' to Africa's traditional polities that we can trace the beginnings of a more systematic examination of the relationship between political and cultural identity in pre-colonial Africa. For J. S. Furnivall[20] who coined the term in the ethnically heteregeneous context of Dutch Indonesia the 'plural society' was one of colonial domination with a medley of peoples who 'mix but do not combine'. In the pre-colonial African context, Smith distinguishes culturally plural states such as Rwanda, Barotse, Zande, Ndebele, Nupe, Hausa and Tswana and heterogeneous 'empires' such as Mali, Songhay, Dahomey and Ethiopia. These are contrasted with homogeneous states such as Ashanti, Benin, Yoruba and BaGanda, while a third category of 'homogenizing' states such as the Zulu, Ngoni and Swazi etc are transitional between the two extremes. There are clearly at least two possibilities in the transitional situation. One is that what today would be described as 'nation-building' is in progress, as a dominant caste or ethnic group seeks to consolidate its position by extending its culture in melting-pot fashion to embrace the entire population.[21] The other is that the politically dominant group is engaged in the reverse process, of making itself as culturally distinct as possible from those it governs and so transforming power into an ethnic monopoly. Here the trend is towards pluralism, rather than towards ethnic homogeneity.

These comparative studies by anthropologists of pre-colonial African political structures tend to follow the 19th century radical political philosopher, John Stuart Mill, in seeing a connection between cultural homogeneity and democracy on the one hand, and cultural pluralism, hierarchy and autocracy on the other. However, this is obviously not necessarily the case since, as we have just seen, some highly centralized and far from democratic societies possess a homogeneous common culture. Indeed, as P. L. van den Berghe[22] points out, democracy and despotism flourish in *both* culturally homogeneous and heterogeneous societies. Thus the association of pluralism with despotism which derives originally from Furnivall's work in Indonesia seems fortuitous. In fact, I would suggest that, over the last decade, the term 'pluralism' has acquired an increasingly favourable connotation – suggesting harmonious tolerance of a variety of life-styles. Thus it is probably significant that South Africa has recently adopted the idiom of 'pluralism' (to the extent of restyling its former Minister of Bantu Affairs, Minister of Plural Affairs) in its quest for more favourable publicity for its modified 'new' version of *apartheid*.

My concern here, however, is not to attempt to assess the currency of democratic political structures in Africa before the imperial partition of the continent. All I seek to demonstrate is the co-existence, both in hierarchical state systems like Buganda and uncentralized polities like the Nuer or Somali, of culturally homogeneous as well as heterogeneous political formations. Thus the pre-colonial 'map of Africa' included true (culturally homogeneous) nation–states, 'non-state' nations and pluralistic heterogeneous Hapsburg-empire style states. Particularly in view of homogenizing trends, it would, I believe, serve little purpose to speculate on the relative preponderance of culturally homogeneous or culturally heterogeneous political formations in pre-colonial Africa. I have simply sought to demonstrate that here 'traditional' Africa enjoyed a mixed political economy.

Colonial and Post-Colonial Africa

It is a remarkable irony that the European powers who partitioned Africa in the late 19th century when the idea of the nation–state was paramount, should have created in Africa a whole series of Hapsburg-style states, comprising a medley of peoples and ethnic groups lumped together within frontiers which paid no respect to traditional cultural contours. This general process of 'balkanization' in which divisions of the same people were parcelled out amongst different Colonial territories is highlighted in the case of the Somali who were fragmented into five parts: one (in Jibuti) under the French, one (the Ogaden) under Ethiopia, another (Somalia) under the Italians, and two under British rule (British Somaliland and the Northern-frontier district of Kenya). This is no doubt an extreme case, but it illustrates the general process which gave an entirely new complexion to sub-Saharan Africa. Pluralism was in the ascendant and the pluralist Hapsburg style states which had formerly represented *one* style of African polity became the prevailing mode for the whole continent.

It was perhaps fortunate for African nationalists, although this can hardly have been foreseen, that the European powers who thus enshrined pluralism as the dominant political strain in the continent, referred to their colonial subjects as 'tribes' rather than 'nations'. Thus, in the struggle to achieve independence from the European colonizers, African political leaders appealed to the transcendant 'nationalism' which colonization kindled amongst subject populations irrespective of their tribal identity. Tribalism which had developed considerably under the *pax colonica*, particularly in urban contexts where competition for resources and power was acute, was inevitably cast in the role of a negative atavistic force impeding the growth of national solidarity. 'Tribalism' like 'nationalism' in common with other forms of group identity is notoriously reactive. So in pluralistic African colonies, 'tribalism' – as John Argyle[23] has so effectively demonstrated – developed in much the same way and with almost all the same characteristics as 'nationalism' in 19th century Europe. Such divisive, particularistic forces had to be thrust into the background in the urgent nationalist campaign to gain independence.

The achievement of independence by Europe's ex-colonies perpetuated the pluralist multi-ethnic state or 'state–nation' whose virtual monopoly is readily seen by contrast with the few exceptions: Botswana, Lesotho, Somalia. Whereas metropolitan connections had helped to differentiate African states in the colonial period, in the post-colonial era, there were fewer distinguishing features and states tended to become identified with their heads of state. The other obvious basis of demarcation lay in the boundaries separating one state from another. So the colonial boundaries which balkanized Africa and provided the foundation for its modern independent states, are today appropriately enough the subject of what amounts to religious veneration. This I refer to as 'frontier fetishism'.

To conclude, I have argued here that there are two pre-colonial styles of African polity, one based on ethnic identity, the other culturally pluralist. In the widest African perspective, both can claim equal legitimacy and 'authenticity'. Colonization and de-colonization, however, have changed this traditional pattern in favour of pluralism. This process might be called the 'Ethiopianization' of Africa, making it not inappropriate that the

Organization of African Unity should have its headquarters in Addis Ababa. The price of the monopoly held by this form of 'state–nation' (rather than 'nation–state') is the inevitable boost it gives to its internal erstwhile 'tribal', but now increasingly canonized as 'national', divisions. Confounding all the highly artificial and tendentious distinctions drawn by political sociologists and others between them,[25] 'tribes' have literally become 'nations' (or 'nationalities') almost overnight. Nowhere in Africa is this better understood than in contemporary Ethiopia. The pervasive force of such inter-active cultural identity is testimony to the universal appeal of ethnic nationalism which, for better or worse celebrates the notion of the naturally created and ideally autonomous community with its special claim to a unique heritage.

References

1. Cf P. H. Gulliver (ed), *Tradition and Transition in East Africa* London, 1969, p 8.
2. M. Fried, 'On the concept of "tribe" and "tribal society"' Transactions of the New York Academy of Sciences, Ser II, 28, 4, pp 527–540.
3. E. R. Service, *Primitive Social Organization*, New York, 1962.
4. M. Sahlins, *Tribesmen*, New York, 1968.
5. S. Larose, 'The meaning of Africa in Haitian Vodu', in I. M. Lewis (ed) *Symbols and Sentiments*, London, 1977, pp 85–116.
6. A Southall, 'Amin's Military Coup in Uganda: Great Man or Historical Inevitability,' *Third International Congress of Africanists*, Addis Ababa, 1973.
7. P. H. Gulliver, *op cit* p 14.
8. A. L. Kroeber, 'Nature of the Land-holding Group', *Ethnohistory*, 1955, pp 303–314.
9. M. Godelier, *Perspectives in Marxist Anthopology*, Cambridge 1977, p 96.
10. R. N. Ismagilova, *Ethnic Problems of the Tropical Africa: Can they be solved*, Moscow, 1978, p 10.
11. E. Evans-Pritchard, *The Nuer*, Oxford, 1940.
12. P. Bohannan, *Tiv Farm and Settlement*, London, 1954.
13. I. M. Lewis, *A Postoral Democracy*, London, 1961: see also 'Problems in the comparative study of descent' in M. Banton (ed) *The Relevance of Models for Social Anthropology*, London, 1965.
14. W. J. MacKenzie, *Politics and Social Science*, Harmondsworth, 1967.
15. E. R. Leach, *Political Systems of Highland Burma*, London, 1954.
16. I. Schapera, *The Tswana*, London, 1953.
17. S. F. Nadel, *A Black Byzantium*, London, 1942.
18. I. Cunnison, *History on the Luapula*, London, 1951.
19. L. Kuper and M. G. Smith (eds) *Pluralism in Africa*, Berkeley, 1971. See also J. F. A. Ajayi, 'A Survey of the Cultural and Political Regions of Africa at the beginning of the 19th Century' in J. C. Anene and G. Brown, *Africa in the 19th and 20th Centuries*, 1966.
20. J. S. Furnivall, *Netherlands India: A study of Plural Economy*, Cambridge, 1934.
21. R. Cohen and J. Middleton (eds), *From Tribe to Nation in Africa*, Pennsylvania, 1970.
22. P. L. van den Berghe, 'Pluralism and the Polity' in Kuper and Smith (eds) *Pluralism in Africa*, pp 67–84.

23. J. Argyle, 'European nationalism and African Tribalism' in P. H. Gulliver (ed) *Tradition and Transition in East Africa*, 1969, pp 41–58.
24. This term was coined to refer to the new states of the Third World which, while possessing sovereignty, lack an integrating national culture. For a discussion see A. D. Smith, *Theories of Nationalism*, London, 1971, pp 189–190.
25. The insistence that 'tribes' are based on kinship whereas nations are not, is clearly perverse to say the least. To argue that they lack 'in-group sentiment' and 'external relations', as A. D. Smith does so, according to him, differentiating them from 'ethnics' and 'nations' compounds the confusion.

SELF-DETERMINATION AND THE OAU

James Mayall

If a Somali or Eritrean nationalist was asked to comment on the OAU's attitude towards the question of national self-determination he might well reply that the OAU was against it. Somalia, after all, raised the question in relation to the Somalis living in Ethiopia, Kenya and Djibouti at the founding meeting of the OAU in May 1963, and was accused on all sides of acting against the spirit of Addis Ababa. Her isolation on this issue was further underlined when, after the border fighting with Ethiopia at the end of 1963, the first Council of Ministers passed a resolution in Cairo in April 1964 binding all African states to respect the territorial integrity of their neighbours: that territory, it was now made clear, was to be defined in terms of the colonial inheritance, no less (no enclaves were to be carved out for neo-colonial or other purposes) but also no more.[1]

The Charter, and the Cairo resolution against boundary revision, together provide a powerful support for the territorial *status quo*. Subsequent Somali attempts to argue (rightly) that the OAU has nothing to say about boundaries that were in dispute at the time of the colonial succession and indeed that these are not bound by this resolution, or (more contentiously) that the dispute in the Horn is analogous to the special case of minority colonial rule in Southern Africa rather than to other inter-state conflicts in Africa have received little support in the international community as a whole and less in Africa. But the Somalis are not alone in their failure to resuscitate the principle of national self-determination in post-colonial Africa; neither the Southern Sudanese nor the Biafrans were any more successful in establishing their right to an independent existence. In both cases the principle of *uti possidetis* was successfully invoked to preserve the territorial integrity of the state.

From this point of view the Eritreans are in an even worse case. Since, by convention, the OAU does not discuss the internal affairs of member states unless they agree, the Eritrean question has never featured on the agenda either of the Council of Ministers or the annual Assembly of Heads of State. A certain scepticism about the OAU, therefore, seems fully justified: it is an organization which claims to support the self-determination of all African peoples but which in practice is committed to the existing state order.

Why has the OAU adopted this restrictive definition? The answer to this question I believe involves two sets of considerations: the first concerns the emergence in the contemporary international order of national self-determination as *the* principle of international legitimacy in general; the second the process by which pan-African ideology was 'domesticated' in African diplomacy after 1960. I shall discuss these considerations first. In the final section of the paper I shall examine two arguments that can be advanced for holding that, despite the general bias of the international community against territorial revision, the Somali and Eritrean claims should be regarded as special cases.

Self-determination and International Legitimacy

In the introduction to his study of what he calls the modern ideology[2] Louis Dumont asserts that there is no more a society of nations than a science of sciences. Insofar as his purpose is to argue that there has never been an international society in the way that there is a British or a Somali society, he is no doubt correct. But as a self-conscious historical construct of the states themselves there undoubtedly is an international society. Its present form was first developed in Europe after the wars of religion and subsequently exported around the world as a consequence first of European expansion and then of decolonization. The evidence for the existence of this society is to be found in the conventions of inter-state behaviour, the codification of international law, the institution of diplomacy (and its progressive institutionalization) and the development of functional international agencies, none of which would have been possible in a truly non social or anarchic world.[3] On the other hand, precisely because this society represents a deliberate historical creation, entry is not a birth-right. It is more like a club with qualifications for entry, from which it is possible to be excluded as Turkey was until 1856, or black-balled as China was until 1974, and to some extent South Africa is today. By international legitimacy, therefore, I mean the principles which have to be satisfied for entry into the community of states and which are generally considered appropriate to govern state-succession, the break-up of empires (or even existing states) and the consolidation or integration of existing states into some new and larger unit.[4]

I do not mean to suggest, however, that these principles are somehow to be considered separately from the general principles of political thought. On the contrary a debate about international legitimacy has always echoed the debate about the legitimate exercise of political power in general. In a world of dynastic Christian rulers, dynasticism provided the entry ticket to the Western society of states. After the French Revolution it gradually become necessary to justify the exercise of authority according to a popular principle; and since in a political and diplomatic sense Christianity was now merely a cultural residue rather than the essence of the Western system, the way was open for the emergence of a global society of states also constituted according to a popular principle. Although now as then dynastic states do survive, it is impossible in general to claim a prescriptive right to sovereignty.

To some extent it is an historical accident, however, that the principle of national self-determination has been universally accepted as the legitimate formulation of the popular principle. The concept was developed in the context of Western liberal thought; but it was elevated tentatively by the League of Nations, then conclusively by the United Nations to become the central legitimizing principle of contemporary international society. There were two reasons for this elevation: first it was the governments of the Western liberal democracies, the most powerful states in the contemporary system, which were largely responsible for the framing of these documents; secondly, since the concept of national self-determination entails the notion of government by consent it has generally been held to imply majority rule. Whether this is a strictly logical implication is doubtful; but majoritarianism does seem to be entailed by the popular principle however it is represented.

However suitable it may be for a notionally egalitarian world, self-determination is notoriously more ambiguous as a general ordering principle than was dynasticism. Although in the dynastic world there was a long tradition of thought, originating in mediaeval Christendom, about both just rebellion and war, since the ruler exercised power by prescriptive right, domestic and international legitimacy were fairly easily reconciled. With the principle of self-determination, however, this reconciliation is not automatic. The basic ambiguity arises because of a latent conflict with the principle of sovereignty. This conflict can, perhaps, best be expressed in a question: is a sovereign state to be recognized as one where the people have already by definition exercised the right of self-determination and which must be proofed therefore against external interference, or is there some public test of popular consent in the absence of which an oppressed population not only has the right of rebellion (that right after all will be exercised and resisted whatever the rest of the world thinks about it) but which allows outside powers legitimately to come to its assistance?

The marriage between nationalism and the essentially individualistic concept of self-determination did nothing to resolve this ambiguity either in Europe where many 'historical' nations did not fit conveniently into the states that were created following the dismemberment of the Hapsburg and

Ottoman Empires, or in Asia and Africa where the creation of states in many cases preceded the development of nationalism in any firmly anchored sociological or psychological sense.

In principle a solution is available but it is rigorous and, from a practical point of view, implausible. Only if it can be safely assumed that the successful exercise of national self-determination could dispose (and could be seen to have disposed) of the problem of popular consent once and for all would the tension between internal and external self-determination be dissolved. Obviously no such assumption can be made. At San Francisco the framers of the UN Charter made some attempt to provide a public test. In order to avoid blatantly fictitious expressions of the popular will of the kind employed by the Axis powers it was agreed that 'an essential element of the principle in question is a free and genuine expression of the will of the people'. As Trusteeship powers, Britain and France also conducted plebiscites in the Cameroons and Togo where there was a question of independence or union with neighbouring states and, once the goal of decolonization had been conceded, held elections in their own colonies – most recently, finally and symbolically in Zimbabwe – to decide the composition of the successor governments. But although at San Francisco the Western powers insisted that self-determination was to mean *real and genuine choice*, it was also subordinated to (and indeed conceived as an instrument for achieving) the primary goal of friendly relations and peace between the states. For this reason it was ruled out in principle that an appeal to the principle of self-determination could authorize secession.[5]

In other words long before a majority of African states achieved independence or the OAU was established, the concept of national self-determination had been established as a 'generic right to self-government' but under fairly restrictive conditions. It prescribed the route by which the European empires were to be dismantled and in this respect entailed a public demonstration of internal legitimacy, but said nothing about what was to happen thereafter or about how peoples were to be protected from authoritarian oppression. Indeed, in contrast to Wilson's approach after 1918, the post 1945 interpretation of the concept gave no comfort to dissatisfied national minories within existing states. Statehood was to provide sufficient evidence of self-determination, and statehood entailed most importantly the right of non-interference in domestic affairs of other states. National self-determination was already tied in time and space to European decolonization.

The Domestication of Pan-Africanism
Within the African context however it was not self-evident during the independence period that statism would prevail in the struggle to establish

a post-colonial order. Only three African states – Liberia, Ethiopia and South Africa – had been members of the League of Nations. The rhetoric of African nationalism, moreover, emphasized Pan-African solidarity rather than territorial identity: amongst the elites throughout the continent there was an assumed identity of all Africans in the face of colonial and racial dominance. The appeal of Pan-African doctrine, as Nkrumah understood better than most of his contemporaries, was to the young, relatively well-educated and largely urban populations which had been up-rooted from traditional society by the colonial experience without being fully co-opted into the modernizing colonial state. He made this appeal in the name of unitary government and the surrender of sovereignty by existing independent African states.[6] So startling a proposal was resisted by political leaders in Africa as it would have been anywhere else. Since they all used the language of Pan-African solidarity, however, it became necessary to 'domesticate' the concept of African unity by giving it an official and statist interpretation. It was this need which led to the setting up of the OAU.

The argument for the creation of pan-African political institutions rested on two foundations: on the desire for modernization, for the economic development which had for the most part been neglected in the politics of decolonization; and on the alleged 'artificiality' of African boundaries. In both cases the ground proved far from solid. Since politics in independent Africa was from the start intimately involved with patronage, the claim that self-determination involved unification for the sake of development, that is the surrender of the instruments of patronage, to a new body which did not represent any visible constituency, was bound to be unpopular. And, in fact, even regional economic integration schemes (eg the East African community) which both employed an internationally approved means of economic co-operation (ie the creation of a common market) and which made minimal in-roads into state authority, have failed to take root in Africa.

Boundary revision was even more unpopular than integration. Perhaps the most common charge of African nationalists against the colonial powers in the pre-independence period was that they had 'balkanized' Africa. At the Congress of Berlin, Africa has been partitioned in an exercise of boundary drawing which paid scant attention to African geography or ethnography, and none to African interests. The 'balkanization' thesis implied (fictitiously it is true) a pre-colonial unity which was to be restored at independence. In anti-colonial thought there were two versions of this restoration. One version, reflected for example in the AAPC resolutions up to and including the 1958 meeting in Accra, had called for wholesale boundary revision alone lines to be provided by indigenous cultural, linguisitic and economic criteria.[7] Nkrumah's alternative version was based on his view that, as a mobilizing ideology, Pan-Africanism had to have a goal: unity had to be defined either by going back to some past of assumed tribal harmony, which was plainly incompatible with modern development, or forward to the creation of a continental state, the goal which he favoured.

In May 1963 against the sole complaint of the Somali government, both of these views were firmly rejected. African Unity was now defined in static rather than mobilizational terms: self-determination was made synonymous with independence from European colonial rule and the achievement of statehood. Despite the plebiscite which the British had previously held in the NFD, the Kenyan Government's insistence on maintaining its territorial integrity, and its riposte to the Somalis that if NFD Somalis wanted to express their right of individual self-determination they could do so by moving to the Somali Republic,[8] were both in line with OAU orthodoxy. In other words the domestication of Pan-African ideology (ie the creation of an institutional framework based on state supremacy) brought African practice in relation to self-determination into line with international practice generally. In Addis Ababa as well as in New York national self-determination was now tied formally in both time and space to European decolonization.

The forging of this link had two implications for the practical treatment of questions of national self-determination by the OAU. Since for African, as in this respect also for socialist, states self-determination means only "external" self-determination and only for peoples subject to colonial or racist rule or to foreign, ie non-African occupation, it established territorial integrity and non-interference as the governing principles of African inter-state relations. Secondly, it meant that the energies of the Organization were focused on Southern Africa where colonial and racist rule denied the right of self-determination to the African peoples.

In 1963 the 'domestication' of Pan-African ideology was considered necessary because unrestrained political warfare between regimes which claimed monopoly rights over the correct interpretation of the ideology had created an atmosphere of endemic insecurity and widespread fears of subversion. By the same token, however, preoccupation with security and with safeguarding the independence which they had so recently acquired, led African governments to commit themselves unequivocally to confrontation with the white South. For this reason, inter-African disputes further north have always been regarded by those not immediately involved as almost frivolous diversions from the central business.

However, the OAU position on self-determination in inter-African relations – in particular the insistence on the colonial land settlement –

itself had further implications for OAU policy towards Southern Africa. (The converse is also probably true.) South Africa's attempts since 1963 to break out of the diplomatic isolation which the African states imposed on her, have been based on the policy of separate development. This policy has domestic as well as external origins, but apart from other justifications, South African leaders have always maintained it to be a legitimate form of de-colonization. On this view, if Lesotho, Botswana and Swaziland could be granted independence and admitted to the United Nations and OAU, despite their incorporation in the South African customs union and virtual total dependence on the Republic, why not Transkei, Bophutatswana, Venda and the rest?

The OAU has never accepted the legitimacy of these creations, nor have their leaders succeeded in obtaining any kind of recognition from individual African countries. (Nor it might be added, has the one homeland leader, Chief Gatsha Butelhezi of Kwa Zulu who may with some justification claim to have a genuine political following in South Africa). There are two reasons for the OAU line on South African's homeland or bantustans. One is that in no sense have they been created in response to nationalist demands for self-determination (the nationalists who made such demands are all in exile or in prison), rather they have been created in response to the dictates of the Afrikaner nationalist ideology and represent therefore an exercise in 'other determination'; secondly their recognition would breach the OAU policy on the territorial issue – independence within the limits imposed and demarcated by the colonial powers or not at all.

South Africa is thus conceived of as one country, just as is Ethiopia and the fact that, in terms of its historical identity the Transkei has as much right to exist independently as Lesotho, is irrelevant. The future of the Transkei cannot be considered independently of the transfer of power to the majority in South Africa of which it is a part. Lesotho's right to self-determination, on the other hand, derives from the fact that Moshesh put Basutoland under British imperial protection in 1962. I shall return to the Somali argument that Ethiopia is as much an imperial power as was Britain shortly. In the meantime it is sufficient to point out that the orthodox 'statist' definition of self-determination in the OAU has been adopted to protect African states in general from secessionist claims by disaffected ethnic minorities. On this view if secession was conceded anywhere it would lead to similar claims throughout the continent and would weaken the case for resisting the partition of South Africa along ethnic lines.

The OAU's refusal to contemplate ethnic, as distinct from racial majoritarian criteria for self-determination is currently under test in Namibia. Despite its refusal to place South-West Africa under UN trusteeship, and its rejection of both World Court judgements and the UN General Assembly resolution withdrawing the mandate, South Africa has never denied its international responsibilities towards the territory, and since 1972 has made a series of slow, awkward and largely cosmetic moves to prepare it for independence. The initial policy was to use South-West Africa as a kind of international proving ground for the policy of separate development and only when it became clear that there was no chance at all of international recognition for the eleven new ethnic states which the South Africans proposed to carve out of the territory did they concede that South West Africa should proceed to independence as a single polity, although still with a political system based on ethnic constituencies. In the negotiations between the five Western powers and South Africa which led to the abortive Geneva Conference on Namibia in January 1981, it was conceded in principle that the issue of state succession should be tested in an election between the DTA (the alliance based on ethnic constituencies) and SWAPO (the nationalist party whose support is predominantly Ovambo but which has always rejected the ethnic principle). At present the outcome, or even whether the election will ever take place, is uncertain: but so far at least the sequence of events (and South African concessions) has vindicated the orthodox OAU interpretation of the application of self-determination doctrine.

There is however one intriguing difficulty. Namibia, it is generally held, can only function as an independent entity if it retains its one developed port, Walvis Bay. SWAPO insists that Walvis Bay is an integral part of Namibia. But Walvis Bay is, and has been since 1854, a part of South Africa. In the UN negotiations the issue has been left open, but on a strict application of OAU doctrine it seems fairly clear that it should remain in South Africa unless of course both countries agree otherwise. If, as seems likely, the OAU supports SWAPO in its claims to Walvis Bay they will presumably do so by denying the legitimacy of any South African claim and by appealing to arguments about geographical propinquity, economic viability and the previous administration of the territory including Walvis Bay as a single unit. But such arguments undoubtedly offer hostages to fortune. If South Africa's territory is not to be inviolate then should not the OAU support Lesotho's historical claim to much of the Orange Free State, a position which quite apart from the practicalities of the matter, the African States would certainly not wish to endorse. And if economic viability is the criterion then what about Gambia's position vis a vis Senegal? And so on. The comparisons that can be drawn are endless and it is precisely to prevent such special pleading, to impose some minimum of diplomatic order on the continent as a whole, that the OAU adopted its limited and restrictive definition of self-determination in the first place.

To summarize: since 1945 national self-determination has been established as the fundamental ordering principle of the international community with the important proviso that it cannot be invoked to legitimize secession. For their part the African states have not only accepted this general and restrictive usage, which amounts to equating the principle of self-determination with anti-colonialism, but they have explicity ruled out territorial revision following the transfer of power from European to African governments. Of course secessionist movements regularly attempt to invoke a more permissive interpretation of the concepts whenever they appeal for international recognition, but while they may attract covert support from sympathetic governments whose interests coincide with their own, sustained public support for a right of seccession is extremely rare. During the Nigerian Civil War (1967–70) the orthodox OAU interpretation was subjected to its most penetrating test; but although four governments (Tanzania, Zambia, Ivory Coast and Gabon) recognized Biafra the Federal Nigerian Government won the diplomatic struggle within the Organization before it secured victory on the battlefield so that the final result was to strengthen rather than weaken the orthodoxy.[9]

Self-Determination in the Horn of Africa
It remains to ask whether, despite the general bias of the UN and the OAU against territorial revision there are any objective grounds for holding that the Somali and Eritrean claims constitute a special case which might lead to their obtaining a more sympathetic hearing from the OAU in the future than in the past. Two arguments are worth considering from this point of view. The first is that Ethiopia is itself a colonial power which established its present frontiers by participating with the Europeans in the partition of Africa; the second that the Islamic world in general, and the League of Arab States in particular, have never unambiguously accepted the concept of national self-determination as the ordering principle of international society.

The first argument was formally adopted by the Somali Government at the time of its invasion of the Ogaden in support of the West Somali Liberation Front (WSLF) in 1977/8. When Somalia raised the question of its neighbouring Somali communities in 1963 it demanded boundary revision – as indeed it was bound to do by the terms of the Somali Constitution – on the basis of common nationality of all Somalis and declared its willingness 'to abide by the results of the plebiscites testing the allegiance of the people in the areas to which they laid claim.'[10]

As we have seen this demand was never accepted by the OAU. Consequently all Somali governments have been faced with choosing one of three alternatives. They could accept African mediation and attempt to normalize their relations with their neighbours in the hope that the process of negotiation might soften their initial resistance to Somali irredentism; they could attempt to contain popular irredentist demands by changing the nature of Somali society and concentrate on alternative social and political goals; or they could change the basis of their claim to bring it into line with the anti-colonial interpretation of the principle of national self-determination. Broadly speaking the civilian governments pursued the first course between 1964–1969 while Siad Barrè's military government pursued the second from the Revolution in 1969 to the confrontation with Ethiopia over the Ogaden in 1977. Whether, as Ahmed Egal has persuasively argued, it was Siyad Barrè's failure to achieve the transformation of Somali society at which he allegedly aimed which forced him to resurrect the irredentist issue in order to secure his personal rule[11] or because the collapse of central authority in Ethiopia presented opportunities which no Somali government could have resisted, the change of policy in 1977 clearly required a new international justification.

The argument which was now advanced was in line with the third alternative listed above. The new Somali line held that the inviolability of frontiers applied to sovereign but not to colonial states and that since Ethiopia was a colonial state the Ogaden Somali had the same rights to rebel against colonial authority and to solicit the support of friendly states in their just liberation struggle as had, for example, the oppressed peoples of pre-independence Mozambique and Angola. After the Somali invasion of the Ogaden had been repelled the Somali government continued to insist that it supported the right of Ogaden Somali to independence, just as they had accepted the independence of Djibouti, without insisting that it should merge with the Somali Republic. The new approach is reflected in the 1979 Constitution which commits the State to support 'the liberation of Somali territories under colonial oppression' but merely encourages subsequent unification of the Somali people 'through their own free will' (my italics).

The claim that as the beneficiary of Menelik's conquests Ethiopia was on a par with Britain, Italy and Portugal has been resisted as strongly by the Ethiopian Dergue as the earlier nationalist claims were resisted by the government of Emperor Haile Selassie. But more important for the present argument, the new Somali position has received almost as cool a reception from the OAU as the old. It is true that following Somali complaints of Ethiopian air attacks on her territory in March 1980 the late President Tolbert of Liberia, then Chairman of the OAU, sent an official message to President Mengistu expressing his concern over these reports.[12] An ad hoc OAU Commission on the Somali/Ethiopian dispute was also set up following the annual Heads of State summit in Freetown. But as rapidly became clear when the Commission met in Lagos in August 1980 African concern was mainly with the threat to African security from growing super-power involvement in the Horn (Somalia concluded an agreement with the United States immediately after the meeting under which the Americans took over the port facilities at Berbera vacated by the Soviet Union in 1977, in return for military and financial assistance) rather than with the justice of Somalia's claim. Despite an impassioned restatement of the colonial thesis by Somalia's foreign minister,[13] the Commission adopted a six-point resolution which not only upheld 'the inviolability of frontiers as obtained at the time of independence' but also expressed 'the strongest possible opposition to any encouragement of subversion against the government of another country',[13] a barely veiled reference to Somali support for the WSLF although admittedly one which applies equally to Ethiopian support for dissident Somali groups, eg the Somali Salvation Front. Predictably the Somali Government rejected the recommendations as biased and the Ethiopian Government hailed them as a diplomatic victory. There the matter rests: whatever the historical plausibility of the Somali thesis the OAU is not at present prepared to jeopardize its existence by reclassifying one of its member states as a colonial power.

At first sight the anti-colonial argument would seem to apply with more force to Eritrea which was an Italian colony between 1890 and 1942 when it was conquered by the Allied Forces. In 1952 it was federated to Ethiopia under an United Nations agreement only to be unilaterally incorporated into the unitary state of Ethiopia ten years later. It was this act, one year before OAU was established, which led to the liberation struggle. But although the Eritrean liberation movements have been more successful than the Somalis in attracting international support from neighbouring countries their struggle has never come up for debate within the OAU. It threatened to do so in the middle 1970s when President Numeiri of the Sudan openly backed the Eritrean cause; but when he became Chairman of the OAU he was evidently persuaded that to raise the issue at the summit would damage rather than enhance his standing in Africa. In any event he sought not for the first or last time to normalize his relations with Addis Ababa by withdrawing at least public support for the Eritreans during his tenure of office.

To the extent that the Eritreans have been successful in attracting international support for their cause it probably has more to do with the second argument to which I referred earlier, namely the ambiguous attitude of Arab and Islamic states to the principle of national self-determination when it conflicts with other loyalties and interests.

The emergence of self-determination as a central legitimating principle of international society accompanied the increasing secularization of

Western societies and the consequent elevation of secular principles in their international relations. In this context non-interference in domestic affairs is a modern equivalent of the principle *cuius regio eius religio* with which the European state system was inaugurated in the seventeenth century. This process of diplomatic secularization has arguably been less firmly implanted in Islamic civilization than elsewhere. In Islamic legal theory the world was originally divided into two domains, *Dar Al-Islam*, which comprised all Muslim and non-Muslim territories under Islamic sovereignty, and *Dar Al-Harb*, the domain of war, which lay beyond the Islamic pale and which was to be reduced through *Jihad* as and when opportunity and prudence dictated. When such opportunities did not exist it was possible for Islamic authorities to enter into diplomatic negotiations with non-Islamic states as a practical matter but this did not imply recognition or reciprocity.

It is difficult to establish how far, if at all, these concepts have survived into the modern period. On the surface, the Charter of the League of Arab States, like that of the OAU, rests on Western intellectual foundations. Indeed according to at least one student of Islamic international relations 'Twentieth Century Islam found itself completely reconciled to the Western secular system.'[14] Certainly claims that the Eritreans have been able to solicit international support on religious grounds need to be handled with circumspection: not only is a substantial minority of Eritrea not Muslim, including many of those involved in the liberation struggle, but inter-Arab rivalries, in the past the link between Emperor Haile Selassie's Government and Israel and the desire to establish the Red Sea as an Arab lake, have arguably all been more important than religion in determining the pattern of external support.[15] Nevertheless there is evidence that the Arab League has been involved with the Eritrean struggle since the beginning – in 1969, for example, the ELF Secretary-General attended the League summit held in Rabat as an observer – while individually Afro–Arab states which are members of both the OAU and the Arab League have often been less sensitive to charges of interfering in the internal affairs of other states than the countries of sub-Saharan Africa.[16] At different times Libya and the Sudan have been vocal champions of Eritrean seccession; similarly Egyptian support for Somalia, which could be explained originally as part of Nasser's campaign against the British in Kenya and elsewhere, also survived the post-colonial period when this defence was no longer available.

Perhaps the most that can be claimed is that when considerations of narrow national interest and calculations of prudence do not intervene the Arab world is less obviously restrained from publicly supporting co-religionists or Arab minorities than are those African states which see the orthodox definition of national self-determination as a necessary support of their fragile defences. For the moment, however, the chances of the Eritreans establishing their right to an independent existence seem hardly better than those of the Somalis. The Ethiopian Dergue has signed a military co-operation agreement with South Yemen[17], once a major conduit through which the Eritrean movements were supplied with Soviet and East European armour; Libya has reversed its traditional alliance with the Eritreans to support the Soviet line after the Revolution, and even Sudan which has traditionally provided the liberation movements with sanctuary and which since 1977 has been in open dispute with the Ethiopian Government over the Eritrean issue agreed in March 1980 to normalize relations and to 'scrupulously respect the principles of sovereignty, territorial integrity, national unity and non-interference in each other's internal affairs.' Any accommodation between the rival Eritrean movements and the Dergue – and many have been rumoured – is still likely to be mediated by the Sudan which retains some leverage through its partial ability to control the refugees; but it looks increasingly unlikely that any political settlement will concede an Eritrean secession. The conclusions seems inescapable: as with Somalia (on which the Sudan has also turned its back) so with Eritrea; in both cases the attempt to establish their claims as legitimate exceptions to the official interpretation of national self-determination has failed.

It would be easier to condemn the Ethiopian Government for its systematic denial of the rights of the Eritreans and Ogaden Somali if the concept of national self-determination was not itself intrinsically so problematic. Because it attempts to combine the values of individual freedom, social identity and social order, it represents an ideal with which it is difficult not to be in sympathy. Moreover when groups such as the Eritreans or Somali have been in intermittent revolt against the state for over 20 years their claims deserve to be taken seriously on this ground alone. But such sustained rebellion has not been sufficient to establish these claims in practice. Nor, it must be said is it sufficient in theory. Who, in the last analysis, can claim to speak for the nation in Eritrea and Somalia? In Eritrea, the ELF and EPLF have sometimes succeeded in uniting but have also frequently come to blows. In Somalia, opponents of the President are either in exile or in prison. There is nothing unique about this pattern; indeed it represents the rule rather than the exception in the history of nationalist movements. But that is not the point. Because no truly 'objective' criteria exist for establishing the identity or limits of the nation, or even for ascertaining unambiguously the national will, it is impossible to distinguish in general terms between those secessionist or irredentist movements whose rebellions against the established order are justified and those that are not.

It is for this reason that international organizations have accepted the priory of state autonomy without probing its ultimate moral basis. Thus Article 1(2) of the UN Charter calls on member states to develop friendly relations 'based on respect for the principle of equal rights and self-determination of peoples' but qualifies this by Article 2(7) which expressly forbids intervention 'in matters which are essentially within the domestic jurisdiction of any state'. The OAU, as we have seen, restricted the application of the principle within Africa still further. That the theoretical problem which arises as a result of basing the international order on the principles of national self-determination is insoluble is implicitly recognized even by states and liberation movements which seek to redraw the political map. This is clear from the importance they themselves habitually attach to the doctrine of sovereignty. Although, in a very loose way, one can speak of an international of liberation movements (they frequently co-operate in order to secure arms) it is their own particular claims with which they are concerned not those of all groups which are dissatisfied with the existing dispensation. Somali governments for example have not sought allies, with the partial exception of Eritreans, amongst the various disaffected minorities elsewhere in Africa.

There is, I fear, not much more that can be said. To take the question further would require an exercise in political theory rather than the examination of the use to which a political concept has been put in international organization and diplomacy which has been attempted here. But it is not my intention to conclude that because the Somali and Eritrean claims have been ignored by the OAU there is no justice in them, merely that an appeal to the right of national self-determination as a matter of principle cannot itself establish that right.[18]

So long as we lack a strong sense of international community with methods for settling disputes between subordinate groups then such disputes can only be treated on their merits. The problem of what constitutes the merits of particular cases is of course itself intractable, but given the recent origin of many African states, the heterogeneity of the groups they contain and the persistence of certain revisionist national claims in defiance of the OAU Charter, there is a strong case for arguing that the OAU should, in its own interest, attempt to be more discriminating in its handling of the self-determination issue. Where there is empirical evidence that claims of self-determination express 'grievances against injustices *flowing from deep and relatively fixed features* of the social and political life of a group'[19] (my italics), as in both the cases under review, there is surely a case for OAU mediation the results of which are not, as at present, a forgone conclusion.

Like all operational principles those on which the OAU Charter is based will only survive if they are interpreted flexibly and with attention to the particular circumstances of individual cases. The alternative is that the Charter will continue to be honoured in the breach rather than the observance and that 'oppressed communities' will seek liberation on the battlefield and with the assistance of external patrons who have their own interests for intervening in African affairs. Perhaps this will be the pattern of the future as it has been of the past but it need not be regarded as inevitable. In any event for an organization whose members regularly bemoan the damage done to Africa by nineteenth century partition it represents a challenge to their nascent diplomatic order which deserves urgent attention.

Notes

1. This resolution was subsequently confirmed at the 1964 Summit. The operative paragraphs rule that 'the borders of African states on the day of independence constituted a tangible reality . . .

    1. As a consequence the Heads of State solemnly reaffirm the strict respect by the all-member states of the Organization for the principle laid down in paragraph 3 of Article II(i) of the Charter of the Organization of African Unity.

    2. solemnly declare that all-member states pledge themselves to repect the border existing on their achievement of national independence',
    OAU Doc KHG/RES16(1).

    In response to objections by the Somali representative, President Nyerere of Tanzania who had introduced the resolution as referring to 'new border disputes', confirmed that the adoption of the resolution 'should not prejudice . . . discussion already in progress'. The Somalis assumed this rider covered the negotiations then taking place between themselves, Ethiopia and Kenya and confirmed this in a note verbale circulated to OAU member states on 1 August 1964.

2. Louis Dumont, *From Mandeville to Marx: the Genesis and Trials of Economic Ideology*, University of Chicago Press, 1977, Chap 1.

3. I have discussed the expansion of these institutions beyond Europe in, 'International Society and International Theory', M. D. Donelan (ed), *The Reason of States*, (Allen and Unwin, 1978), pp 122–141.

4. See Martin Wight, 'International Legitimacy', *International Relations*, Vol IV, No 1, 1972.

5. For a discussion of the role of the concept of national self-determination in the UN Charter, see Antonio Cassese, 'Political Self-Determination Old Concepts and New Developments' in A. Cessese (ed), *UN Law/Fundamental Rights*, (1977), pp 137–65.

6. See K. Nkrumah, *Africa Must Unite*, (1963).

7. The 1958 Resolution stated: 'As a first step towards the attainment of the broad objective of an African Commonwealth, the independent states of Africa should amalgamate themselves into groups on the basis of geographical contiguity, economic inter-dependence, linguistic and cultural affinity . . .' 'whereas artificial barriers and frontiers drawn by Imperialists to divide African peoples operate to the detriment of Africans and should therefore be abolished.'

8. For the text of the memorandum of the KANU Delegation to the Addis Ababa Conference in 1963 see C. Hoskyns, *Case Studies in African diplomacy* (Oxford University Press, Dar Es-Salaam 1969).

9. The high point of the African challenge to the OAU orthodoxy came with Tanzania's *Memorandum on Biafra's Case*, a document which President Nyerere circulated privately to his fellow Heads of State at the 1969 OAU Summit Conference. It failed to win further adherence to the Biafran cause but made sufficient impact to persuade the Nigerian Federal Government to make an official refutation. For both documents see A. H. M. Kirk-Greene (ed), *Crisis and Conflict in Nigeria*, Vol 2, (London, OUP, 1971). pp 429–38.

10. See Sally Healy, The Principle of Self-Determination – Still Alive and Well, *Millenium Journal of International Studies*, Vol 10 No 1 pp 14–29.

11. Ahmed Egal, 'The Real Causes of the 1977/78 War and Super Power Switch in the Horn of Africa', unpublished manuscript.

12. *Africa Research Bulletin*, March 1–31 1980, p 5604.

13. *Ibid*, August 1–31 1980, pp 5763–64.

14. See Majid Khadduri, 'The Islamic theory of International Relations and Its Contemporary Relevance', J. Harris-Proctor (ed), *Islam and International Relations*, London, Pall Mall Press, 1965, pp 24–39.

15. This is the view taken by J. Spencer Trimingham. See, for example, *The Influence of Islam on Africa*, (London, Longman's, 1980, 2nd ed), Chapter 6 (4).

16. See M. O. Ojo, *The African States and the Arab world: the Development of Afro-Arab Relations, with special reference to the OAU and the League of Arab States*, unpublished PhD thesis, London University, 1977, pp 123–38.

17. *Africa Research Bulletin*, January 1–31 1980, pp 5541–42.

18. For a theoretical discussion of this point, see Stanley French and Andres Gutman, 'The Principle of Self-Determination', in Virginia Held, Sydney Morgenbesser and Thomas Nagel (eds), *Philosophy, Morality and International Affairs*, (London, Oxford University Press, 1974), pp 138–53.

19. Charles R. Beitz, *Political Theory and International Relations*, p 115.

THE CHANGING IDIOM OF SELF-DETERMINATION IN THE HORN OF AFRICA

Sally Healy

The normative principles of the international political system are generally characterized by their pragmatism. The agreed principles of non-interference in the internal affairs of states and the preservation of territorial integrity are practical rules for co-existence which are inherently conservative and aspire to order before justice. One of the few exceptions is the principle of national self-determination, which not only possesses an ideological foundation but has also been espoused by both East and West for over 60 years.

Some realists have hoped that the idea of self-determination might go away:

Stalin wrote in 1921:

> We parted with the nebulous slogans of self-determination long ago and there is no need to revive them.[1]

Begin said in 1980:

> Self-determination is not mentioned in the Camp David agreement. That is not a coincidence. We don't want to play with words.[2]

But however unsatisfactory its implementation the idea of self-determination is still deeply entrenched in the international political system. It is likely to remain so for as long as nationalist movements develop within any of the existing states of the world.

Self-Determination and the International Political System
Nationalists seek international support by appealing to the principle of national self-determination. It is not merely that approval is sought for nationalist goals which have been developed in response to specific conditions within a state. International support is integral to any nationalist movement which aspires to full succession. If the legitimacy of the nationalist cause is denied by other powers the resources (in the form of

external assistance) which the central authorities can call upon to resist the nationalist movements are theoretically limitless. Even if the nationalists can gain control of the territory which they seek by force of arms the recognition of other states is essential before they can participate as independent states in the international system.

The longevity of the principle of self-determination and its almost universal acceptance is largely attributable to the fact that there has never been full agreement on the precise meaning of the term. Different generations of nationalists have supplied different answers to the questions which the principle begs – namely 'what is a nation?' and 'what form should self-determination take?'. Three distinct phases many be identified:

(i) 19th century Eastern European nationalism which achieved expression in the Versailles settlement of World War I (1918)

(ii) Anti-colonial nationalism which developed after 1945 and found expression in the granting of independence to the European colonies after 1960.

(iii) The new wave of nationalism which has developed in some of the multinational ex-colonial states and has not yet found an adequate institutional expression.

The Eastern European nationalists conceived the nation as a group of people bound together by a common history, language and culture. Where questions of statehood were at issue the ideal method of applying the principle of self-determination was through the use of the plebiscite to ascertain under which authority each nation wished to live. In the words of Martin Wight:

the plebiscite came as near as may be to an impartial method of self-determination in the peace settlement of 1919–20 . . . The post war plebiscites tested the allegiance of ill-defined districts of heterogeneous population which were the debris of the collapsed Central Empires. These plebiscites were at the limit of what is technically feasible in consulting popular wishes.[3]

The result of these plebiscites, however, was not the creation of a series of nationally exclusive states but a collection of multinational states in which the rights of national minorities were recognized and protected constitutionally.

With the emergence of anti-colonial nationalism after 1945 the meaning of national self-determination was radically changed. The nationalists conceived the nation not in terms of cultural exclusivity but as a group of people bound together by a common experience of colonialism, in spite of their diversity in other respects. The word 'national' began to be dropped from the term National self-determination. Race was a central feature of the nationalist identity which was asserted against the European colonial authorities. The plebiscite was not regarded as a necessary feature of the application of self-determination and the protection of minorities was regarded with suspicion as a means to entrench the political influence of white settlers in some colonies. The preservation of territorial integrity and majority rule became the new order of the day and the granting of full political independence on this basis the only satisfactory expression of self-determination.

The nationalism which has developed in some of the multinational states which resulted from de-colonization combines some of the features of both the previous types of nationalism. There is a return to the conception of the cultural nation in many cases with emphasis on the unique history, language and culture of each group. However cultural exclusivity is regarded as neither a necessary nor sufficient basis for nationalist demands. In every case the nationalists emphasize the existence of oppression within the state which resembles a colonial relationship between groups. This nationalism remains at the struggling phase so it is not possible to say what form self-determination should take to satisfy the demands of its exponents. The nationalists usually demand full political independence as the anti-colonial nationalists did before them. It is not inconceivable though that arrangements guaranteeing the recognition and protection of national minorities might not prove satisfactory in principle at some stage in the future.

Nationalists do require the acquiescence or support of external powers for the achievement of their goals. Although the principle of self-determination is well established in the international political system its meaning tends to reflect the conceptions of the most recently successful nationalist movements. It is too easy to forget that not thirty years ago the United Nations was dominated by acrimonious debates as to whether the term self-determination could be applied to colonies at all. The European powers clung to the earlier conceptions of nationhood to deny that the colonial populations constituted nations. They argued that the anti-colonial powers were interfering in their internal affairs in demanding changes which would damage the territorial integrity of the European Empires themselves. An enraged critic wrote in 1955:

> Thus self-determination is to be applied only to colonies and is identified with anti-colonialism – a sad comedown for a noble principle once thought applicable to all mankind . . . The (anti-colonial) movement has no standards, no common sense, indeed no clear objective.[4]

The debate of the 1950s over the meaning and significance of self-determination was brought to an end by the 'Declaration on the Granting of Independence to Colonial Countries and Peoples' (UN Res 1514(XV) of December 1960). This amounted to a victory for the anti-colonial interpretation of the right to self-determination endorsed by the votes of 89 states. Those who had previously resisted this interpretation marked their acquiescence by abstaining from the vote. The Declaration recognized:

> that the peoples of the world ardently desire the end of colonialism in all its forms and manifestations

It continued:

> Convinced that all peoples have an undeniable right to complete freedom, the exercise of their sovreignty and the integrity of their national territory, solemnly proclaims the necessity of bringing to a speedy and unconditional end colonialism in all its forms and manifestations
>
> And to this end
> *Declares* that . . .
>
> 2 All peoples have the right to self-determination; by virtue of that right they freely determine their political status and freely pursue their economic, social and cultural development.

The declaration was qualified by the contradictory assertion:

> 6 Any attempt aimed at the partial or whole disruption of the national unity and the territorial integrity of a country is incompatible with the purposes and principles of the charter of the United Nations.[5]

With this Declaration the anti-colonial powers established the idea that the loss of colonies did not affect the territorial integrity of a European state.

The demands of the nationalists today confront the newly established wisdom that European colonies held overseas are the *only* cases suitable for the application of the principle of self-determination. Any other demands are an unwarranted intrusion in the internal affairs of states and threaten the principle of territorial integrity which is essential to international order. Attempts to have the question of self-determination re-opened in the OAU bear many similarities to the fact of the early anti-colonial nationalists at the United Nations. There is the added disadvantage that no external power with a voice in this forum has yet shown itself willing to advocate their cause.

Some illustrations of the changing conceptions of self-determination can be drawn from the propaganda of the various groups currently demanding self-determination in the Horn of Africa. It could be argued that the unusual history of this region makes many of the rules constructed for other situations rather inappropriate. In Ethiopia we find a conquest state which resisted colonization and achieved international recognition in 1896 on the basis of its indigenous power relations; in Eritrea an Italian colony which achieved not independence but federation, and later absorption into Ethiopia; in Somalia a rare example of African nationalism which was based on national characteristics of language and culture rather than anti-colonialism; in the Oromo a majority population denied access to power. Nonetheless the peoples involved must function in an international environment not of their own making and therefore try to make their cases by appealing to the norms prevalent in international society.

Ethiopia and Somalia: competing nationalisms

Immediately after World War II the European conception of self-determination was still dominant. Thus in submissions to external powers both Somalia and Ethiopia emphasized cultural national factors:

The Somali Youth League
'We wish our country to be amalgamated with the other Somalilands and to form one political, administrative and economic unit with them. We Somalis are one in every way. We are the same racially and geographically, we have the same culture, we have the same language and the same religion . . .

'The existence of several foreign official languages within the several territories, is enough, in itself, to make aliens out of brothers of the same race, religion and country . . .

'By this union only can we have the opportunity to give full expression to our national spirit and work out our destiny as a nation of normal human beings . . .

'Union with the other Somalilands is our greatest demand which must take priority over all other considerations.'[6]

Memorandum presented by the Imperial Ethiopian Government
—On the return of Eritrea and Somaliland.

'In view of the abject misery of the Eritrean and Somali populations under the fifty years of Italian occupation which forced them to suffer the indignity of being treated legally as an inferior race in their own country as compared with the lot of other nationals, it cannot be suggested that their lot would be worse under the regime of their

Ethiopian brothers . . . There is no question whatsoever of their being afforded a proper place in the Government of the Empire for the simple reason that they are not being accorded it . . . it is futile to separate this one nation . . . Ethiopians and Eritreans are incontestibly one and the same people . . . The history of Eritrea has been one with that of Ethiopia . . . The race is the same, the language, except for dialectical differences, is the same. The culture and habits are identical . . . Similar considerations of historical, racial and cultural ties likewise apply . . . to the relations between Ethiopia and Somaliland . . . It is firmly claimed that with the forfeiture of Italian rule, Eritrea and Somaliland should revert to their mother country. To provide for such a return would be merely to recognize the realities of the existing historical and other ties which bind them integrally to Ethiopia.'[7]

During the 1950s African nationalism in its anti-colonial form was still being worked out. It was not a foregone conclusion that territorial integrity would become the sacred norm that it has to prevent any new political configurations on the continent. The validity of past history was being asserted, the sense of African Unity was strong and the radicals at least envisaged a restructuring of the continent.

Thus in 1958 the All Africa Peoples Conference (not a state organization) passed a Resolution on Frontiers, Boundaries and Federations stating:

(In the context of advocating regional groupings of states towards the ultimate goal of an African commonwealth)

'Whereas artificial barriers and frontiers drawn by imperialists to divide African peoples operate to the detriment of Africans and should therefore be abolished or adjusted:

'Whereas frontiers which cut across ethnic groups or divide peoples of the same stock are unnatural and are not conducive to peace or stability . . .

. . . the conference

(a)   denounces artificial frontiers drawn by imperialist powers . . .
(b)   calls for the abolition or adjustment of such frontiers at an early date
(c)   calls upon the Independent States of Africa to support a permanent solution to this problem founded upon the true wishes of the people.[8]

The Somali desire for unity was specifically endorsed at this conference. By 1960 such ideas, which had never been suported by the conservative states were already on the wane. The AAPC of 1961 declared in its Resolution on Neo-colonialism:

> This conference denounces the following manifestations of neo-colonialism in Africa:
> (c)   Balkanization as a deliberate political fragmentation of states by creation of artificial entities, such as, for example, the case of Katanga, Mauritania, Buganda, etc.[9]

The creation of the Organization of African Unity confirmed this trend with the agreement of the principle:

> Respect for the sovereignty and territoral integrity of each state and for its inalienable right to existence. (Article III 3) of the OAU Charter.)

Since 1963 the OAU has set itself firmly against any attempts at secession and refused to consider self-determination in any light other than that of straightforward de-colonization from European control. This inflexibility has prevented the OAU from dealing effectively with this problem in Africa. As one writer has noted:

> 'The OAU's commitment to the absolute preservation of the territorial status quo in Africa would make sense only if it were supplemented by a serious effort to come to grips with the problems that underlie and breed secessions.'[10]

The newly agreed norm for Africa clearly suited Ethiopia's situation. Note the change in emphasis between Haile Selassie's Ogaden speech of 1956 and his comments on African Unity in 1963:

> We remind you finally that all of you are by race, colour, blood and custom, members of the great Ethiopian family[11] (1956).
>   We know that unity can be and has been attained among men of the most disparate origins, that differences of race, or religion, of culture, of tradition are no insuperable obstacle to the coming together of peoples[12] (1963).

For the Somali Republic the new development was a serious set back. Since independence in 1960 they had sought the unification of all Somali inhabited territories. This aim was included in the constitution:

'The Somali Republic shall promote by legal and peaceful means the union of the Somali territories and encourage solidarity among the peoples of the world and in particular among African and Islamic people.'[13]

The case for unification was made with reference to the principle of self-determination using the European conception of cultural nationhood. The President made this plea at the inaugural meeting of the OAU:

> The most serious obstacle to African Unity originated from the artificial political boundaries which were imposed on large areas of the African continent by Colonialist Powers . . .
>
> Those who oppose the reunification of the Somali territories attempt to portray the Somali people's desire for unity as a form of tribalism. Such opponents use every means at their disposal to rank the Somali people as an ordinary tribe without any rights to nationhood. The Somali are a nation in every sense of the word.
>
> A nation has been defined as 'a people usually inhabiting a distinct portion of the earth, speaking the same language, using the same customs, possessing historic continuity, and distinguished from other like groups by their racial origins and characteristics.' The Somali people share all these common bonds, and in addition share a common religion . . . This concept of nationhood is profoundly felt by all Somalis . . .
>
> The people of the Republic cannot be expected to remain indifferent to the appeals of its brethren. The Somali government must therefore press for self-determination for the inhabitants of the Somali area adjacent to the Somali Republic . . .
>
> . . . On OTHER important issues, we share the strong feeling of all Africans that the liquidation of the last vestiges of colonialism from the African continent must be accelerated.[14]

This view no longer carried weight in a forum committed to the newer anti-colonial conception of self-determination. The Ethiopian reply denied the nationhood of the Somali and emphasized the need to respect colonial boundaries:

> Ethiopia has always existed in history for centuries as an independent state and as a nation, for more than 3,000 years. That is a fact. Second fact: the historical frontiers of Ethiopia stretches from the Red Sea to the Indian Ocean including all the territory between them. Third fact: there is no record in history either of a Somali state or a Somali nation.

That too is a fact. I apologize for stating it . . . It is in the interest of all
Africans now to respect the frontiers drawn by the former colonizers,
and that is the interest of Somalia too, because if we are going to move in
this direction then we, too, the Ethiopians will have claims to make: on
the same basis as Somalia, and for more on historical and geographical
reasons.[15]

Today a rather more sophisticated argument is advanced by the Ethiopians
to deny Somali nationhood. In outline this relies on the Marxist–Leninist
formulation that the nation is a form of community associated with the rise
of capitalism. Since the Somali have not reached this stage in socio-
economic development 'It follows' in the words of one, 'that the Somalians
are at most a tribal community and not developed further'.[16]

Arguments over whether or not the Somali constitute a nation were
really of little significance in the African context. More forceful was the
comment of the KANU delegate to the 1963 OAU meeting:

'If anyone wishes to exercise his right of self-determination let him
exercise that right by moving out of the country if necessary but not
seek to balkanize Africa any further under the guise of so called self-
determination. The principle has relevance where FOREIGN
DOMINATION is the issue. It has no relevance where the issue is
territorial disintegration by dissident citizens'.[17]

Opposition to 'balkanization' was and remains the theoretical justification
for refusing to reconsider the question of self-determination in independent
Africa. In 1962 the Somali president had made the case that Somali aims
did not constitute a form of balkanization:

'The principle of self-determination, when used properly to unify and
enlarge an existing state with a view towards its absorption in a federal
system of government is neither balkanization nor fragmentation. It is a
major contribution to unity and stability and totally consistent with the
concept of Pan-Africanism'.[18]

This argument had lost its force by 1963. The institutional form adopted by
the OAU as a state based organization adhering to the more conservative
rules of international behaviour demonstrated that the idea of Pan African
federations had passed into the realm of distant aspirations.

Nationalist Movements in the Horn of Africa
The conditions which give rise to nationalist demands for self-determination

are not, of course, resolved by debates in the OAU or elsewhere. Nonetheless, external support is still required for the achievement of nationalist goals, so these forums cannot be ignored. It was clearly established during the early 1960s that any plea which employed a European conception of self-determination was doomed to failure, especially in African circles where the anti-colonial interpretation for self-determination was supreme. Thus in the 1970s demands for self-determination from nationalists have been couched in anti-colonial terms.

This can be illustrated in the statements and literature of the various liberation movements which have emerged in the Horn of Africa. Certain features of Ethiopia's history make it peculiarly susceptible to the charge of colonialism, but it would be mistaken to regard it as uniquely so. For example, in 1967 the secessionist movement in the Southern Sudan posed their case to the OAU as follows:

'As the people of the Southern Sudan were denied their inalienable right to self-determination the great challenge to the OAU in this question is whether inherited colonialism should be condemned or not.'[19]

Patterns of 'inherited colonialism' exist in many independent states of Africa, even where nationalist movements have not emerged to challenge them.

Ethiopia was unique in retaining a political system based upon traditional legitimacy but this ceased with the revolution of 1974, since when Ethiopia has shared most characteristics of the ex-colonial African state. Yet it is since the removal of the Imperial sustem that the most serious demands for the 'de-colonization' of Ethiopia have been made.

The case for Eritrean independence has always conformed to the anti-colonial interpretation of self-determination because it was an Italian colony. It is worth recalling that in 1952, when its federation with Ethiopia was enacted, the meaning of self-determination for colonies was still a disputed issue internationally. The 'national' argument advanced by Ethiopia (see above) was not yet absurd and many European colonial powers were insisting that measures of self-government short of full independence could be regarded as adequate expressions of self-determination. By the time this view had been routed, Eritrea was absorbed into Ethiopia and fell victim of the new sanctity attached to territorial integrity. The special prestige of Ethiopia in Africa militated against making a special case of Eritrea.

Eritrea is unusual in being able to make a strong legal case under prevailing international law:

One of the oddest spectacles in the world is that of otherwise serious and sensible people who affirm that the colonized people of the Ethiopian Empire, just because the Ethiopian Empire is African, are not to be allowed to be free to decide and govern their own national identity.[20]

According to all juridical logic the Eritrean people have the right to self-determination and independence because they have been colonized and they are struggling against foreign domination.[21]

The second pillar of their case rests on their identity as a colonial people:

(Eritreans are) a colonial people deprived of their right to govern themselves democratically, oppressed by a foreign power . . . The identity of the Eritrean people is quite simply denied . . . (through the) . . . suppression of fundamental freedoms . . . the disappearance of Eritrean institutions and the imposition of Amharic as the official language.[22]

It is strange to find that the Ethiopian government refutes the nationhood of the Eritreans by reference to criteria which the Eritreans themselves do not employ:

A people constitutes a nation when it has unity based on common history, common territory, common language, common psychological make-up and culture and is a stable community formed on the basis of an advanced economic life . . . Eritrea is not a nation . . . there are no less than 8 nationalities in the administrative region of Eritrea.[23]

The argument that Eritrea has been re-colonized by Ethiopia is refuted by the use of a narrow Leninist formula which identifies imperialism with the export of surplus capital. Eritrea cannot be regarded as a colony since:

The simple truth in the case of Ethiopia is not that capital was exported from the rest of Ethiopia into Eritrea, but exactly the reverse.[24]

Ethiopia finds it necessary to refute the Eritrean case because it is such a well developed literation struggle which attracts a considerable amount of sympathy and support from outside powers. This is not the case for the Oromo liberation movement which continues to be unacknowledged outside the Horn of Africa. The Ethiopian government is therefore free to employ less subtle means than propaganda to oppose this movement. The Oromo must however press their case in the outside world.

The Oromo can and do emphasize a nationhood based on the traditional criteria.

> The Oromo nation is the largest single nation in the Horn of Africa (18m).It has a common national character that constitutes a common language, a common determination, a common territory, a common psychological make-up, a common economic life, a common history and culture . . .[25]

The development of the Oromo language is an important element in their programme:

> The Oromo Revolution demands the freeing of Oromo society from foreign language domination.
> (Programme includes) To adopt the Latin alphabet for the Oromo language . . . To develop the Oromo language and bring it out of the neglect that colonialism has imposed on it.[26]

The anti-colonial dimension of self-determination is strongly emphasized by the Oromo Liberation Front. In addition to their identity as a cultural nation they are also a 'colonized' people. In spite of the demand for an independent state of 'Oromia' their plea extends to self-determination for all the nationalities within Ethiopia.

> The liberation of all people living under the heel of the Ethiopian Empire will not be realized until and unless this colonization is negated and all oppressed nations are liberated . . . The fundamental objective of the struggle is the realization of national self-determination for the Oromo people and their liberation from oppression and exploitation in all their forms . . . by the establishment of the People's Democratic Republic of Oromia.[27]

> It was an is a historic duty for the union and its members to take up a firm position in defence of the national honour of the Oromo people, who are putting up fierce resistance against the barbarous and savage Abyssinian colonialism, and its patron world imperialism.[28]

They have also taken issue with the Ethiopian definition of colonialism as a feature of monopoly capitalism which Ethiopia could not have been guilty of since it had not reached that stage of social-economic development:

> The Abyssinian chauvinists claim that there was no colonialism before the rise of monopoly capitalism . . . (but) Lenin explicitly, clearly and

directly teaches us that colonialism existed before capitalism . . . The
national question and colonial question define the relations between two
countries or between two nations. It defines that colonialism begins
with the violation of the sovereignty of a people and occupation of their
country. The solution . . . is the recognition of the colonized nation's
right to self-determination including its separation from alien national
bodies and formation of an independent state.[29]

The most dramatic change in the idiom of self-determination is to be found
in the manner in which the case of the Somali population of Ethiopia is
presented. The development of the Western Somali Liberation Front is of
great significance in this. Their case is made entirely on the grounds of
anti-colonialism and their stated aim is independence for the territory.
National similarities with the population of Somalia are not stressed so
much as their similarities with other oppressed nationalities in Ethiopia.

We are colonized and we do not see why we should be different from the
rest of the world in securing our dignity and right of emancipation.
(Regarding union with the Somali Republic) The people will decide but
one thing is certain – Western Somalia is just part of the divided Somali
nation and it has been the dream of our people to come together one
day.[30]

The attainment of independence by the member states of the
Organization of African Unity has been an inspiration, as has the
development of armed struggle by the people of Africa against the
former Portuguese empire and the achievement of self-determination
and independence . . . by former subject peoples throughout the world.
The changes we see when our country is eventually liberated will be
fundamental and based on self-determination and self-government for
the people and the victory of their armed struggle.[31]

The Somali Republic itself no longer talks of national unifaction but endorses
the anti-colonial interpretation of WSLF. The constitution of 1979 states:

'The Somali Democratic Republic, adopting legal and peaceful means,
shall support the liberation of Somali territories under colonial
oppression and shall encourage the unity of the Somali people through
their own free will.'[32]

Historical justifications are provided to explain the colonial character of
Ethiopian rule in the area:

(Extract) Following historical accounts of Ethiopian occupation of the Ogaden in 1890s . . .

Can one doubt that had (these accounts) been describing the activities of a fourth colonialist power from Europe, world opinion, the UN and OAU would long since have insisted that the anomaly be put right through the application of the universally accepted principle of self-determination? We Somalis, wherever we live, do not understand why they have not done so, for neither the geographical proximity of Ethiopia to Somali territory nor the colour of the skin of her people should blur the otherwise straightforward issue of decolonization . . . As long as Ethiopia continues to rule through force and to deny the right of self-determination, it remains an Empire and an anachronism in the contemporary African and world scene . . .

The Somali Democratic Republic respects lawful boundaries and the principle of territorial integrity, as we respect the right of self-determination and all other relevant rules of international law in the resolution of current problems. On the other hand the Ethiopian position is simply imperial.[33]

This interpretation of history has been challenged in Ethiopian writings:

European designs on the coast forced Menelik to write his famous circular latter to the European Powers in 1891, defining his country's boundary. According to Somalian leaders he should have remained indifferent and quiet – very much like their tribal chiefs who were indifferent and quiet when they were being sold cheaply. Minilik's staunch political and military resistance to colonialism is perverted by Somalian leaders as participation in colonialism . . .[34]

On the whole it has been easiest for the Ethiopians to refute the WSLF case by ignoring the autonomous role of the liberation movement and treating it as puppet of the Somali government in pursuit of its previous 'expansionist' goals on the discredited basis of 'tribal' nationalism. The commitment of Somali forces during the Ogaden war did much to foster this interpretation in Africa in spite of the explanation given by the Somali Foreign Minister at the time:

The principle of the inviolability of frontiers does not apply to Somali territory colonized by Ethiopia. This principle concerns sovereign states and not colonial states. Ethiopia is a colonial state. She took part in the Berlin conference in the division of Africa in 1884. The population of the Ogaden has the right to self-determination.[35]

Finally the Ethiopian government does not deny the validity of the principle of self-determination. It is recognized in the programme for the revolution thus:

> The right to self-determination of all nationalities will be recognized and fully respected. No nationality will dominate another one since the history, culture, language and religion of each nationality will have equal recognition in according with the spirit of socialism . . .
> (Each nationality) within its environs has the right to determine the contents of its political, economic, and social life, use its own language and elect its own leaders and administrators to head its internal organs.[36]

The point at which this differs from the conception of self-determination employed by the liberation movements is the insistence that adequate expression of self-determination can only be sought within the present territorial limits of the Ethiopian state.

Nation or colony?

Although expounded in both East and West the principle of self-determination has never been upheld as an absolute. In liberal–democratic thought it was seen as the basis of international justice but its application was always qualified by considerations of world order and security. In Marxist–Leninist thought it supplied the basis of opposition to imperialist (capitalist) domination but was qualified in its application to socialist states. The European colonies were the only case where both USA and USSR (as the powerful exponents of the ideologies of West and East) agreed upon the application of the principle and the anti-colonial states joined them in declaring the principle of self-determination to be the ideological justification for ending the European colonial system.

However fortuitous the link between the idea of self-determination and the process of decolonization the connection of the two has become orthodoxy in international society. This is reflected in the change of idiom employed by those groups who appeal to the idea of national self-determination. Where the central question used to be 'what is a nation?' it has shifted now to the question 'what is a colony?' Where claims to self-determination were once based on such features of nationhood as a common language, customs, tradition and history they are increasingly based on opposition to political oppression which may be said to resemble a colonial relationship between the groups.

The linking of the principle of self-determination with de-colonization was a major clarification, at the international level, of those situations where the principle should be applied. The clarity gained at the international level, however, was at the price of still greater obscurity as to the meaning of the principle within independent states. Qualifying, if not abandoning, consideration of national exclusivity arising from historic and linguistic factors, appeals for self-determination now take their starting point from oppression within the state.

Notes

1. J. Stalin cited by Mesfin Wolde Mariam in *Somalia: Problem child of Africa* (Addis Ababa, 1977) p 62.
2. Menachem Begin quoted in the *Times* February 1980.
3. M. Wight 'International Legitimacy' International Relations Vol IV No 1 1972 p 7.
3. C. Egleton 'Excesses of Self Determinationi' *Foreign Affairs* Vol 31 No 4 1953 p 597.
5. UN Resolution 1514(XV).
6. Somali Youth League Memorandum to the Four Power Commission 1948.
7. Memorandum presented by the Imperial Ethiopian Government to the Council of Foreign Ministers in London, September 1945.
8. All Africa People's Conference 1961. Resolution on Frontiers, Boundaries and Federations.
9. Africa People's Conference 1961. Resolution on Neo-colonialism.
10. O. Kamanu. 'Self-determination: an OAU Dilemma' *Journal of Modern African Studies*, 1964.
11. *Ethiopian Observer* December 1956.
12. H. Selassie. 'Towards African Unity' *Journal of Modern African Studies*, 1963.
13. Somali Constitution 1960 Art 6 Para 4.
14. Address of Aden Abdulla Osman to the inaugural OAU 1963.
15. Reply of Tsehafi Taezaz Akilu Habte Wolde at inaugural OAU 1963.
16. Mesfin Wolde Mariam (as above) p 52-3.
17. KANU Delegation to the inaugural OAU 1963.
18. A. A. Osman during Kenya Somalia negotiations July 1962. cited by C. Hoskyns.
19. Memorandum presented to the 4th OAU Summit Conference (1967) by the Azania Liberation Front on the problem of the Southern Sudan.
20. *Eritrea Information* N4 Oct 1979 (Basil Davidson).
21. *Eritrea Information* N4 Oct 1979 (Alain Feret).
22. *Eritrea Information* N4 Nov 1979.
23. Mengistu Haile Mariam: Nationwide address on the situation in the Administrative Region of Eritrea June 1978.
24. Mengistu Haile Mariam: Nationwide address on the situation in the Administrative Region of Eritrea June 1978.
25. *Segalee: Oromo Journal of the Union of Oromo students in Europe*, Aug 1978.
26. *Ibid.*
27. Oromo Liberation Front Programme (1976).
28. *Segalee Oromo* (as above).
29. *Segalee Oromo* (as above).
30. Ahmed Husain Haile (WSLF Exec) *The Times* Aug 1977.
31. Abdellahai Hassan Mahamud (WSLF) in 'Go From My Country' (1978).
32. 1979 Constitution of the Somali Democratic Republic.
33. 'Self Determination and the Somali Nation' Advertisement in *New African* (March 1977) by the Min of Information Mogadishu.

34. Mesfin Wolde Mariam (as above).
35. Rahamn Barre quoted in *Le Monde* Aug 1977.
36. Programme of the National Democratic Revolution of Ethiopia (1976) Article 5.

COMPETING VIEWS OF NATIONAL IDENTITY IN ETHIOPIA

Alessandro Triulzi

Before the Ethiopian Revolution most discussions on regional separatism, ethnic nationalism and subject groups' identity in Ethiopia were confined to limited circles, mostly student unions and a few radical circles outside Ethiopia, particularly in Europe and the United States. These were, and to a certain extent still are, taboo topics among *éthiopisants* and had no place in their public meetings and scholarly publications. The same held true, basically, for all those who intended to live in Ethiopia or to conduct research in that country. One was simply not supposed, and not expected, to become involved in any in-depth study of ethnicity in Ethiopia. The old Haile Sellassie I University student papers which dealt with regional groupings and their expressed discontent towards the Ethiopian polity, though accepted by the University authorities in fulfilment of the requirements for a BA, were normally not accessible to other students or to foreign researchers.[1] All in all, the myth of a culturally united 'Greater Ethiopia', even before Levine's recent assessment,[2] appeared to the ruling élite in Ethiopia and to most *éthiopisants* as a durable and unshakable 'article of faith'.[3]

Nevertheless, the debate on what was then called 'regionalism' and the 'national question' in Ethiopia went on among student circles and a few foreign expatriates in the country, as well as among Ethiopian radical groupings outside it. The debate was at first associated with another, no less important issue, concerning the nature of Ethiopian 'feudalism' and its impact on the country's subject peoples. Although the discussion was an extremely lively one within the Ethiopian student movement, it was generally agreed until the late 1960's that regionalism was merely a symptom of the feudal system of the *ancien régime*, and that in order to defeat the former one only needed to fight the latter: 'If it is granted that regionalism is an offspring of feudalism, it follows that the latter must be combatted in order for the former to be eliminated: only thus can both evils be removed.'[4] The logical consequence of this statement appeared not to be in doubt:[5]

The way out from the dangers of divisive regionalism and ethnocentricity is to adopt socialism which by definition is one and the same act as being opposed to feudalism and imperialism. Only by aiming at the higher level of socialist theory and practice can the seemingly insoluble problems of regional, ethnic and religious antagonisms be solved. Only through socialism can exploitation be ended and national aspirations become vehicles for the attainment of national liberation.

The issue of self-determination was by and large absent from the theoretical debate then going on within the student movement. When it was raised, as it was done in the Eritrean case, it was answered mainly in the negative. Andreas Eshete, in his 'theoretical considerations' on the problems of regionalism and religion in Ethiopia, opined that[6]

> a number of the historical conditions under which the principle of self-determination was applied were not to be found in Ethiopia . . . Most of the anachronistic historical contexts and corresponding meanings of the principle of self-determination have and, no doubt, will continue to be appealed to by way of justification when questions of regionalism and religion arise in Ethiopia. Therefore, examining them will make it plain that those drawing upon them for support are perpetrating a fraud.

The rationale for such a clear-cut position appeared to be the long-term strategy which was then devised by the student movement 'to advance the Ethiopian people's struggle for liberation'. It should be recalled in fact that the students were attempting at that time to establish a nation-wide political organization which was meant 'to mediate between revolutionary theory and practice, between the rural and the urban struggles, [and] between the various fronts of the national struggle'. All attempts at individual solutions, involving separate struggles, were seen therefore as dangerous since they 'might undermine the effort to bring about a unified national struggle'.[7]

The Marxist Debate
Things however took a different turn in the early seventies when the debate over the national question in Ethiopia became a dividing issue within the student movement whose established leadership and official line were openly challenged during the 19th Congress in 1971. On that occasion the majority of the Congress upheld the applicability of the principle of self-determination to Ethiopia's oppressed nationalities thus repudiating 'the unscientific and social-chauvinist position of its ex-leaders'.[8]

Although several causes may be ascribed to the 1971 split over the national question (a split which affected in particular the old leadership of ESUNA, the American branch of the Ethiopian student movement) it is probably unfair to describe it merely as a 'generational' (ie, non-ideological) revolt of the younger students against 'the authoritarian rule of their seniors', as the Ottaways seem to believe,[9] or as an ethnocentric and nihilist plot aimed at dismantling the Ethiopian student movement, as claimed by Hagos Gebre Yesus.[10] Ever since the bloody 1969 confrontation between the students and the imperial government in Addis Ababa, which gave rise to new forms of militancy in the country and to the exodus of several student leaders towards Europe and North America, the national question in Ethiopia, ignited by the Eritrean demand for self-determination, became a major cause of *ideological* friction among the students. The applicability of the principle of self-determination to oppressed nationalities in the country was now openly debated.

Thus, within two years, the old debate on 'regionalism' had transformed itself into a major ideological and political clash. Furthermore, the 1971 fissure within the Ethiopian student movement was not to remain within the circumscribed limits of a family quarrel. After the coming to power of the Dergue, it was to be transferred to national politics when many of the former student leaders joined the Dergue's ranks and helped in the formulation of its internal policies.

The issue of self-determination in fact kept kindling the discussions within the Ethiopian left, and was to determine further splits in the mid-seventies, as by then 'the debates within the left had begun advancing towards divergent and competing lines with irreconcilable ideological differences'.[11] What these 'differences' were became clear in the years 1976-78 when the apparently unanimous stand in favour of 'self-determination up to and including secession' supported by the umbrella organization *Emaled* (Organization for the Unity of Ethiopian Marxist-Leninists) broke down into two opposite positions, one held by *Meison and Echaat* in favour of a gradual ('step-by-step') implementation of this right, and the other held by the rival *Woz* League and *Seded* who opted for 'regional autonomy' within the Ethiopian state – this last one being also the official position of the Dergue.[12]

A third position, close to the first one, but ideologically more articulate, was expressed by the post-1971 ESUNA leadership. According to this position, although the *right* to self-determination was theoretically recognized to all oppressed national groups and minorities in Ethiopia, the *exercise* of this right was to be limited to the existence of some 'necessary' preconditions. What these preconditions were became clear in 1976 when ESUNA's journal, *Combat*, published a special issue dedicated to 'The National Question in Ethiopia'.

The new ESUNA leadership, politically close to the Marxist–Leninist Ethiopian People's Revolutionary Party (EPRP), claimed that 'the problem of national liberation is inseparably linked with the problem of class emancipation', therefore: 'the national question is essentially one of the emancipation of the broad masses of exploited people of all nationalities'.[13] It followed that not all liberation struggles were to be supported: 'the question of whether a given demand for secession is expedient or not is basically a question of whether the demand promotes or retards, strengthens or weakens, advances or undermines the revolutionary class struggle of the proletariat.'[14] Along the same line, *Combat* stated that the only path of liberation for the oppressed nationalities in Ethiopia was to be sought in class contradictions and class struggle rather than in bourgeois forms of petty nationalism. The 'New Democratic Revolution' in Ethiopia meant therefore a ' "two-folded" task which the Russian proletariat carried out as a "corresponding" stage of its revolution', namely:[15]

(1) To combat nationalism of every kind, above all (big nationality) chauvinism; to recognize not only fully equal rights for all nations in general, but also equal rights in regards to policy, ie, the right of nations to self-determination.
(2) At the same time . . . to preserve the unity of the proletarian struggle and the proletarian organization into a closely knit international association, despite bourgeois strivings for national exclusiveness.

While the intellectual debate developed in rather abstract ideological terms, the turn of events in the country brought about dramatic changes which demanded a reconsideration of the theoretical debate and its practical implications. On one side the Dergue's internal policies raised increasing doubts and criticism which focused particularly on its handling of the national question; and on the other a host of old and new liberation movements, each demanding self-determination and independence from 'colonial' Ethiopia, came up from almost every corner of the country. The debate was taken up again, this time involving specific demands made by the liberation movements while for the first time more critical questions were posed by a few 'liberal-spirited' scholars and *engagé* groups and individuals of various origin and persuasion. The debate is worth summarizing, in my view, as it provides the basis for the laying out of opposite ethnic identities as well as underlining the importance of some general, yet crucial issues both for the practical solution of the problems at stake and for the no less important theoretical aspects they reflect.

The debate may be said to have focused around three major issues, all closely related to one another: the nature of Ethiopian 'feudalism', the extent to which Ethiopia acted as a *de facto* 'colonial' state towards its possessions in the south, and the quality of 'Amhara domination' over the subject peoples of the Empire; or, to put it in more general terms, the nature of centre-periphery relations in a multi-ethnic centralized African state.

Feudalism or Colonialism?

Pre-1974 Ethiopia was often labelled in the past as a 'feudal' state, a label which, for lack of better definitions, was somehow uncritically attached both to the traditional 'Abyssinian' state of the pre-Menelik period and to the loose empire he put together at the end of the nineteenth century, as well as to the centralized state which Haile Sellassie ruled up to 1974. The term 'feudal' or 'semi-feudal' is equally applied to present-day Ethiopia by most of its critics. Although some authors recognize that the term feudal was 'often applied impressionistically to Ethiopia in the past' and that its use as a conceptual category 'is fraught with unresolved difficulties',[16] feudal and feudalism are still widely used nowadays both in scholarly works and in political pamphlets concerning Ethiopia. The Ottaways, for example, claim that the 1974 revolution meant 'the destruction of the imperial, feudal system of government',[17] and most radical publications and progressive movements declare their 'anti-feudal' character and origin.

A few recent authors, however, do make important distinctions within Ethiopian 'feudalism'. Markakis and Nega distinguish between Northern (highland) and southern 'relations of production' and allege that tribute in kind and labour services which made up for the 'unpaid surplus labour' existing in the feudal foundation of the *ancien régime* was greater in the south than in the north. Thus they emphasize the 'qualitative difference in the situation of the southern producers', namely 'the irreparable loss of possession and the reduction of the southern peasantry to tenancy'.[18] This 'qualitative difference' has recently been emphasized in a long essay on Ethiopia's 'modes of production' published in the newly-born *Ethiopian Marxist Review*, the theoretical journal of EPRP. The author, Negatu Alemu, while arguing against 'the almost-canonized characterization' of pre-1974 Ethiopia as predominantly feudal, calls for a reappraisal of the *various* modes of production as this [ie, feudal] mode varied from North to South and even from province to province'. According to this author:[19]

The land holding system in the North basically lay on what was known as *rist*, generally land that is owned by an extended family, hereditary but non-saleable, and in fief-like imperial grants known as *gult*, while in the South, many areas of which were occupied by Menelik in a clear military feudal conquest, the method of land appropriation (forceful occupation of the land of different nationalities) and the epoch it occurred in (the late 19th century) put an indelible stamp on the features of the relationship between the owners and the direct producers.

Along similar lines of enquiry, Addis Hiwet had previously described the late nineteenth century process of empire-building in Ethiopia as 'the creation of a typical pre-capitalist empire-state' which was markedly different from the 'agrarian feudalism' of historic Abyssinia, loosely organized around 'a number of kingdoms, principalities and feudal baronages'. This process of conquest, which the author defines as 'military-feudal-colonialism', resulted in 'a major and extensive alienation and confiscation of the land of the subject nationalities'. Thus, in post-conquest Ethiopia,'feudal landlordism' became inextricably linked with national oppression:

> An extensive process of land confiscation and the enserfment of the indigenous peasants took place. The religious, cultural and linguistic differences between the feudal conquistadors and the indigenous peoples gave the process of enserfment a still more brutal dimension – the aspect of national and religious oppression accentuated the more fundamental aspect of class oppression. Out of the incorporated areas emerged a distinct class of feudal landed aristocracy. Hence the designation that the oppressed nationalities constitute the bulwark of feudal landlordism.

Henceforth, military-feudal-colonialism was 'the direct product of the empire-building process of the last decades of the 19th century' in Ethiopia.[20]

It is no wonder, then, that the alleged feudal nature of the Ethiopian polity had become a burning political question in which scholarly discussions may have little to offer. To put it bluntly, the feudal issue conceals a second and more important question, that of the alleged *colonial* nature of post-conquest Ethiopia. The issue is not a new one, but it has assumed dramatic overtones in the Eritrean and Ogaden (Western Somalia) cases which were both presented by their respective liberation movements as anti-colonial wars for which the universally accepted decolonization principles stand to be applied. The same claim was more recently advanced by other nationalist movements in the country, notably the Oromo Liberation Front (OLF).[21]

The question, clearly, has become a central one. Andreas Eshete was obviously aware of the broader implications of the feudal/colonial issue when he wrote:[22]

> It has been contended that certain regions in Ethiopia have been subject to Ethiopian colonization and hence can appeal to the principle of self-determination . . . But this rationale is unavailable because it rests on mistaken analysis. Colonialization, even in a primitive form, requires manufacture production. In its purer forms, it demands industrial production and capital. Certainly, feudal Ethiopia did not possess any of the prerequisites which were components of more advanced stages of social and economic organization. With feudalism, one can speak of conquest not colonialization; and this is quite a different matter.

The issue was more recently taken up in *Combat* in no less equivocal terms: 'It must be stated at the outset that whether to view the Eritrean question [or any other] as a colonial question or whether to reject this view is not an academic question but one of principled significance.' Yet this 'principled significance' cannot just be, as *Combat* states, 'a question of whether one opposes or upholds the Marxist–Leninist concept of "colonialism"' since the matter has been debated and resolved in totally opposite terms by different groups all of whom have used, or claim to have used, Marxist and Leninist principles and terms of reference.[24] ESUNA's recent analysis changes little on this point:[25]

> Thus, in the Marxist–Lenininst politico-economic sense, old-style colonialism is and can only be a product of the pre-monopoly stages of capitalism and new-style colonialism is and can only be a product of monopoly capitalism. Such being the case, it is a self-evident truth that a colonial relationship does not (and cannot) possibly exist between oppressor and oppressed nationalities in Ethiopia. Therefore . . . Ethiopia at present is not a multi-national colonial empire but a semi-feudal and semi-colonial country suffering imperialist oppression.

The matter seems however not to be so 'self-evident' to Eritreans or Oromo who, often using the same technology and quoting from the same passages, reach different conclusions, namely that Ethiopia acted as a *de facto* colonial power and that colonial violence was used in incorporating adjacent territories and in colonizing its peoples in spite of some obvious but not crucial differences with European colonialism. Typical is the following plea, made recently by the OLF:[26]

> The Ethiopian colonialists have consistently tried to confuse world

public opinion by trying to distinguish between European colonialism and Ethiopian black settler colonialism . . . they have been arguing that they are non-European with their territory adjacent to that of the colonized (Oromo) land and that they had (at the time of colonization) a feudal agrarian economy . . . However this argument is without any basis . . . The fact that Ethiopian colonizers were of the same colour as those they colonized could not hide the colonizers' domineering and racist attitudes and behaviour as evidenced in their colonial settlements and policy of forced assimilation . . . The fact that the Ethiopian colonies are adjacent to the country of the colonizers (Ethiopians/ Abyssinian Kingdom) should have made it easier for the colonizers to go home earlier than the distant Europeans . . . The fact [that] the Ethiopians had a feudal economy also does not conceal the existence of economic necessity (the quest for fertile land, grain, cattle, coffee, hides and skins, slaves and serfs, minerals, etc) for colonization and the sharing (with European colonial powers) of the territory of the Oromos and other neighbouring sovereign peoples.

Again, scholarship may fit awkwardly in this kind of debate especially since, as Paul Baxter and Hector Blackhurst have put it, 'liberal-spirited scholars have felt uneasy about recognizing the Ethiopian Empire for the mini-colonial State that it was, populated by colonized subjects rather than citizens'.[27] Besides, one feels that the debate, so far conducted exclusively in ideological terms and reciprocal accusations of non-orthodoxy, risks to obfuscate the very experience of the people who were part of this process both in the oppressor's and on the oppressed side – what Lévi-Strauss would call the 'native model' both for the colonizer and the colonized.

The nature of Amhara domination
In effect, the colonial question leads the debate to an analysis of what has been called 'Amhara domination' particularly over the southern and western parts of the country since their incorporation within the Ethiopian state at the end of the nineteenth century. This is, and has been in many ways, a controversial subject until very recently. Even Ethiopian radicals have been somehow reluctant to talk of 'Shoan or Amhara domination' within the Ethiopian empire-state alleging that 'such elements of truth as exist are commonplace characteristics of the social system itself over which no particular region of ethnic group has a monopoly'.[28] Indeed, the Ethiopian 'ruling cliques' were said to be, as in the case of Gondar, 'a veritable tutti-frutti comprising Muslims, Christians, Gallas, Amharas, Tigreans, etc. In the ruling classes, there is no such animal as a 'pure' Galla, Amhara, Tigre, Gurage, etc in the Ethiopian museum'.[29] No one would, I

think, dispute the mixed origin of the Ethiopian leadership, past and present. But this begs the question of a sociological and political definition of what it means to be an 'Amhara' in the Ethiopian context, and what the term means, and has traditionally meant, to the non-Amhara peoples of Ethiopia.

'The typically Ethiopian', wrote Mahteme Selassie not long ago presumably referring to his own peer group, 'knows by instinct what he is, what is the exact measure of the place which he occupies within his family, and at what height is found the level occupied by his family in the social scale. He is convinced that it is Good God himself who put him where he is and put the others where they are . . .'[30] This being the Amhara 'native model', other people such as the Oromo have their own. Their 'portrait of a colonizer', as depicted by an 'Oromo sympathizer', runs as follows:[31]

> From an Oromo viewpoint an Amhara is anyone who is either born into Amhara society and culture or anyone who chooses to enter them, by speaking Amharic in domestic situations, by adopting an Amharic lifestyle and by acting in public situations in support of Amharic values . . . An Amhara is one who, all in all, assumes that Amharic culture is so obviously superior to the other cultures of Ethiopia that all Ethiopians should seek to acquire that culture.

The striking resemblance between the two 'models' should not conceal the fact that they reflect two different historical experiences which neither a class analysis alone or one merely based on ethnic ground can help to understand.

The issue is further complicated by the so-called Amharization process by which several Oromo have 'become' Amhara by adopting the political and cultural code of their overlords. Yet, although one may easily 'pass as an Amhara' by adopting the victor's set of values, the basic reality remains unaltered. In the words of Karl Knuttson: 'The "political" language is without question Amharic . . .' so, 'to act the part of a *poor* Amhara would be of little avail since one of the basic ingredients in the Amhara ethnic status is its very connection with economic and political superiority.'[32] The important factor, therefore, is not so much that we, as scholars and/or motivated individuals , define Amhara domination in epistemologically adequate terms but that we understand what it means to the people themselves.

The view from Wallagga
Judging from my own experience in western Wallagga, to the Mao, the Bertha and the Oromo of the region, the Amhara did appear as the

colonizers and the oppressors. In Wallagga, Amhara is a synonym for *naftaanya* (lit, gun-carrier, ie, armed settler) and is used in particular for the haughty and harsh rule of the *gondaré* troops of *ras* Damissaw, the military ruler of the Shoan-Amhara soldiers who were settled in the region by Menelik and who were assigned Oromo land and peasants for their upkeep – literally carriers of wood and haulers of water.

In Wallagga, as in other southwestern regions of Menelik's Ethiopia, the indigenous population not only found itself on land confiscated by the state and distributed according to the law of conquest – about one third (*siso*) was given to the traditional rulers (*balabbat*), the rest apportioned between the crown, the conquering generals and their armed retainers – but was divided up and allotted to the soldiery of the newly built garrison towns or *katama*, formerly as tribute-payer (*gabbar*) but in practice mere serfs. The *gabbar* in fact[33]

> bore all the brutalities and the degradation of both the process of conquest and the post-conquest social-economic structure of military-feudal-colonialism; landless, treated as nothing more than a chattle by *neftegna, melkegna* [local governor] and *balabbat* alike. The *gebar* tilled the landlord's plot, erected the house of the *neftegna* and also provided the household of the latter with food, drink, and fire-wood. The *gebar* continued to serve the family of a *neftegna* even after the latter's demise. Indeed the feudal obligations imposed on the *gebar* were on all counts intensive and onerous.

In effect the exploitation of the *gebbar*, in spite of the 1901 proclamation which introduced a tithe (*asrat*) on the harvest of landed proprietors to try and lift from the peasants the burden of provisioning the soldiers' garrisons, was total and enduring. The moving description by Asbe Hailu, a liberal Ethiopian of the 1920's, of the onerous duties of a *gebbar* 'working on a patch of *gasha* land' in the central highlands, may help to describe the usual lot of any Oromo or otherwise 'colonized' subject of the Ethiopian south: [34]

> three times in a year he surrenders 15 *quna* [baskets] of ground flour to the *melkegna*, tribute in honey, and a tenth of his produce to the state. No sooner the peasant had unloaded the tribute due to the *melkegna* that the latter 'congratulates' the peasant for having come just at the right time to be sent to the *melkegna's qelad* [measured land] somewhere beyond the Awash from where the peasant is supposed to bring a load of *téf* [grain]. The toil-torn peasant supplicates, pleads and laments: 'Oh, Sire, it is harvest time in our area and if I don't do the harvesting now,

before the approaching rains, Sire I will be finished, evicted, uprooted! Oh, Sire!' No heeding to his pleadings and lamentations. He must go to the *qelad* and collect the load of *téf* as the *melkegna* ordered! The peasant has no choice and he submits. Cursing, like the Biblical Eyob, his birthplace, ie, his very existence, he takes to his heels in the direction of the Awash. At the *qelad* the inevitable happens. The *mislené* [the governor's representative] engages the peasant in the renovation of the *melkegna*'s house on the *qelad*. That takes a good whole week's work. Only then does the peasant reach Addis Ababa with the load of *téf*. At Addis, another task, another order! Endless! The peasant now collects the whole lot of grain – the one from the Awash *qelad*, which he would have had grounded into flour, and the one he himself had brought in earlier – and stores them properly. While he does this he runs out of his own provisions and in the hope of keeping his belly full gorgeously moves after feast places – and comes back exhausted, sick and diseased. Like a sick old dog with his head resting on a heap of animal dung the peasant passes his last torturing and agonizing days below the fence of the *melkegna*'a compound. When at last he dies, the *melkegna's* household servants carry the body on a stick and after a few scratchy digs they 'bury' him in a ditch. Oh, the donkey! No problem, somebody has helped himself to it as the peasant lay dying below the fence. A lady living nearby asks a lady of the *melkegna*'s household: 'Sister, I saw a dead body leaving your household for burial today. Who could he possibly be?' asks the lady from the neighbourhood. 'Don't mind him, Sister,' reports the lady from the *melkegna*'s household, 'he is not of human born, he is only a *gebar*.'

Whether one agrees on the colonial nature of Greater Ethiopia or not, there is little doubt that to the people themselves, as Paul Baxter reports, 'Ethiopia was a ramshackle . . . Empire of which all the members were subjects rather than citizens but in which almost all the Oromo [or any other people from the conquered regions] were *colonial* subjects.'[35]

Why this should be so had been described at length elsewhere and need not be recounted here. The harsh reality of *pax amharica* meant for most people in the newly conquered parts of the empire the alienation of their land and a brutal system of 'colonial violence' which was institutionalized in the *gabbar-naftaanya* relationship.[36] The fact that some of the traditional rulers of the south and west collaborated with the new overlords, as some of them did, is no indication of the benevolence of the system but rather of its cooptative nature. It is to be regretted that very few studies have been made of specific instances of *natfaanya* rule over the southern peoples. Were they available to us today, the debate over the feudal and/or colonial nature of post-conquest Ethiopia would probably be discussed in different terms. Nevertheless, a few points can be made here, as they have been usually neglected in the recent literature on the topic.

First, the armed settler system was widespread throughout the south and west of the newly formed empire: military colonies of *naftaanya* were settled after 1893 among the Leqa and the Gudru of Wallagga, in Limmu, Kafa, Sawro and Ilubabor in the west, and among the Arussi, Sidamo, Walamo and Borana of the south, to name only a few notable instances. These armed settlers were by and large confined to strategically situated military garrisons or *katama* which were located in the midst of the conquered regions. It was from the *katama* that the new imperial rule was administered with its own set of oppressive regulations: the exaction of tributes and taxes, daily services, corvées, and the humiliation of being subjected to a law of conquest which had all the characteristics, except the name, of a colonial one. In the words of a French contemporary:[37]

> Among the Arussi, Sidamo, Walamo, Borana, Kaficho and other Negro peoples who inhabit these southern provinces, the garrisons of the Shoan soldiers who occupy the katamas constitute Abyssinian colonies ... These katamas have served the interests of Menelik in the partition of East Africa's territories which took place at the end of the nineteenth century ... Menelik's position would have been weaker were he to oppose to the ambitions of the neighbouring European powers only a vague historical right. Instead he oppposed the effective occupation of the contested territories: military posts and, in these posts, men under arms.

Second, the *naftaanya* system was not just an administrative device applied to recently conquered areas, nor was it a new system created *ad hoc* by Menelik II. What was new was the extent to which the system operated, an extent which was dictated by the accelerated expansion of the state at the end of last century. The *naftaanya* were in fact not just the main defenders of *pax amharica*: they were part of a general process of forced incorporation of alien peoples within the state structure.

Enrico Cerulli, who visited the *worwari* (lit 'spear-thrower', one of the *naftaanya* corps) colonies in Limmu in southern Ethiopia in 1927, clearly saw this when he wrote that the real aim of the armed Amhara settler communities in the region was 'to localize the *worwari* in the country' so that after some thirty years the children of the Amhara settlers, now married to local women and maintained by the local *gabbar*, will 'tend gradually to become a local aristocracy, uniquely privileged in the law and ... in a few generations, through new marriages, they will claim foreign origins and will trace their genealogies back to their Abyssinian ancestors, the first conquerors of Limmu.'[38] Cerulli also claims that the very 'ethnic and political history of Ethiopia' has been shaped by similar colonization processes so that different parts of the country, like Kafa, Dawro or Guarage land, 'have no different origin than that which in a few generations will have the descendants of the *worwari* in Limmu; and, in general terms, the establishment of troops named ceuà [tchawa] in recently conquered frontier areas must have happened in much a similar way as the assigning, after Menelik's conquest, of the Limmu or Leqa *gabbar* to the *worwari* or *gondaré* troops.'[39]

The situation today

In the light of these considerations, it is not surprising that people who suddenly became 'Greater Ethiopians' in the late 1880's side today with those movements which earnestly demand the withdrawal of the Amhara *naftaanya* and 'the right of the colonized to self-determination'.[40] Nor is it a wonder that the Oromo in particular – who according to the Ottaways favoured the Dergue's takeover at first and were allegedly among 'the main beneficiaries' of the Dergue's policies[41] – became increasingly disaffected with its inability to maintain its own pledges such as the 'right to self-determination of all nationalities' or the 'full right to self-government' which were formally accorded to each nationality in the 'Programme of the New Democratic Revolution' of 20 April 1976.

Not only, in fact, does the Programme appear not to have been implemented but the respect it claimed for each and every nationality of the empire seems to be contradicted. The recent report to the effect that 'over two million Amhara were to be resettled in Oromo regions over the next three years', the first 80,000 having already been moved and a further 50,000 undergoing 'military and political training' at the Tatek Military Camp near Addis Ababa,[42] if proved to be true throws serious doubt on the motives of such huge 'resettlement' schemes and raises the spectre of the *tchawa* soldiers and *naftaanya* military colonies of olden times. The fact that the first resettlement areas appear to be located in the Bertha-inhabited Asosa area of northwestern Wallagga and among the Anuak of the Gambeila region – two classical spots of troublesome Shanqella along the Ethio–Sudanese border – as well as in the Oromo-inhabited regions of Bale, Arussi and Harar, suggest a political and strategic logic which can hardly be ignored.

This logic was, in a different context, assessed, by Conti Rossini back in the early 1900's when he noted that the settling of 'loyal' troops or *tchawa* along the frontiers of the expanding kingdom was a traditional process of military colonization dating back to the times of Amda Tseyon (1314–1344) and increasingly uséd in times of difficulty:[43]

... such establishments – Conti Rossini later commented – were a rather frequent device to which the *negus* resorted in order to occupy with his own trusted people strategically important sites after a rebellion or some other trouble had taken place, or in order to keep under control restless populations. Historical documents and traditions relate about these [establishments] and still in our days can we follow the development of these colonies, whose components ended up by constituting in the course of time the bulk of the population of entire districts.

The Asosa project may be taken as a good case in point. It was started in March 1979 when some '6,000 heads of families' (involving presumably a bigger number of people) from Wollo were moved to Hoha in the Asosa province 'to be settled for a better livelihood'. In the appraisal of the Settlement Authority, the area selected for the project, totalling some 10,921 hectares, is said to be 'relatively sparsely populated' and is described as 'virtually virgin land where wild animals roam'. No mention is made of the existing, mainly Bertha, population although it is acknowledged that 'hunting and bee-keeping are being carried on in the area by some of the peasants in the vicinity'.[45] This description fits very awkwardly with my own recollection of the Asosa habitat back in the early seventies when I did my field-work in the area. As for the hope of a 'better livelihood' which is proposed for the displaced Wollo settlers, the project is said to be 'suitable for mechanized, rainfed agriculture' although the following 'constraints' are listed as a dubious *caveat* to the smooth running of the operation: [46]

There is malaria in the area. This is a constant problem to the inhabitants and the intended settlers. It is also known that other human diseases are endemic in the area ... Tse tse flies infect the area and are known to carry trypanosomes which causes trypanosomiasis in cattle. A few, apparently resistant, local cattle can be found in the area but it will not be possible to introduce improved cattle breeders. Rinderpest has also been reported ...

These being the prevailing environmental conditions it seems surprising that the area should have been selected for a resettlement project. Asosa refugees in Khartoum have claimed that, since the beginning of the project, 'over three thousand [local inhabitants] have fled to Sudan' and that, upon the arrival of the Amhara settlers, 'villagers were forced to build houses for them and to supply them with free grain until they had been able to reap their first harvest. This left the local people very short of food.

Most of the settlers were men and many were armed.'[47]

The tragic irony of this 'exercise', as the Settlement Authority describes the project, is that, in analogy with the first settling of the northern soldiers in the newly-conquered southern regions which took place after the 'great famine' of the late 1880's, today the Amhara settlers came mainly from the northern regions which have been most badly hit by the recent drought in the region.

However questionable it might seem on humanitarian grounds, this relocation of poor northern Amhara settlers in equally poor, mostly Oromo-inhabited, regions in the south, seems bound to encourage new outbursts of ethnic resentment and new processes of competing national identities in the region.

References

1. Such, for instance, was Aberra Ketsele's 'The Rebellion in Bale, 1963–1970', BA thesis, HSIU 1971.
2. Donald Levine, *Greater Ethiopia. The Evolution of a Multi-ethnic Society*, The University of Chicago Press, Chicago & London, 1974.
3. See P. T. W. Baxter and Hector Blackhurst, 'Vercingetorix in Ethiopia. Some Problems Arising from Levine's Inclusion of the Oromo in his Delineation of Ethiopia as a Culture Area', *Abbay*, Cahier 9, (1978), p 159.
4. Hagos G. Yesus, 'Problem of Regionalism in Ethiopia', *Challenge*, XI, 1 (1970), p 28.
5. *ibid*, p 32.
6. Andreas Eshete, 'The Problem of Regionalism and Religion: Some Theoretical Considerations', *Challenge*, XI, 1 (1970), p 5.
7. *ibid*, p 7.
8. ESUNA, 'The National Question of Ethiopia: Proletarian Internationalism or Bourgeois Nationalism?', *Combat*, V, 2 (1976), p iv.
9. Marina and David Ottaway. Ethiopia. *Empire in Revolution*, Africana Publishing Co., New York, 1978, p 115.
10. Hagos G. Yesus, 'The Bankruptcy of the Ethiopian 'left': Meison-ERPR, a two-headed hydra – a commentary on the ideology and politics of national nihilism'. Paper presented to the Fifth International Conference of Ethiopian Studies, Nice, 19–22 December, 1977, p 6.
11. Tsegaye Atnafe, 'In Defence of Me'ison against the ideologists of Amhara National-Socialism'. Cyclostyled publication distributed by the Oromo Students in Europe, Zagreb, Yugoslavia, May 1979, p 10.
12. See *ibid*, pp 42–46; see also Walleligne Mesfin, 'La "Giunta" e la fine dei gruppi "reformisti" in Ethiopia', *Altrafica*, Rome, 7/8 (1980), pp 112–17.
13. See ESUNA, 'The National Question . . .', pp 21, 24.
14. *ibid*, p 50.
15. *ibid*, p 82.
16. John Markakis and Nega Ayele, *Class and Revolution in Ethiopia*, Spokesman, London, 1978, p 25. For a general discussion, see Gene Ellis, 'The Feudal Paradigm as a Hindrance to Understanding Ethiopia', *Journal of Modern African Studies*, 14, 2 (1976), pp 275-95.

17. M. and D. Ottaway, *Ethiopia* . . . , p 11.
18. Markakis and Nega, *Class and Revolution* . . . , p 25.
19. Negatu Alemu, 'On the Modes of Production in Ethiopia', *Ethiopian Marxist Review*, 1 (1980), p 10.
20. Addis Hiwet, 'Ethiopia: From Autocracy to Revolution', *Review of African Political Economy*, Occasional Publications N 1, London, 1975, pp 30–31.
20. See, for instance, Association of Eritrean Students in North America, *In Defence of the Eritrean Revolution*, New York, 2nd edition, May 1978, especially pp 59–78; Western Somali Liberation Front, *Information Bulletin*, Mogadishu, Somalia, June 1978, pp 1–24; oromo Liberation Front, *Oromia shall be free*, June 1978, pp 1–9.
22. Andreas Eshete, 'The Problem of Regionalism . . .' p 15.
23. ESUNA, 'The National Question . . .' p 147.
24. See, for instance, *In Defence of the Eritrean Revolution*, p 60, where ESUNA's stand – it is claimed – 'crudely distorts the Marxist–Leninist analysis of colonialism, and particularly, the colonial policy of finance capital.' Equally, the Fifth Congress of the Union of Oromo Students in Europe, in its Resolution on 'Colonialism and National Liberation Movements', claims to have adopted 'the correct interpretation of colonialism and the national question given by Lenin . . .' See *Sagalee Oromo*, V, 1 (1979), p 19.
25. 'The National Question . . .', p 59. The same concept has been restated recently by Negatu Alemu, 'On the Modes of Production . . .', p 10, fn.
26. *Oromia shall be free*, p 7.
27. 'Vercingetorix in Ethiopia . . .', p 22.
28. Hagos G. Yesus, 'Problem of Regionalism . . .', p 22.
29. *ibid*, p 26.
30. Mahteme Selassie Wolde-Maskal, 'Portrait de l'éthiopien typique'. Paper presented at the Third International Conference of Ethiopian Studies, Addis Ababa, 1966, p 6.
31. P. T. W. Baxter, 'Ethiopia's Unacknowledged Problem: the Oromo', *African Affairs*, vol 77, 308 (1978), p 289.
32. Karl E. Knuttson, 'Dichotomization and Intergration: Aspects of inter-ethnic relations in southern Ethiopia', in *Ethnic Groups and Boundaries*, ed F. Barth, Allen & Unwin, London, 1969, pp 96, 98.
33. Addis Hiwet, *Ethiopia* . . . *', p 33.*
34. *Berhanenna Selam* (Amharic), Addis Ababa, vol 3, 29 (July 1927). I have used here the English translation of Addis Hiwet, cit, p 20.
35. P. T. W. Baxter, 'Ethiopia's Unacknowleged Problem . . .', p 286.
36. 'This landed [Amhara] élite imposed upon an oppressed class of tenant farmers a colonial violence, in which [the latter] had no legal, political, or economic rights.' P. Schwab, 'Haile Sellassie: Leadership in Ethiopia', *Plural Societies*, 6, 2 (1975), p 20.
37. Henri Dehérain, 'Les Katamas dans les provinces méridionales de l'Abyssinie pendant le règne de l'Empereur Ménélik', *Bulletin de la Section de Géographie*, Comité des Travaux Historiques et Scientifiques, Ministère de l'Instruction Publique et des Beaux Arts, T XXIX, 1914, Paris, Leroux, pp 240–41.
38. Enrico Cerulli, *Etiopia occidentale*, Rome 1933, Vol I, p 137.
39. *ibid*, p 138.
40. *Oromia shall be free*, p 4.
41. M. and D. Ottaway, *Ethiopia* . . . *', p 28.*
42. Mary Dines, *Ethiopia: Aid and Human Rights*, London, nd [1980], p 2.
43. Carlo Conti Rossini, 'Gli Atti di Abbâ Yonâs', *Rendiconti Reale Accademia Lincei*, 1903, pp 7–9; and 'Uoggeràt, Raia Galla e Zobùl', *Africa* (Naples), LVI (1938), offprint, p 4. On the meaning of *tchawa/čawa/, see the definition by J. Perruchon (Les chroniques de Zar'a Yâ'qôb et de Ba'eda Mâryam*, Paris, 1893) 'signifie "soldat" an amharique, mais il

paraît désigner dans les chroniques soit un corps de troupes affecté à la demeure du roi, soit une garnison placée dans une province pour y maintenir l'ordre' (p 31).

44.   OLF, *Oromia Speaks*, vol I, 1 (1979), p 4.
45.   Provisional Military Government of Socialist Ethiopia, 'Hoha Settlement Project (Physical Plan)', Settlement Authority, June 1979, p 6.
46.   *ibid*, p 5.
47.   Dines, *Ethiopia: Aid . . .*, p 9.

THE PROBLEM *OF* THE OROMO OR THE PROBLEM *FOR* THE OROMO?*

Paul Baxter

The frontiers of Ethiopia have been restored to their old Imperial limits, and ethnic minorities in Eritrea and the Ogaden which were seeking to break away are on the defensive. The difficulties that Ethiopia has been enduring in the Horn have received fairly full news coverage, because the fighting zones have been accessible to reporters and the interests of the Great Powers and their satellites have been involved. European newspaper readers feel vaguely sympathetic towards Ethiopia. Memories of European perfidy to Ethiopia in the 1930's perhaps still tug a little at the consciences of the elderly, while the young question why it is that, whereas the technology of the rich nations could only be tardily organized to alleviate the famine which finally toppled Haile Selassie, it can quickly be organized to airlift tanks to Jigjiga and to distribute machine guns to penniless peasants. But the efflorescence of feelings of common nationhood and of aspirations for self-determination among the cluster of peoples who speak Oromo has not been much commented upon. Yet the problems of the Oromo, or Galla people have been a major and central one in the Ethiopian Empire ever since it was created by Menelik in the last two decades of the nineteenth century, and an old nagging problem from long before then. If the Oromo people obtain only a portion of the freedom which they seek then the balance of political power in Ethiopia will be completely altered. A unified Oromo would necessarily constitute a powerful force. The Ethiopian regular army and the militia depend heavily on Oromo for their other tanks. If an honest and free election was held and the people voted by ethnic blocs, as experience of elections elsewhere in Africa suggests that they well might do, then around half the votes would be cast by Oromo for Oromo and only about one-third for Amhara. There are many more Oromo than Somali and Eritreans put together.

'Amhara' is the name commonly given to the peoples of the northwestern corner of Ethiopia which is coincident with the old Kingdom of Abyssinia. During the scramble for Africa the Amhara conquered, or acquired by the default of the other colonial powers, the territory which became the Ethiopian Empire of Menelik and later of Haile Selassie. They have since ruled it for their own benefit. Amhara have continuously provided almost all the holders of government offices and still appear to dominate the revolutionary military junta. It is not possible to be precise about ethnic identities but the following statement, if not absolutely accurate, clearly indicates that Amhara domination continues and is seen by non-Amhara as continuing:—

'The Amhara-dominated military Junta has not even dropped the pretence that "No nationality will dominate another". (This was a popular slogan at the time of the revolution.) This can be deduced from the composition of the Commission which is supposed to organize the party of the Working People of Ethiopia (COPWE). Of the 123 central committe members, 109 are from the Am(h)ara nationality . . . Of the 7 Executive Committee members, only one is non-Am(h)ara . . . 13 of the 14 Chief Administrators of Ethiopia's regions are Am(h)ara.'[1]

In many other ways old forms of domination have survived the revolution. While Comrade Chairman Mengistu reviews his subjects seated 'on the gold and red velvet eighteenth century armchair favoured by the Emperor Haile Selassie',[2] his government follows centralist policies similar to those of the old Emperor.

The almost unbroken and absolute political domination and cultural dominance of the Amhara has resulted in the public presentation of Ethiopia as a state with a much more unitary culture than, in fact, it has. Foreign scholars and travellers have come to accept Ethiopia, at the evaluation of its own sophisticated and charming élite, as a nation-state whose Christian core is dedicated to civilizing the brutish pagan and Muslim peasantry. There is a distorted truth in this myth insofar as much of the history of Ethiopia can be viewed as a struggle between the Amhara and the Oromo; compared to which the chroniclers of the dynastic struggles of the petty northern chiefdoms, which have so preoccupied historans, represent a *1066 and All That* sort of diversionary tale.

The Oromo
Until recently the Oromo have been better known outside Ethiopia as 'the Galla', but that is a name which none use of themselves and which they resent. Galla is an Amharic word which entered the written literature in the second half of the fifteenth century. This pedigree does not justify the use of this term today since it has acquired pejorative connotations and is rejected by those to whom it is applied. The Oromo are made up of a number of branches, of which the best known are the Raya, Wollo, Karaiyu, Afran Kallo, Leqa, Mecha, Tulama, Guji, Arussi and Boran, but

there are several others. I have worked amongst Arussi and Boran. Some Oromo are Muslim, some are Monophysite Christians and some are Roman Catholic or different Protestant denominations (as is the martyr Gudina Tumsa), and others maintain their traditional religion. There are great ecological variations in Oromo lands, and hence great variations in modes of life and modes of production from pastoral nomadism to itinerant trading to hoe agriculture.

The cradleland of the Oromo was probably in the grasslands of southern Ethiopia where they lived as pastoral stockmen. In the early sixteenth century, triggered by demographic and ecological changes which we do not yet understand (and possibly also by the introduction of the saddled horse), there was a population upsurge and Oromo spread rapidly. They took over most of the territory which they still farm or graze. They absorbed the peoples they overran, and drove out the garrisons and religious houses from those parts of the south which Amhara had briefly colonized during the previous century. The expansion of the Oromo was approximately coincident in time with (and indeed in part may have been a consequence of) the *jihad* led by Ahmed Gran (1506–1543) which, to contemporaries at any rate, appeared likely to destroy the Christian Abbysinian state.

The different Oromo tribal groups have evolved quite different political systems, which vary from small acephalous clusters of agnatically connected neighbours to quite complex kingdoms. Oromo have never yet been politically united and, in the past, have possibly expended as much blood and energy fighting each other as they have in fighting and resisting Amhara. But most Oromo have maintained, at least in their values and ritual observances, elements of their famous *gada* or *luuba* system of age – and generation – grading. Also, and importantly, each of the several Oromo groups cherishes, as part of its oral traditions, descent from an eponymous ancestor or family stock named Oromo or Orma; so that they are each and all *ilman Orma* ie literally 'children of' or 'descendants of' *Orma* or the Orma family. So that all the Oromo speaking peoples therefore, however they may have since been divided by disputes and fights are, at any rate in opposition to non-Oromo, all of one origin or, literally 'one womb', (*gara'tok'*) or 'one family' (*Worra tok'*). The word Orma itself is used as their only name by the most southerly of all the Oromo people who live to the south of Tana River in Kenya, and who are more widely known as the Worra Dai, which is the name given to them by their Somali and Boran neighbours. These memories of common origins and shared customs and language are being refurbished as the basis for revised national identity; so for example the common name 'Oromia' has been created by young Oromo nationalists for the independent state to which they aspire or, more modestly, the state which could be an equal partner in a federation of

Ethiopian states on the Nigerian model. The name Oromia thus serves the same purpose and is as justified as 'Ghana', 'Benin', 'Mali' and 'Zimbabwe'.

Bahrey, the Abyssinian ecclesiastic who wrote *A History of the Galla* towards the end of the sixteenth century, selected *luuba* or *gada* as the organization which harnessed Oromo valour into an undefeatable force. It grouped men by age and genealogical generation into a combined ritual, political and military organization of considerable complexity which maintained a strongly democratic and egalitarian ethos and restrained the exploitation of office, wealth and power. Under the rules of *gada* no office-holder, nor set of elders in office, could retain office for longer than a ritually prescribed period, usually of eight years. Some Oromo nationalists hope to reconstruct a form of *gada*, which they see as a unique constitutional invention, as the political basis for the new Oromo state they seek to establish. *Gada*, I think, is unlikely to provide a practical working model which can deal with the complexities of a modern nation state, but it is an ideal mythical charter in which to enshrine Oromo values.[3] Oromo are brought up to resist authority based on wealth or political position. Traditionally political power was transient and was not associated with the possession of wealth or position in Oromo society. In this the Oromo differ greatly from the Amhara whose political organization has long rested on the principles of rank and hierarchy.[4]

Disinterested nineteenth century travellers among the Oromo were impressed by their culture and its underlying unity. D'Abbadie wrote of 'les Oromos grande nation africaine',[5] and the great missionary explorer Ludwig Krapf suggested that 'Providence has placed this nation in this part of Africa for very important reasons. It is the Germany of Africa'.[6] Krapf, perhaps naïvely and certainly ethnocentrically, saw the Oromo as the dynamic nation which would, if only they accepted Christ, lead their less fortunate and less numerous neighbours militarily, economically, spiritually and culturally. But, in the event, it has taken the shared experience of Amhara imperialism to create an Oromo national consciousness.

Relations with the Amhara
Their preservation of a subtle literary and Christian cultural tradition in beleaguered isolation in the Ethiopian Highlands is an achievement of which the Amhara are very properly proud. The ruling élite seems to have been very confident of the superiority of its own culture and its duty to impose it on any who sought near equality with it. But, since the sixteenth century, fears of Islam and of the Oromo have dominated the political consciousness of the Amhara ruling élite, and the thought of the two in combination has been a recurring nightmare.

The Amhara have seen their problem as how to first hold off and then later to subjugate and exploit the Oromo. For them it has been the problem of the Oromo. But for the Oromo it is the Amhara who have been the problem. In competition for land and grazing the Amhara have conquered and occupied the land traditionally inhabited by the Oromo, and have imposed their own political control and their religion. The struggle between the two ethnic groups precedes the establishment of European colonies in the last century and the efflorescence of the new African nationalisms in this one,[7] and it continues.

Very little is known about early conflicts,[8] but in the earlier centuries it was as often the Amhara who felt threatened as it was the Oromo. Bahrey[9] (whose 'History of the Galla' has been mentioned already) was concerned to explain how it was that Christians could be defeated by pagans. He states that between 1530 and 1546 the Oromo had overrun Bale and the lowlands of Dawro and were menacing the Highlands. Indeed both Kings Galawdewos (1540-1559) and Susenyos (1607-1632) sought foreign assistance in their struggle with the Oromo. (As the present government does.) But from the mid-nineteenth century, when the northern chiefs and kings obtained fire-arms, Christian Amhara domination spread. Tewedoros (1855-1869) and Johannes IV (1872-89) campaigned against the Oromo but it was Menelik (1867-1913) who effectively extended his Shoan Kingdom to incorporate the Oromo into his colonial empire.[10]

Amhara policies have continuously provoked, and thereby confirmed, those very responses which they feared. For example, the mass acceptance of Islam by the highland Arussi of Arussi Province[11] in the 1930's was, in part, a mass demonstration of anti-Amhara sentiment and rejection of all the values of their Amhara colonizers. This confirmed Amhara beliefs that many Oromo were, basically, uncivilizable because they rejected Christianity so passionately.

In action the policies of northern administrators have veered between treating Oromo as pagans or as Muslims to be pillaged on the one tack, and as treating them as inferiors who might nevertheless be 'Amharized' and incorporated into Ethiopia as full citizens on the other. The latter option has never been open to the black negro (Shanqella) peoples of the southwest, and it must be acknowledged that Oromo treatment of those they have overcome in the southwest has been no better than their own treatment by their conquerors.

Pre-revolutionary Ethiopia, to Oromo and other southerners under the yoke was not, as it is described by the ruling military junta and their sycophants, a 'feudal state'. The term 'feudal' may have a limited applicability to the traditional northern Amhara and Tigrean states, but if it is applied to the south or to the Empire as a whole it is only a term of abuse which obscure analysis.[12] Ethiopia was a ramshackle, though rapidly changing and developing, Empire of which all the members were subjects rather than citizens, but in which almost all the Oromo were *colonial* subjects. Hence the Oromo movement towards liberation can be viewed as part of the continental movement towards decolonization.

The Naftaanya: 'armed settlers'

The officials who administered Oromoland for the Empire were often self-made men with little formal education who had fought their way up the patronage-ladder of the Ethiopian administrative system. Few members of the cultivated Amhara aristocracy, whom European visitors often found so charming, ever served in the south except at, at lowest, provincial governer level. If policy was made by staff officers in Addis Ababa, it was interpreted by made-up rankers in the field. Their behaviour moreover was hardly inhibited, as was that of colonial officials in other Empires, by respect for a powerful metropole to which principle could sometimes outweigh expediency. Provincial officials were poorly paid, and it was anticipated that they would supplement their salaries by using the opportunities offered by office. I doubt whether many of the officials in Kofele, for example, lived on their official pay and might even have risked dismissal for not living at the level expected of those in their positions. A local magistrate whose salary approximated £30 a month ran a Landrover, drank imported Scotch and maintained three children in fee-paying colleges. No one thought this exceptional. The university graduates and liberal-minded civil servants which Haile Selassie's education programme had produced were seldom sent to the provinces: there was not one graduate employed in the Arussi provincial administration. It is in such terms that the Amhara claim to civilize and rule must be assessed.

Officials were feared and usually disliked, as any rate in Arussi and Hararghe, as were the Amhara settlers who had been given much of the best land which had been taken from the indigenous population. (Most officials were also settlers, but most settlers were not officials.) Many Oromo, particlarly those living in the more fertile areas, were transformed by conquest (or later on by government allocation of their land to landlords) from free farmers into poor share-cropping tenants. From the beginning a major rallying cry of the Oromo Liberation Front has been the eviction of the foreign settlers (*naftaanya*), many of whom reportedly remained in Oromoland despite Proclamation No 31 of 1975, 'To provide for the Public Ownership of Rural Lands'.[13] Indeed the Dergue apparently soon realized that the elimination of many *naftaanya* landlords, and the consequent dispersal of their armed retainers threatened their control in the region. The interests of *naftaanyas* have to coincide with those of the central government because they entirely depend on that centre. Certainly landlords in Arussi were haunted by fear of another collapse at the centre, because they recalled that in 1936, between the flight of Haile Selassie and the establishment of Italian rule, they had had to flee north or remain and be killed by their subject tenants. (Indeed for an initial period the Dergue because of its dispossession of landlords was thought to be pro-Oromo![14]) but the Dergue subsequently set out to establish plantations in the south, of loyal, armed northern peasants. This was described as 'Rehabilitation' and frequently involved the bewildered assistance of EEC and UNDP/ FAO. One example involves the vast stretches of the banks of the Webi Shebelle which have been taken over to settle poor northerners and urban proletariat. It is wrongly claimed that the local Arussi do not use, or require the land.[15] Another case in point is the Hoha Settlement Project which seeks to settle, initially, 6,000 northern families in Asosa Sub-Province in Wallagga. The Settlement Authority claims that the '10,921 hectares is virtually virgin land where wild animals roam', but at the same time puzzlingly records that 'the bamboo in the area is being extensively used for building and handicrafts by local people'.[16]

Accurate population figures for Ethiopia are not obtainable. Mesfin Wolde-Mariam,[17] quotes an official estimate of the total population in 1968 as 26.4 million while John Markakis[18] quotes another official estimate for 1970 as 24.3 million, with an annual growth rate of 2.5 per cent. These gross indicators will, however, suffice for our purposes. Estimates of Oromo population vary from Levine's, in 1974, of 7 million[19] to that of the Oromo Liberation Front, in 1978, of 18 million.[20] It was not in the interest of the Imperial Government to collect and publish accurate data on the ethnic, linguistic and religious diversity of Ethiopia. Hence, as Markakis remarks 'the relative strength of the major ethnic groups remains a matter of guesswork. Such conjectures as have been advanced are politically motivated and therefore of little value'.[21] The Atlas of Ethiopia, for example, prepared for student use, has a map (No 46) which shows the distribution of mules, and tables which list the most trivial manufacturers, but does not attempt to present accurate or comprehensive data on the different tribal, linguistic or religious groupings of the Empire. Yet, almost certainly, the Oromo are the largest ethnic group in Ethiopia and make up somewhere between a third and a half of its population. A reasonable estimate would be ten million and it could be as high as fifteen million. (A further hundred thousand Oromo are citizens of Kenya.) Certainly there are very many more Oromo than there are Cubans in Cuba, Irish in Ireland, or members of many of the minority nationalities in the USSR. There must be as many Arussi or Leqa or Guji Oromo as there are Somali in the Somali Republic.

The Oromo Language

There are many differences of pronunciation, vocabulary and syntax between the dialects of Oromo but an intelligent and eager native speaker of one dialect can make himself understood in any other, and soon become fluently at ease in it. Oromo speakers in Ethiopia extend, though not uninterruptedly, from Wollo in the north (approximately 13°N) to the southern frontier and from past Harar in the east to past Dembi Dollo in the west. The distance between the most northerly Oromo in Ethiopia and the most southerly in Kenya is about 1,200 kilometres. Oromo is also very widely spoken as a second language and is probably as widely spoken as Amharic even in towns. For example, in Kofele, where I lived for a year the only Ethiopian residents I can recall who claimed not to be able to speak any Oromo were the Police Officer and the telephone operator: I was assured that both of them were surpressing the truth because they thought it demeaning to speak Oromo to a foreigner. Oromo must have been less studied and have less printed material available in it than any language in the world which has a comparable number of speakers.

The criterion of language is important in distinguishing who is an Amhara and who is an Oromo. Amhara society is, at its fringes, fairly open and, in the past, certainly many Oromo have become Amhara or 'passed' as Amhara. It is commonly said that the late Emperor Haile Selassie was by pedigree or 'blood', as much Oromo as Amhara, but no one would ever have classified him as an Oromo. Comrade Chairman Mengistu is also Amhara by culture, it seems, rather than by descent. The crucial criteria are cultural. One may pass as an Amhara by adopting the observances of the Coptic Church, an Amharic name and lifestyle and, particularly, by using the Amharic language as one's first tongue. Indeed the Amharic script is a symbol of national identity and Amharic the language of political power. Fluent Amharic and an Amhara way of life have always been, and still are, pre-requisites for entry to government employment; and government was, and is, almost the only employer of schooled labour. For most officials 'to civilize' was to 'Amharize'. Census figures were employed by Imperial officials to show that Amharic was driving out the other languages of the Empire, and particularly Oromo, by a sort of inverted linguistic Gresham's Law! There has been little change since the revolution. In 1976 an Oromo doctor who had been educated overseas and did not write Amharic was refused employment because of that. Students say that they are afraid to write home, and their kinsfolk do not write to them in anything other than Amharic for fear of the censors reporting them as 'tribal counter-revolutionaires'.

Until the final days of the Empire, Oromo was denied any official status and it was not permissible to publish, preach, teach or broadcast in any

Oromo dialect. In court or before an official an Oromo had to speak Amharic or use an interpreter. Even a case between two Oromo before an Oromo-speaking magistrate had to be heard in Amharic. I sat through a mission church service in which the preacher and all the congregation were Oromo but the sermon, as well as the service, was given in Amharic, which few of the congregation understood at all, and then translated into Oromo. To have preached in Oromo would have resulted in the preacher being fined or imprisoned. Every Oromo child, like every child in Ethiopia, had to start his primary school studies in Amharic. Every child who sought higher education had to pass an examination in Amharic even though he would be instructed in English. It is as if every English child had to use Russian in primary school and switch to Turkish for his secondary schooling. But many Oromo were inspired by the very difficulties which confronted them and, like Ewe or Welshmen, sought through education an entry into salaried employment.

During the all too brief dawn which followed the fall of Haile Selassie's government, an Oromo newspaper (*Bariisu*: Dawn) did appear written in Amharic script. Some further issues have appeared and some underground papers have appeared in Oromo. Educated Oromo bitterly resent being deprived of the use of their native language for anything but domestic purposes, and particularly so when it is the first language of a nation of some ten million or so people. After land reform, the main impetus among the masses of Ethiopia towards the revolution was an upsurge of local culture nationalisms. So traditional Oromo *Gada* rituals were revived in the country, and in Addis Ababa attempts were made to publish in Oromo. Hayle Fiida, an Oromo emigree student leader who returned as an enthusiastic revolutionary was associated with the Oromo efflorescence and his political faction became known as an Oromo group. He soon disappeared from public view and was rumoured to be in prison or dead. Interest in non-Amhara cultural activities may be classified as counter-revolutionary and is extremely dangerous.[22]

Official ethnic affiliation, then, had to some extent been optional for the educated, ambitious and mobile, except that few Muslims could contemplate changing their religion. (There are a few Muslim Amhara.)

Perception of the Amhara

From an Oromo viewpoint, an Amhara is anyone who is either born into Amhara society and culture or anyone who chooses to enter these by speaking Amharic in domestic situations, by adopting an Amhara lifestyle and by acting in public situations in support of Amhara values, in particular by following the fasting rules of the Coptic Church. In rural Arussi, the maintenance of different fasts and rules about slaughtering and feeding and alcoholic consumption are major markers of ethnic differences. It is extremely difficult for Christians and Muslims to be convivial together.

For the Oromo an Amhara is one who assumes that Amhara culture is superior to the other cultures of Ethiopia and that all Ethiopians should seek to acquire that culture. Amharic is 'civilized' *siltane*, all else is backward and uncouth. This does not mean that all subjects were encouraged to become *evolués*. No more than the French Empire could the Ethiopian have given equal citizenship to all its members. As McClellan points out, 'northerners firmly believed that acculturation of the indigenous population served only to undercut and destroy the system of domination and exploitation that had been erected.[23]

I do not suggest that these criteria are the only ones which Amhara themselves, or students of Amharic culture, would always use; clearly mine are partisan. My endeavour here is to present the Oromo view. For Arussi at any rate, 'Amhara' and 'self-satisfied dominant élite' have become convergent categories. The Amhara peasants in their own homelands were also abused and exploited by government. But the fact that there were a number of migrants from the north who lived in poverty did not impinge much on Arussi consciousness – just as the presence of poor whites in the American south, or whites living on social relief payments in South Africa, does little to diminish black awareness of white dominance. What Arussi experienced were the slights and hardships and exactions which were imposed on them by a foreign ruling élite. An élite, moreover, which appeared to look down on them and to discriminate against them as cultural and political inferiors.

The cheery middle-aged magistrate whom I got to know fairly well, and have mentioned before, will serve again to illustrate this. He had spent over thirty years in government service and had acquired an extensive knowledge of Ethiopian law in practice but he did not pursue his duties in a learned way. He did not own, nor have access to, a single law book, not even to a copy of the laws of Ethiopia. As the laws were very readily interpreted in favour of the rich, powerful or open-handed, this was not much of a disability in daily life. Arussi did not bring cases to him; so most of the few cases he heard were between Amhara and Amhara or Amhara and Arussi. He did not let his prejudices hamper his self-interest, and any Arussi who was substantially richer than the Amhara with whom he was in dispute had a good chance of winning his case. He insisted to me that he was an Amhara. Arussi classified him as such but also said that he came of Christian Oromo stock from Shoa (I do not know if this was so). He used Amharic as his domestic tongue. Certainly, he perceived Arussi culture to be inferior to Amhara culture. His amused response to my research was similar to reactions I had experienced among the more insensitive Europeans in other parts of colonial Africa. He assured me that I was wasting my time studying Arussi culture, because they had none and were 'uncivilized'; in support of which he instanced that those Arussi who owned wellington boots continued to wear them even in the dry season!

Local resistance and rebellion

Until the time of the Italian invasion, there were sporadic, local outbreaks of rebellion against particular harsh governors or landlords, but little that hinted of concerted Oromo action. The Italian invasion in 1936 lead to local outbreaks of violence and there were some attempts to create locally autonomous units. In Arussi and Bale the people seem to have been content to chase away or kill their local *naftaanya*. In Wallagga and Jimma (where the Italians were welcomed as liberators), there was a series of attempts to create a Western Oromo Federation which would break away and place itself under British mandate. But this came to nothing.[24] There was a comparable movement in Harar in 1947. When Haile Selassie returned to Ethiopia during the Second World War with Allied military backing, he was able to strengthen his grip on the country remarkably, in part because those who had opposed him were tainted by accusations of collaboration and treason.

The first Oromo rebellions which had national reverberations were those led by Arussi patriot-cum-brigands such as Wako Guto in Bale in the 1960s. With some Somali support, these succeeded in pinning down substantial units of the regular Army and demonstrated that determined Oromo could wage effective guerilla warfare against the Addis Ababa authorities. Probably more important for the development of Oromo national consciousness, were the unanticipated consequences of the Imperial Government's own creation of a strong, centralized administration which ignored local differences in custom and culture, coupled with the imposition of Amhara culture. Both these developments increased resentment and promoted reactive, positive feelings of nationalism. As more Oromo became civil servants, Army officers and NCO's and more Oromo schoolboys became undergraduates, and as more Oromo members of parliament managed to get elected, the various Oromo groups found that, in addition to humiliating experiences, they shared a common language and similar values. The new pan-Oromo consciousness was largely generated by the army, the University and the Parliament itself. For example, when I was looking for one of the members from Chilalo constituency in the lounge of Parliament I was directed, by an usher, to a corner where 'the Oromo members usually sit together'.

Those who achieved success in the national arena, and hence influenced opinion at home, discovered just how numerous, extensive and similar the Oromo peoples were. The most conspicuous manifestations of this new self-consciousness was the Macha–Tulama Self Help Association which, founded in 1965 by an Oromo civil servant, immediately attracted an enthusiastic membership. I met some of its leaders in the club house in 1967 and it was clear that the movement was flourishing. It even persuaded an Amharaized general, Tadessu Biru, to become its active patron. It was impossible to measure precisely the support the association gathered but it so alarmed the government that, using a bomb explosion in a cinema as a pretext, it imprisoned the general and the association's key members and dissolved the association. As elsewhere in Africa, as for example among the Ibo, Akan, Somali or Kalenjin, increased education, trade and mobility fostered wider ethnic sentiments and affiliations; whereas wider national and narrower class consciouness have more frequently been subjects for political rhetoric than realized action or organization.

Each of the Oromo peoples has a distinctive history but all share comparable experience of the imperial system. I select a few instances from Arussi Province to illustrate these.

The view from Arussi

The Arussi people extend far beyond the boundaries of Arussi Province, which takes their name, into Bale and Sidamo. They wee finally subjected by Shoan gunpower in 1887 after six different annual campaigns which R. H. Kofi Darkwa, the Ghanaian historian of Menelik's reign, summarizes as 'perhaps the most sustained and the most bloody which Menelik undertook'.[25] Four years after their conquest, the observant traveller Donaldson-Smith passed among the Arussi and was appalled by their reduced condition, recording that: 'The Arussi Galla here, as elsewhere, were regarded as slaves and were even sold in the market as such'.[26] Arussi in the 1960s spoke of this Amhara conquest as the commencement of an era of miseries, after which life had not run as God intended, but out of true. Boran likewise divide their history into two eras, 'before' and 'after' colonization: the first of which is good and the second bad. John Hinnant reports that the Guji Oromo also tend to 'blame all social problems on their incorporation into Ethiopia'.[27] This reflection of Amhara colonization is aggravated by such acts of arrogance as the naming of the only secondary school in Arussi Province after Ras Darge, who is bitterly remembered for his brutal conquest of the Arussi Highlands.

After the conquest, much of the best Arussi grazing land was given as booty to the soldiers and the clients of Ras Darge. Where, as in the Rift Valley or on the better agricultural land, these new settlers had acquired most of the land near a garrison town and were sufficient in numbers to give each other mutual support, they put down local roots and expanded. Those however who had been allocated land in areas best suited only to grazing which also tended to be furthest from the garrisons encountered serious hostility from their Arussi tenants. Many exchanged the land they had seized for livestock which they then took back to Shoa. Some landlords who stayed on were killed or driven out during the Italian occupation.

During my research in 1969, many Arussi elders in Kofele and Gedeb districts reminisced nostalgically about the brief period of Italian rule as a time during which they had been free to kill Amhara and, free of exploitative and apparently random impositions by officials had been able to earn money and had been encouraged in the practices of Islam. It was not so much that they had enjoyed Italian rule but rather that they had found it much less oppressive than that of the Amhara. Moreover, the Italians had broken the power of local Amhara landlords so that they had never been able to completely re-establish themselves as rifle-armed autocrats over their tenants. I several times heard elders tell younger men that, however harsh the Amhara appeared to be, their rule was much more moderate than it had formerly been. Former *banda*, Italian irregulars, were still often praised in song.

I worked in Kofele District which had the smallest proportion of Amhara settlers and landlords in Arussi Province, and even there it was difficult to see anything at all that the population had gained from their incorporation in the Ethiopian Empire. To the people, it seemed that all they received in return for taxes and exactions were yet more officials to extract more taxes and exactions and bribes. Although the people of Kofele did not appear to be as totally 'pauperized' as their fellow tribesmen of the Rift Valley floor,[28] they were mostly extremely poor even though they farmed and pastured their cows on well-watered hills.[29] The land was becoming severely over-grazed and barley yields had dropped, in many places to a level at which it did not justify ploughing and sowing. The agricultural crisis was masked by the increased cultivation of that hardy carbohydrate producer, the false banana (*ensete edulis*). Many children had kwashiorkor, yet a large proportion of the butter that was churned was bought and exported from the district by traders from the north. Cash was in extremely short supply and opportunities for wage-labour were negligible. Migrant labour did not create social problems because there was no work to which young men could migrate.

There was a chasm between the 'Amharized' and the Arussi which only a handful of young, schooled and determined young men sought to cross. Even the handful of wealthy Arussi landlords or headmen (*balabbats*) only maintained courteous and formal (or 'joking') relations, but never easy nor intimate ones, with local Amhara. Almost all the school places above

Primary III in the Province were filled by the children of settlers, officials and migrants. Only 4 out of 57 senior officials listed in the official Handbook of Arussi Province were not classified by Arussi as Amhara. I don't think even a single Arussi was employed in an equivalent post outside the Province. Only about 5 out of 30 or so low-level government employees in Kofele District were Arussi. The Islamic Kadi who dealt exclusively with disputes or religious affairs between Muslim Arussi was even allotted a Christian Amhara clerk!

Similar discrimination occurred, and apparently continues in the much more populous province of Harar where Oromo make up around 60% or more of the population and produce most of the export crops and tax revenues.[30] A heavily disproportionate number of school places were occupied by the children of alien administrators and settlers and, by 1977, less than a hundred Oromo had completed secondary schooling and some dozen proceeded to University. Few Oromo held even lowly posts in the provincial administration. Even in predominantly Oromo-speaking sub-provinces the numbers were negligible as the following figures for 1977 illustrate:— Chercher none out of 28, Harar Zuria 4 out of 30, Gursum 1 out of 22, Garu Mulleta 7 out of 20, Dire Dawa 3 out of 40, Oborra (Weberra) 2 out of 21, Habro 1 out of 23. The three Oromo officials from Oborra and Habro were executed in 1978, and have not been replaced by Oromo. None of the judges and only one high school teacher and one nurse were Oromo. Oromo are accustomed to such discrimination. A similar incident to the one I describe below for Kofele occurred in 1969 in Deder in Hararghe Region. The Governor with the agreement of the ministry of the Interior, merely disallowed one of the Oromo candidates who had been elected to Parliament and declared an Amhara elected in his place. The disqualified candidate, Mohammed Abdo, was killed in 1978 reportedly by order of the Dergue. Generally, the allocation of Parliamentary seats was biased to favour Amhara areas: Menz and Geshe sub-provinces, for example, returned as many MP's as provinces such as Arussi and Illubabor.

The Muslim religion was discouraged in large and small ways. The *Arussi Provincial Handbook* listed 216 churches but only 59 mosques in an area in which almost every settlement had a hut reserved as a mosque. The churches and priests had land and tenants granted to them and received donations from the state; mosques did not. Every seller in Kofele market, almost every one of whom was a Muslim Arrusi paid a market toll. Almost all the revenue was absorbed in the wages of the Christian Amhara clerks, but the small surplus was used to pave a road to the church which was only used fully twice a year, while the market remained a foul quagmire throughout the rains. Only I was astonished at this decision. The officials assumed that no better use would be found for the money, and Arussi assumed that market tolls were just another exaction from them to benefit their rulers.

During the cholera epidemic of 1970–71 the great annual pilgrimage to the tomb of Sheikh Hussein (the Muslim patron-saint of southern Ethiopia) was banned because it would spread infection, but that to the Christian shrine at Koluubi was allowed because the prayers of Christian pilgrims should diminish the epidemic. To add insult to injury, the church at Koluubi itself (an Oromo name meaning 'wild garlic') had been deliberately erected on an Oromo site of blessing and pilgrimage in order to Christianize it.

I could heap up incidents of Amhara arrogance but brief versions of two others must suffice.

One Friday afternoon in 1969 a Police Land-rover brought an Arussi prisoner to Kofele to be hanged in the market place on the next day. It was the only police vehicle to visit the district during the twelve months I lived in it. The condemned man had been under sentence for over ten years, for participating in the shooting and killing of the adult son of his Amhara landlord. There had been a violent quarrel over the calculation of the share of crops due to the landlord. One of those sentenced with the prisoner had escaped from prison and another had died in prison. The Landlord had refused to accept compensation, and hence have the death sentence commuted, so the sentence was to be carried out. The prisoner, who had been provided with clean clothes for the event, told me that he had been sent for execution because the prison in Asella was so overcrowded.

What looked like a rugged set of football goal posts had been erected in the market place. The policeman who had accompanied the prisoner put the noose around the prisoner's neck, threw the loose end over the crossbar, tied it to the front bumper, reversed sharply and jerked the man up. They then untied the rope from the bumper hitched it to a stout peg and left the corpse dangling. They drove back directly to Asella but left instructions that the corpse was not to be removed before dusk. The late Ato Saddo, an Arussi mission convert and teacher and a most gentle man, had the body cut down and buried at his own expense. The gibbet was still standing months afterwards. The reasons for the delay in carrying out the sentence, and the crudeness of its performance could tell us much about the mixture of humanity and Old Testament harshness which compose Amhara Law, but that is not our present concern.

The Arussi were numbed and outraged. Those who had heard the news waited by the paths to inform those coming to market; the women turned back wailing as they do at a mourning and the men were silent and angry; the market was completely boycotted on that day, and on the following Saturday, except by curious children and northern settlers and migrants.

Arussi rightly or wrongly, were convinced that if it had been an Amhara who had shot an Arussi then the most that could have happened was that the killer would have been ordered to hand over some compensation, and the kin of the victim ordered to accept it. Again and again, as if it was a refrain, I was told: 'This is the way the Amhara destroy us. Are we like bush animals?'

At the Parliamentary Elections in 1969 the two-seat constituency of which Kofele District formed a part returned two Arussi members. Arussi made up the overwhelming majority of the electorate, but this was the first time that two Arussi had been returned; and that was simply because more Arussi had been persuaded to register and to vote. The Governor however regarded the result as subversion of the proper political order and had one of the candidates disallowed (the other was thought to be protected by Swedish Aid patrons) and ordered a fresh poll. During the second poll Arussi voters were threatened, some imprisoned and the majority prevented from voting so that a Christian northerner was declared elected.[31]

Most Arussi in the District had demonstrated only the slightest interest in the Election up to the time of the Governor's intervention. They tried to avoid any contacts at all with government agencies which all, in their experience, exsisted only to hold them back; they regarded Parliament, not entirely justly, as another Amhara trick. But irregularities in this election roused passionate Arussi if not Oromo, feelings. They were angry not just because Arussi were repressed, they were familiar enough with that, but because they were so openly humiliated. Protests such as 'The Amhara are trying to kill us': 'The Amhara are trying to destroy the Arussi' 'It is better to live like Tigre' (ie in open revolt as in Eritrea): or 'It would be better to follow Wako' (the leader of a guerilla force in Bale), were reiterated again and again. Men retold nostalgic stories of Italian times when they had had the freedom to kill Amhara. The defeated candidate was transformed from a traditionalist and Government time-server into an Oromo martyr. A consequence, which surely the Governor could not have wished, was that poor peasants and wealthy pastoralists learned that Parliament must have some importance if the Governor was so anxious to cheat Arussi out of a representative. A small group of schoolboys and primary school teachers had always been embarrassingly eager to discuss national affairs with me, but the great mass of the rural population had been quite unconcerned. After that incident I was constantly asked, even by elderly women, about how elections, etc, were carried out in Europe. This particular act of Amhara arrogance struck just at the time it could set off a reverberating chord.

Oromo nationalism since the revolution.

The collapse of Haile Selassie's autarchy has obviously unleashed a variety of repressed forces throughout the Ethiopian Empire,[32] of which nationality appears to be the strongest, most passionate and enduring. Certainly among the Oromo, many of what were local, sullen resentments have been converted into national aspirations, and a nationalist struggle has developed which has now been temporaily repressed by the intervention of foreign forces. The breech-loading rifle helped Menelik to subjugate and hold down the Oromo, as it did many other African peoples in other Empires. It still remains to be seen whether the repressive concommitants of the Kalashnicov will achieve the same effect. It is doubtful whether the bloodshed of the last few years, in which thousands have died in wars and massacres and in the streets and prisons, can be interpreted simply as inevitable, if bloody stages in a revolution or a class war. In part at least, what appears to be involved is a process of decolonization in which the grip that the Amhara have held over the government of Ethiopia for some ninety years is being profoundly challenged.

It is not possible to assess accurately either the extent or the depth of pan-Oromo fervour, nor to estimate the effectiveness of pan-Oromo organization and resistance in Ethiopia since the government allows no testing of opinion nor any free discussion. But clearly both are growing and the Oromo peoples, as distinct from a handful of Oromo individuals, will certainly become an increasingly influential factor in Ethiopian politics. Even though much of the educated Oromo leadership has been killed or exiled,[33] those Oromo who are living and suffering as refugees are quite clearly getting to know and trust each other and are creating a substantial organization. The Oromo Liberation Front since its foundation in 1974 has become a movement and not just a student pastime. Though their magazines and circulars are still written partly in international student idiom, they are working toward a policy for the time when, as they hope, the Dergue will collapse and are waging practical and understandable campaigns for their rights. A nationalism which is rooted in a common language and shared modes of thought and feeling, and which has been nurtured in shared colonial-style oppression, can only be repressed by an extremely efficient as well as ruthless, and strong state. Even with the help of East German internal security police, under the Dergue it is doubtful whether this can be achieved.

Today even a wealthy, secure and benevolent government would find it difficult to woo the Oromo,[34] and the Dergue has shown few of those characteristics. It must remain dependent on the fire-power of its foreign allies unless it can find some more permanent appeal to base itself upon than the 'Somali threat' or the deriding of the old Emperor's ghost; land distribution to peasants can only be a one-off measure.

Oromoland, or 'Oromia,' encompasses Shoa, which is the very heartland of the Ethiopian state and includes the capital Addis Ababa (*Finefine* in Oromo). The soil in the north has been degraded by generations of poor farming and most of its forests destroyed. The most productive farming land of Ethiopia is in the south and much of it is still farmed by Oromo. The south has been the granary of the north and its supplier of meat, butter, sugar, honey (used to make the national drink, mead), and the coffee and even, until the 1930's, of slaves. Addis Ababa and the new towns of Shoa could not be fed without food provided by rural Oromo land and labour. The south also provides almost all the principal exports of coffee, gold, timber and hides and skins. If the Ogaden or Eritrea were detached from it, Ethopia would merely be dimished; but if the Oromo were to detach themselves, then it is not just that the centre could not hold, the centre itself would be part of the detached Oromo land. The Empire, which Menelik assembled and Haile Selassie held together, would fall apart. The Amhara would then be forced back to subsist in their barren and remote hills.

On the one hand their numbers, geographical position and natural resources give the Oromo a strong base from which to bargain or to act but, on the other, the crucial dependence of Ethiopia on the Oromo inclines the central, and Amhara-dominated, government to strike out at any manifestation of Oromo consciousness. Presumably the inertia of the Organization for African Unity and the cynicism of those great powers which have interests in the Red Sea and the Gulf will not permit Ethiopia to split into its national components. Equally, from all reports, Ethiopians of all nationalities and classes are wearied of being kept in order by the troops of foreign powers; for Oromo this is a double yoke. If Ethiopia is not to remain a broken-backed fief state, dependent on foreign arms and handouts, its government must clearly find some way of countering the alienation of the Oromo. But it is difficult to see, at present, any policy the military junta could adopt in order to achieve this as long as it continues to see Ethiopia through Shoan eyes. The junta appears to have taken over Haile Selassie's conviction, though justified by quite different dogmas, that any other cultures must be suppressed and that to grant any devolution is a sign of weakness. Yet, to an outsider, deeply attached both to the ideal of a just and democratic Ethiopia as well as to Oromo aspirations, some form of devolution seems the only humane way, indeed the only practical way, of reconciling Oromo rights with order and peace in the Horn.

As long as a Northern oriented, Shoan-based government persists in defining its central problem as holding down the Oromo by a mixture of brutal oppression for the mass of people and patronage for its own lackeys, it can only aggravate the very basic problem of, or for, the Oromo. As experience in Eritrea, Tigre, the Ogaden (and even the neighbouring southern Sudan) would appear to show, intransigent but not very efficient centralism only intensifies the resistance it seeks to quell.

The slogan of the Oromo Liberation Front is 'Let Oromo freedom flower today!' (*Addi bilisumma Oromo Ha'dararuu!*). The hopes may be over-optimistic but the time of flowering and fruiting cannot be delayed forever. One of the characteristics of 'twentieth century anti-colonial revolutions is the effort to establish a new form of society with substantial socialistic elements . . . (and) throwing off the foreign yoke is a means to achieve this end'.[35] It may be that the Oromo will have to push on their struggle into a bitterness that no-one seeks. But the last decades of this century do not seem to be favourable to empires (even those disguised as socialist nation states) that depend on the subordination of large ethnic groups to smaller ones.

Notes

* This is a revised version of a paper which appeared as 'Ethiopia's Unacknowledged Problem: The Oromo', *African Affairs*. Vol 77, No 208, July 1978 pp 283–296. I am most grateful to the editors for permission to reprint here.
   I am also most indebted to my friend Mohammed Hassan for references, suggestions, contributions and many stimulating discussions. I am also grateful to the SSRC for the research grant which enabled me to carry out field research in Ethiopia.

1. *STORM: Somali, Tigray and Oromo Resistance Monitor* No 2, March, 1981 p 1.
   I am aware that in this essay I grossly over simplify the complexities of ethnicity in Ethiopia; in particular I use Amhara in many instances where Shoan might be more appropriate. See Gerry Salole. 'Who are the Shoans?, *Horn of Africa*, No 3, 1979 pp 20–29 and Hector Blackhurst 'Ethnicity in Southern Ethiopia', *Africa* Vol 50, No 1, 1980 pp 55–65.
2. Victorian Britain. 'Ethiopia eludes Moscow in a Saville Row Suit.' *The Guardian* March 14, 1981.
2. Victoria Britain. 'Ethiopia eludes Moscow and Blackhurst in P. T. W. Baxter and Uri Almagor, editors, *Age, Generation and Time: Features of East African Age Organizations* (London: C. Hurst), for a full discussion of surviving Oromo gada systems.
4. See Donald N. Levine's *Wax and Gold: Tradition and Innovation in Ethiopian Culture.* (Chicago Press, 1965), and *Greater Ethiopia: The evolution of a Multi-ethnic Society* (Chicago University Press, 1974).
5. A. d'Abbadie, 'Les Oromos grande nation africaine,' *Annales de la Societe Scientifique de Bruxelles*, 1879, 2nd partie, pp 167–192.
6. Quoted by Richard Pankhurst in 'The Beginnings of Oromo Studies in Europe,' *Africa: Rivista trimestrale di studi documentazione del'Istituto Italo-Africano*, XXXI No 2, 1976, pp 171–206.

7. Richard Greenfield was perhaps the first writer to point out this central contradiction in the Euthopian state; see his *Ethiopia: A new political History* Pall Mall Press, 1965. Some local observers, such as Consul Erskin in the 1930s, certainly saw the dilemma.

8. See Ulrich Braukamper. 'Islamic principalities in south-eastern Ethiopia between the thirteenth and sixteenth centuries.' *Ethiopianist Notes* Vol 1 No 1 p 17–47, vol 2, pp 1–30, 1977 and 1978.

9. Bahrey 'History of the Galla' in *Some Records of Ethiopia 1593–1646*, trans, and edited by C. F. Beckingham and G. W. B. Huntingford. London, Hakluyt Society. 1954.

10. M. Hassan 'Menilek's conquest of Harrar, 1887 and its effect on the political organization of the surrounding Oromos up to 1900' in *Working papers in society and History in Imperial Ethiopia: the southern periphery from the 1880's to 1974* ed D. L. Donham and Wendy James, 1980.

11. There are no standard ways of spelling Ethiopian place or tribal names in roman script. I use Arussi for the province, which is the usual mode, and for the people, language and land.

12. One might have hoped that E. M. Chilver's 'Feudalism in the inter-lacustrine Kingdoms' In *East African Chiefs*, ed by A. I. Richards (London: Faber and Faber 1960), pp 378–93 had settled the matter, but the debate on the use of 'feudal' in Africa appears to be endless. For a succinct analysis of the use of the term generally and in relation to Ethiopia see Gene Ellis, 'The Feudal Paradigm as a Hinderance to Understanding Ethiopia.' *Journal of Modern African Studies*, 14, 2 (1976), pp 275–295 and 'Feudalism in Ethiopia: A further comment on paradigms and their use.' *Northeast African Studies*. 1.3 1979–80 pp 91–98.

13. *Negarit Gazeta*, No 26, 29 April, 1975; reprinted in 'Rural Development in Ethiopia,' *Rural Africana*, No 28, (Michigan, Fall, 1975), p 145.

14. Marina and David Ottaway. *Ethiopia: Empire in Revolution*, African Publishing Co NY 1978 p 91.

15. Maggie Black 'Rulers who can't forget.' *The Guardian*, 4 June, 1979 and my letter of 5 July, 1979.

16. Provisional Military Government of Socialist Ethiopia. *Hoha Settlement Project*(Physical Plan). Prepared by Settlement Authority Assisted by UNDP/FAO Project. ETH/75/025 June 1979.

17. *An Atlas of Ethiopia*, Addia Ababa, 2nd ed, 1970, p 73. Mesfin Wolde-Meriam distributed some maps, based on IEG Central Statistical Office, Surveys carried out between 1964–68, on language distributions, at the Fourth International Conference of Ethiopian Studies in Rome, 1972. The surveys must have been dreamed up in make-believe land.

18. *Ethiopia: Anatomy of a Traditional Polity* (Oxford, Clarendon Press, 1974), p 51.

19. op cit p 38.

20. Union of Oromo Students in Europe, Press Release, 17 January, 1978.

21. Markakis, op cit p 52.

22. The eagerly awaited Oromo English Dictionary being prepared in Chicago by Professor Gene Craggs is apparently to be printed in the Amharic script at government insistance. If that is true then the volume will be a scholarly curiosity and of little practical use.

23. Charles W. McClellan. 'The Ethiopian Occupation of Northern Sidamo–Recruitment and Motivation' in *Proceedings of Fifth International Conference on Ethiopian Studies*. Session B, 1978, pp 513–523.

24. See Patrick Gilkes, *The Dying Lion. Feudalism and Modernization in Ethiopia*. London: Julian Friedmann, 1974); see his Ch 7 for a fuller account of Oromo national movements.

25. *Shewa, Menilek and the Ethiopian Empire* (London, Heinemann: 1975), p 105-6.

26. Donaldson-Smith. 'Expedition through Somaliland to Lake Rudolf,' *Geographical Journal*, 8 pp 221-39 1896.

27. In 'Gada as a Ritual System: the Guji' in P. T. W. Baxter and Uri Almagor editors, *Age, Generation and Time: Some Features of East African Age Organizations* (London: C. Hurst, 1978).

28. Karl E. Knutsson, 'Dichotomization and Integration: Aspects of inter-ethnic relations in Southern Ethiopia,' in *Ethnic Groups and Boundaries*, ed F. Barth (London: Allen and Unwin, 1969), pp 86-100.

29. See Yilma Kebede, 'Chilalo Awraja,' *Ethiopian Geographical Journal*, 5, 1 June, 1967), pp 25-36.

30. Demissie Gebre Michael, 'The Kottu of Harerge: An Introduction to the Eastern Oromo.' *Bulletin No 68*, College of Agriculture, Dire Dawa Dec 1974 p 30.

31. For a much fuller account of this election see my 'Always on the outside looking in. A view of the 1969 Ethiopian elections from a rural constituency.' *Ethnos* 45 1-2 1980 p 39-59.

32. Allessandro Triulzi, 'Social Protest and rebellion in *gabbar* songs from Qellam, Wallaga,' in Tubiana J. ed *Modern Ethiopia from the accession of Menilik II to the present.* Rotterdam: A. A. Balkema. 1980.

33. Gunnar Hasselblatt. *Schréie in Oromoland.* Radius Bucher, Stuttgart, 1980.

34. Charles McClellan. *op cit* p 521.

35. Barrington Moore Jr *Social Origins of Dictatorship and Democracy* (1966 Penguin Edition 1979) p 113.

SOMALI SELF-DETERMINATION IN THE HORN: LEGAL PERSPECTIVES AND IMPLICATIONS FOR SOCIAL AND POLITICAL ENGINEERING

W. Michael Reisman*

Somaliland, as a geographical term, refers to vast areas in the Horn of Africa, inhabited almost exclusively by the Somali people for centuries. Western Somaliland, the extensive inland area between the mountain ranges of Ethiopia and the plains of the Somali Republic, has been claimed by both countries. It is inhabited almost entirely by Somalis, who appear to identify, to all intents and purposes, with the Somali Republic; ecologically, the area appears to be more integral to Somalia than to Ethiopia. Ethiopia exercises jurisdiction in the area. However, throughout most of this century it has been the theatre of intermittent warfare, sometimes local, but increasingly international.

Any consideration of the legal issues in the conflict in western Somaliland – in particular, to whom it rightly belongs – requires some historical perspective. The dismemberment of Somaliland and the division of its people were effected in the last half of the 19th and the early part of the 20th centuries by four expanding Empires: Great Britain, France, Italy, and Ethiopia. Britain's original interest in Somaliland was as a food source for Aden. By the 1870's, the UK had agreed to Egyptian jurisdiction as far south as Ras Hafun, primarily to prevent other European powers from entering there. Meanwhile the French established themselves at Obock and the Gulf of Tadjoura, while the Italians entered the wings, as it were, at Assab in Eritrea. In 1889, Italy tried to establish a protectorate over Abyssinia. But Ethiopia repudiated the interpretation of Italy's claims and developed its own imperial ambitions, circulated in the letter by Menelik II, in 1891, in which he made allegedly historical claims over vast areas of East Africa.[1]

From 1884 to 1889, Britain concluded protectorate agreements with coastal Somalis in order to fill the vacuum created by Egypt's precipitous withdrawal from the region. In 1896, a treaty with the Ogaden was signed. Comparable agreements were struck with other Somalis by France and

*The first part of this paper was originally published as 'The Case of Western Somaliland', in *Horn of Africa*, vol 1 no 3, 1978.

Italy. Among themselves, the three imperial powers had worked out basic spheres of influence and some boundary agreements.[2] In 1884, for example, Britain purported to establish boundaries with Italy for their respective protectorates. Neither had been authorized to do this under the express terms of the treaties with the Somalis by the local authorities party to the original protectorate agreements.

During this period, the power of Ethiopia increased greatly, partly because of the political acumen of Menelik II and partly because of the cupidity of European arms merchants who supplied his forces with modern arms. In 1896, Menelik decisively defeated the Italian army at Adowa, thus undoing the border agreements which Britain and France had just concluded with Rome. Menelik's strategic importance was magnified by the Mahdist revolt in full flame in the Sudan. Anxious to purchase Menelik's neutrality in that conflict and to discourage his incursions into the Somali protectorate, Britain concluded another border agreement with Menelik in 1897, surrendering large expanses of the British Somaliland Proctectorate to Ethiopia.[3] This treaty was concealed from the Somalis, who apparently could not divine it, in any case, from changes in the minimal local activity by Ethiopian regular and irregular forces. As for the boundary between Ethiopia and the Italian Somali protectorate, an agreement was concluded in 1896, but no copy of it nor record of its terms is extant. The local inhabitants were not again consulted. A joint attempt to demark the boundary in 1908 failed. In the south, Britain established a protectorate over Jubaland which was ultimately extended into that part of Somaliland now administered by Kenya in its Northern Frontier District. Part of this was ceded back to Italy by Britain after the First World War, again, without consultation of the inhabitatnts.

Modern Somali nationalism is said to have commenced with Sheikh Mohammed Abdullah Hassan, the so-called 'Mad Mullah', who sought to drive out the Europeans as well as the Ethiopians at the beginning of the century.[4] He failed and, for the next forty years, the struggles in Somalia were essentially between the four imperial powers. In 1935, Italy occupied Ethiopia and in 1940 British Somaliland as well. Shortly afterwards, the British conquered the Italians in East Africa and, for a short period, virtually all of Somaliland was united under a single colonial power. In 1942, Britain restored Ethiopian sovereignty in the metropolitan areas and confirmed the borders which had been set in 1897; but it retained administration of parts of Somaliland: Ogaden, the Haud and the Reserved Area.

This is not the place to explore the strikingly consistent territorial metaphysics of empires throughout history; however, a brief comment is called for. Empires which have based themselves on an attributed divine authority or some mystical *volksgeist* do not seem to accept the notion of fixed borders. Instead they conceive of what we may call 'perimeters' provisionally demarking their sphere of effective control from that of the 'barbarians'. The perimeter is to be respected by the barbarian but will be pushed back at an appropriate time by the power of the empire. In the interim, imperial designs on the barbarian territory are to be respected by third states. This metaphysics, confounding to the outsider but self-evident to believers, permits the empire simultaneously to demand respect for the perimeter at will, and to retain the right to denounce,with a full righteous indignation, territorial moves by another state in its own intended area as 'aggressive' or 'expansionist'. An insight into this metaphysics can help to explain Haile Selassie's territorial programmes, even before he himself regained effective power. An imperial proclamation of 1941 declared:

I have come to restore the independence of my country, including Eritrea and the Benadir [the Ethiopian name for Somalia], whose people will henceforth dwell under the shade of the Ethiopian flag.[5]

Belatedly, Europeans familiar with the history of the area began to consider the interest of the Somalis. In 1946 Ernest Bevin, then British Foreign Secretary, recommended a Greater Somalia:

Now may I turn to Eritrea and Somaliland. I think that M. Molotov has been more than unjust in stating that we are trying to expand the British Empire at the expense of Italy and Ethiopia, and to consolidate what he calls the monopolistic position of Great Britain in the Mediterranean and Red Sea. In the latter part of the last century the Horn of Africa was divided between Great Britain, France and Italy. At about the time we occupied our part, the Ethiopians occupied an inland area which is the grazing ground for nearly half the nomads of British Somaliland for six months of the year. Similarly, the nomads of Italian Somaliland must cross the existing frontiers in search of grass. In all innocence, therefore, we proposed that British Somaliland, Italian Somaliland, and the adjacent part of Ethiopia, if Ethiopia agreed, should be lumped together as a trust territory, so that the nomads should lead their frugal existence with the least possible hindrance and there might be a real chance of a decent economic life, as understood in that territory.[6]

The proposal failed and, in 1948, the British withdrew from the Ogaden and the Ethiopian Empire seized it. A Somali protest in Jigjiga was suppressed. In 1950, the Italian protectorate was transformed into an

Italian Trust Territory with a pre-determined duration of 10 years. In 1954, the vestige of the Reserved Area was given to Ethiopia without warning, occasioning violent demonstations of protest in the British protectorate. In 1960, the British protectorate and the Italian Trust Territory achieved independence and united, as the Somali Republic.

For their part, Somali leaders consistently refused to endorse the unauthorized disposition of their territory by the Protecting powers. As Lewis writes:

> After independence, the union of Somalia with the British Protectorate added a new complication. In their negotiations with the British government the Protectorate leaders formally refused to endorse the provisions of the Anglo-Ethiopian treaty of 1897 which they were considered to fall heir to in succession to Britain. However questionable in international law, their attitude was that they could hardly be expected to assume responsiblity for a treaty which, without Somali consent and in defiance of prior Anglo-Somali agreements, eventually led to Ethiopia's acquisition of the Haud.[7]

The Somali Liberation Front began operations in the administered territories against Ethiopian forces and established a number of offices abroad.

The available record of Ethiopia's activities in the Somali territories it administers varies from indifference to bursts of violence. From some publications such as the United States *Area Handbook*[8] a picture of benign neglect emerges. But examinations closer to the field reveal frequent instances of official violence, often intended to suppress the political and economic rights of the Somalis. Practices of this sort were heralded by Ethiopian entry into the Ogaden in 1948, when police opened fire and killed 25 members of the Somali Youth League. Nor was this a single instance. A correspondent for the *London Times* who visited the Haud in 1956 reported:

> Individual tribesmen have been brutally treated (it is not possible to describe the intensely painful and humiliating torture) and Ethiopian police have attacked the tribal women. British liaison officers have been threatened by armed police, and attempts have been made to overwhelm and disarm the British tribal policemen. The most recent and serious development has been a blatant attempt to suborn the British tribes. In the case of the Habr Awal, the Ethiopian authorities tried to foist upon it some settled and partly detribalized members as Sultan and elders, a plan that strikes at the roots of the tribal organization and loyalty. At the

same time, an intertribal meeting was called without notifying the British liaison officers, and Ethiopian officials, alternating between threats and promises, tried to persuade the tribesmen to accept Ethiopian nationality . . .[9]

Many other examples are provided by the late Professor Silberman in an unpublished manuscript.[9a] It is difficult to say whether acts such as these represented a policy of official terror or were simply undisciplined outbursts. From the standpoint of international responsibility the distinction may not be important.

The most recent history of western Somaliland has less to do with the issues of substantive law considered in this paper and more with procedures. Hence it may be reviewed briefly. The uneasy stalemate of Somali and Ethiopian claims in western Somaliland was stabilized from 1960 to what appeared to be a reciprocally tolerable level of violence. Whenever that level was exceeded Ethiopia responded with major coercions directed against the Somali Republic. Throughout this period, Somalia contended that its regular forces were not engaged in the belligerent zones, while Ethiopia insisted that they were.

The overthrow of the Emperor by the Dergue in 1974 set loose centrifugal forces throughout the Empire and, as in other parts, the level of fighting escalated in western Somaliland. The increasing success of Somali forces coicided with the expulsion of the Soviets from the Somali Republic and the shift of their support to the Dergue. In addition to material, this support included as many as 10,000 Cuban soldiers reportedly under Russian generals, a force sufficient to turn the tide against the Somalis, most of whose forces appeared to break and retreat to the Somali Republic. Thus, Ethiopian control of the area was re-established. If the pattern in the Horn of Africa persists, the events of 1977 and 1978 will not be the conclusion but only one more chapter in a continuing conflict. The international legal issues are not moot.

1. The Boundary Issue and Ethiopian Claims

The western Somali case is not, at heart, a boundary dispute, but an aspect of the case which is quite unique in the context of African politics is the absence of legal borders between Somalia and Ethiopia. Between Ethiopia and the former Trust Territory, there is only a provisional administrative line which the British established when they transferred the territory to Italy (the UN designated trustee) in 1950; the provisionality of the line was underlined in Article 1 of the Trusteeship Agreement and, in fact, from 1950 until the termination of the Trust in 1960 the General Assembly of the United Nations pressed Ethiopia and Somalia to establish a boundary.[10]

Nor are there binding treaties, for the Somalis are not party to any agreement ceding parts of Somaliland to Ethiopia since they never authorized any European government to cede their territory.

In 1897, an agreement between the Italians and Emperor Menelik II reportedly established a provisional border running parallel to the coast. The terms of the agreement are not known because no documents have survived.[11] But here again there is no indication of Somali privity.

In 1908, another Italian-Ethiopian Convention established the basis for the demarcation of the border,[12] but it was never implemented, partly because it incorporated the 1897 agreement which had vanished. From 1935 to 1948, the Ogaden was merged with Italian Somaliland and administered in sequence by the Italians and the British. Thereafter, the Ogaden was given back to Ethiopia, once again without consulting the wishes of the inhabitants. This latter transfer, it may be noted, was effected after the United Nations Charter and the formal installation of the doctrine of the right of self-determination as a key norm of international law.

Thus, the legal situation with regard to the southern borders is that there is no *de jure* border; all that exists is the 'provisional administration line' established by Britain, Italy and Ethiopia at the time of the establishment of the Trust in 1950. The repeated United Nations efforts to secure a demarcation of a boundary between Ethiopia and Somalia from 1950 to 1960, a well as the language of the Trusteeship Agreement itself, make clear that the official representatives considering the matter in the UN did not believe that the provisional administrative line of 1950 was a legal or *de jure* border.

The complex and confusing web of border claims between Ethiopia and the Somalia Republic in the area of the former British Protectorate can only be unraveled by tracing lines of asserted authority back to their source: the will of the indigenous Somali peoples inhabiting the regions in question. In the 1880s, Great Britain concluded a number of Protectorate Agreements with Somali coastal tribes, the final being with the Ogaden in 1896.[13] These Protectorate Agreements represent the foundation of British authority on the Horn of Africa.

The agreements, with minor variations in formula, reiterate a number of key points. First, the manifest objective of the agreement, as set out in the considerandum, is the maintenance of the independence of the tribe concluding the agreement. Second, the agreements by express language and implication concede the sovereignty of the tribes over their territory. To deny it would, indeed, have undercut the entire purpose of concluding such agreements. Third, the agreements establish a relationship of trust and good faith, hardly less demanding than that of a trustee in private law. Thus Article I of the Agreement with the Warsangeli provides:

The British Government, in compliance with the wish of the undersigned Elders of the Warsangeli, undertakes to extend to them and to the territories under their authority and jurisdiction the gracious favour and protection of Her Majesty The Queen-Empress.[14]

Given the ecological indispensability of the inland areas to the nomadic life, it requires a great leap of the imagination to assume that the Somalis would even imply that Britain or anyone else might alienate that vital territory. Professor Silberman observes:

> . . . the Somalis in signing the 1884, and later, agreements knew full well what they were doing and . . . they had not ceded any right to the Crown to disrupt by treaty the arduously built up mastery of the seasonal ecology of the Horn.[15]

It is this complex of protectorate agreements which formed the exclusive basis of the authority of Great Britain with respect to the Somali territory. Principles of the interpretation of international agreements require strict construction of the terms of the instruments, especially when there may be a partial cession of sovereignty. Lawful performance requires strict fidelity to the explicit terms which have been agreed upon.

In 1884, the British attempted to delimit the inland boundaries of the Somali protectorate with Italy, which purported to have a protectorate over Ethiopia. The agreement of 5 May, 1894 extended the protectorate considerably inland. But Menelik II, the Ethiopian Emperor, refused to acknowledge Italy's asserted protectorate. The subsequent Italian defeat at the hands of Menelik and Britain's difficulties with the Mahdist uprising in the Sudan made London anxious to settle with Ethiopia on terms that would win Menelik's good will.[16] James Rennel Rodd, later Lord Rennel of Rodd, was sent to Addis Ababa in 1897 and concluded a treaty andan exchange of notes delimiting the border.[17] The note of 4 June, 1897, purported to establish the border. In contrast to the agreement with Italy in 1894, Great Britain in the 1897 agreement ceded about 25,000 square miles. Other provisions of the Treaty of 4 June, 1897 made plain that the United Kingdom had struck a 'package' deal, purporting to trade the patrimony of the Somali tribes in exchange for commercial privileges for British traders in Ethiopia and commitments by Menelik to remain neutral with regard to the Mahdist war. As against Britain's breach of the Somali protectorate, there was no countervailing Ethiopian claim of any international legal merit, for as of 1897 Ethiopian claims could not be supported 'by any firm Ethiopian occupation on Somali soil beyond Jigjiga.'[18] The Somalis themselves were unaware of the 1897 Agreement. Lewis reports:

... it was not until 1934, when an Anglo-Ethiopian boundary commission attempted to demarcate the boundary, that British-protected Somali became aware of what had happened, and expressed their sense of outrage in disturbances which cost one of the commissioners his life. This long period of ignorance, far from indicating acquiescence, was facilitated by the many years which elapsed before Ethiopia established any semblance of effective administrative control in the Haud and Ogaden.[19]

Ethiopia's claims for Somali territory adjacent to the former British Protectorate are ultimately based, in international law, upon the 1897 Treaty and the Exchange of Letters which followed it. Insofar as that treaty is null and void, Ethiopia's claims have no legal basis.

As a matter of law and fact, the 1897 Treaty was void because it presumed an authority which the Somalis had never accorded Great Britain. The Somalis gave no authority to the British to transfer Somali territory to another state. Ironically, the British had committed themselves to protect the Somali territory and this was the manifest reason for the Protectorate. In attempting to transfer the land to Ethiopia, the British were acting without competence, exceeding their jurisdiction and concluding an agreement without the participation of the central party. Moreover, the Treaty violated the fundamental trust which was expressed in the Protectorate Agreements on which the British rested their authority with regard to the Somali Territory. Even if the Treaty of 1897 had originally been valid, it would have been invalidated by Ethiopia's failure to perform key obligations. In the *Namibia* opinion, the International Court of Justice held that

> ... a party which disowns or does not fulfil its own obligations cannot be recognized as retaining the rights which it claims to derive from the relationship.[20]

The 1954 Anglo-Ethiopian Agreement, the purported successor of the 1897 agreement, imposed fundamental obligations on Ethiopia, some deriving from the core of the original 1897 agreement. In particular, the 1954 Anglo-Ethiopian Agreement reaffirmed the boundary and grazing rights of the 1897 treaty and so provided for the continued functioning of tribal authorities and police in the areas to be given to Ethiopia 'as set up and recognized by the Government of the Somaliland Protectorate', but 'without prejudice to the jurisdiction of the Imperial Ethiopian Government'. Ethiopia did not comply with these provisions to the satisfaction of its treaty partner, and the British Government formally stated:

many of the actions of the Ethiopian authorities . . . proved to be neither in accord with the letter nor the spirit of the Agreement. . . .[21]

These Ethiopian violations cut at the fundamental provisions of the Treaty and may thus be deemed to be contrary to the basic purposes of the Agreement, thus authorizing the termination of the agreement by Somalia.

The level, not to speak of its quality, of the administration exercised by Ethiopia in western Somaliland was itself inadequate to cure the defects in its treaty claims or to constitute an independent basis for claiming title to the area. In the *Western Sahara* case, the Kingdom of Morocco sought to build its argument on the *Eastern Greenland* precedent, where the absence of inhabitants had led the Permanent Court of International Justice to require only a very low level of administration of satisfying the requirement of effective and manifest control. In rejecting that claim, the International Court remarked:

> But in the present instance, Western Sahara, if somewhat sparsely populated, was a territory across which socially and politically organized tribes were in constant movement and where armed incidents between these tribes were frequent.[22]

In those regions of Somaliland claimed by Ethiopia, the level of control has been sparse and often nonexistent. Nor does it appear that any historical claims can avail:

> 'Tax collecting' forays in the Somali Ogaden country were called off as early as 1915 after the massacre of one hundred and fifty Ethiopian soldiers in January of that year. Since that was the only profitable element in the provincial administration of the Ogaden, this zone, which also included territory to the south of the Somaliland border, was barely occupied by the authorities before the Wal Wal incident.[23]

From the time of its establishment, the Somali Republic has consistently denounced the borders asserted by Ethiopia. Neither words nor deeds after independence can be construed as recognition of the Ethiopian claims. The fact that time elapsed *before* the establishment of Somalia as an independent state during which European states, purporting to act on behalf of the Somali people did not protest the Ethiopian claims, does not contribute to Ethiopian claims to western Somaliland. Nor does this fact in any way preclude or estop the Somali Republic or in any way extinguish its rights; laches or estoppel do not run against a party which has been denied procedural access.[23] If the absence of protest is relevant to the consolidation of a title, it is necessary to provide sufficient notice and sufficient time for, as Judge Huber put it in *Island of Palmas*, 'a reasonable possibility' to react.[24] In short, Ethiopia's claims cannot benefit from a claim of estoppel or preclusion.

Under international law, prior to the installation of the doctrine of self-determination as a fundamental norm, the requisite components for the establishment of a title by occupation were 'an intention to secure sovereignty and the exercise of continuously effective control, the former being derivable from the latter.'[25] Ethiopia certainly fulfills the requirements of the psychological component.[26] But Ethiopia's aspirations have far exceeded her political capacities and she has not fulfilled the all-important requirement of continuously effective control in the occupied Somali territories.

It has been claimed that it is only the most recent international agreement which must be consulted. To the purported disposition of portions of Somaliland, this claim concedes that the 1897 agreement violated the Protectorate agreements of 1884 to 1889, but avers that the violation is irrelevant, since the latest agreement in time prevails.[27] But the internal, domestic doctrine of *lex posterior derogat priori*, ie, a later law prevails over earlier ones, makes no sense and indeed has no application where the competence to make law is derived from, and limited by, some other authority nor is it pertinent in a system which includes peremptory norms or *jus cogens*.

Consider the following example. Mr X's title to property which he has purchased from Mr Y is only as good as Mr Y's title to that property. Mr Y's title, in turn, is only as good as the title of Mr Z from whom Y acquired it. This sequence continues until we encounter some basic or first authority. That first authority in cases of inhabited territory is the will of the indigenous inhabitants. In international law, basic authority in the disposition of territory, as we will see shortly, is the principle of self-determination.

The authority with which Britain disposed parts of Somaliland is found in the complex of protectorate agreements concluded by Britain and the Somali tribes from 1884 to 1889; for it is only in these agreements that the Somali tribes accorded whatever authority the British might have had with respect to the territories. *No authority to transfer was given.* The contention that, this limited authority notwithstanding, Britain could make subsequent agreements violating the authority and trust on a principle of *lex posterir derogat* would defeat the basic policies of international law.

2. Decolonization and the Right of Self-Determination

The traditional search for title in international law is in fact of only secondary interest, because no contemporary consideration of these problems can proceed without reference to the doctrine of self-determination. It is a basic right of contemporary international law which has been given prominence in the United Nations Charter, by subsequent multilateral agreements exhibiting customary expectations, and by numerous resolutions by the General Assembly.[28] Both the International Covenant on Civil and Political Rights and the International Covenant on Economic, Social and Cultural Rights[29] affirm in identical terms the right of self-determination. Article 1 of each instrument provides:

> All peoples have the right of self-determination. By virtue of that right they freely determine their political status and freely pursue their economic, social and cultural development.
> The States Parties to the present Covenant, including those having responsibility for the administration of Non-Self-Governing and Trust Territories, shall promote the realization of the right of self-determination, and shall respect that right, in conformity with the provisions of the Charter of the United Nations.

The most authoritative expression of the right of self-determination is Resolution 1514 (XV), the Declaration on the Granting of Independence to Colonial Countries and Peoples, which the General Assembly adopted unanimously in 1960.[30] The Declaration adopts a functional definition of colonialization, speaking of colonialism in 'all its forms and manifestations'. Thus it does not limit itself, by its express terms, to the subjugation of non-European peoples by Europeans. Rather it undertakes a more functional approach in which the emphasis is upon the *fact of subjugation* by a racially or ethnically distinct group, which need not be European. This crucial point was clarified in Resolution 1541 (XV),[31] which was passed on the same day as Resolution 1514 (XV), cited above, and may be viewed as an authentic interpretation thereof. That Resolution, entitled, 'Principles Which Should Guide Members in Determining Whether or not an Obligation Exists to Transmit the Information Called for under Article 73e of the Charter', was concerned *inter alia* with identifying the features of a non-self-governing territory's status, which would, under Charter obligations, require the annual submission of information by the administering state. Principle IV and V of the Annex provided:

> *Prima facie* there is an obligation to transmit information in respect of a territory which is geographically separate and is distinct ethnically and/or culturally from the country administering it.
> Once it has been established that such a *prima facie* case of

geographical and ethnical or cultural distinctness of a territory exists, other elements may then be brought into consideration. These additional elements may be, *inter alia*, of an administrative, political, juridical, economic or historical nature. If they affect the relationship between the metropolitan State and the territory concerned in a manner which arbitrarily places the latter in a position of status of subordination, they support the presumption that there is an obligation to transmit information under Article 73e of the Charter.

The same functional approach was confirmed in the General Assembly's Declaration on Principles of International Law concerning Friendly Relations and Co-operation among States in accordance with the Charter of the United Nations of 1970:

> By virtue of the principle of equal rights and self-determination of peoples enshrined in the Charter of the United Nations, all peoples have the right freely to determine without external interference, their political status and to pursue their economic, social and cultural development, and every state has the duty to respect this right in accordance with the provisions of the Charter.
>
> Every state has the duty to promote, through joint and separate action, realization of the principle of equal rights and self-determination of peoples, in accordance with the provisions of the Charter, and to render assistance to the United Nations in carrying out the responsibilities entrusted to it by the Charter regarding the implementation of the principle, in order:
> (a) To promote friendly relations and cooperation among states; and
> (b) To bring a speedy end to colonialism, having due regard to the freely expressed will of the peoples concerned;
> and bearing in mind that subjection of peoples to alien subjugation, domination and exploitation constitutes a violation of the principle, as well as a denial of fundamental human rights, and is contrary to the Charter. [32]

The significance of this development was aptly summarized by the International Court of Justice in the *Namibia* case. There the Court said:

> Furthermore, the subsequent development of international law in regard to non-self-governing territories, as enshrined in the Charter of the United Nations, made the principle of self-determination applicable to all of them. The concept of the sacred trust was confirmed and expanded to all 'territories whose peoples have not yet attained a full measure of self-government' (Art 73). Thus it clearly embraced

territories under a colonial regime. Obviously the sacred trust continued to apply to League of Nations mandated territories on which an international status has been conferred earlier. A further important stage in this development was the Declaration on the Granting of Independence to Colonial Countries and Peoples (General Assembly resolution 1514 (XV) of 14 December 1960), which embraces all peoples and territories which 'have not yet attained independence'. Nor is it possible to leave out of account the political history of mandated territories in general. All those which did not acquire independence, excluding Namibia, were placed under trusteeship. Today, only two out of fifteen, excluding Namibia, remain under United Nations tutelage. This is but a manifestation of the general development which has led to the birth of so many new States.[33]

It is obvious that the principle of self-determination will sometimes challenge existing state structures, the maintenance of whose stability is another goal of the international legal system. This coordinate goal is expressed in the UN Charter and in virtually all UN Resolutions which have expressed international policy on the matter of self-determination. There is, in short, a potential conflict between two policies. Which one prevails?

The answer to that question has recently been provided by the International Court of Justice in its important opinion regarding the Western Sahara.[34] That case squarely contraposed the policies of self-determination of a people against the territorial integrity of an existing state. Morocco and Mauritania claimed land to which they had had legal ties which Spain ignored when it occupied the territory in the latter days of its imperial expansion into North Africa. Though the people of the Western Sahara were not present in the Hague, the Court, directed by the reference of the General Assembly, considered their opposing claim that the contemporary will of the people was paramount over past legal claims in dispute of this sort. The Court concluded that both Morocco and Mauritania could demonstrate 'legal ties', but that it was the will of the people which prevailed.[35] These dramatic legal developments may be summarized as follows:

(i) Self-determination is a fundamental right in contemporary international law;

(ii) The right is available to all peoples who are subjugated, ie, functionally subjected to colonialism;

(iii) A situation of subjugation will be inferred from such objective factors as geographical, ethnical or cultural distinctiveness.

Prima facie, the western Somali territory and people administered by Ethiopia are factually in a colonial situation. Their territory is distinct geographically and ecologically from metropolitan Ethiopia, and their racial, ethnic, linguistic and cultural distinctiveness from Amhara-ruled Ethiopia is total. Hence, they would appear to be entitled to the right of self-determination under international law.

3.   Self-Determination and Non-Self-Governing Territories

Self-determination – the notion that people should decide upon their community and its power structure – is the basic principle of political legitimacy in this century. Its predominance, as we have seen, is no where more evident than in the United Nations Charter where it occurs, in grand language, in Article 1, where it is listed among the purposes and principles of the Organization, in Chapters XII and XIII where it is given practical application in the conception of international trusteeship and, in most extraordinary form, in Article 73. It is that provision which introduces the idea of the 'non-Self-Governing Territory', a notion which may well be the most radical political conception in the entire Charter.

Members of the United Nations which have or assume responsibilities for the administration of territories whose people have not yet attained a full measure of self-government recognize the principle that the interests of the inhabitants of these territories are paramount, and accept as a sacred trust the obligation to promote to the utmost, within the system of internationl peace and security established by the present Charter the well-being of the inhabitants of these territories, and, to this end:

(a) to ensure, with due respect for the culture of the peoples concerned, their political, economic, social, and educational advancement, their just treatment, and their protection against abuses;

(b) to develop self-government, to take due account of the political aspirations of the peoples, and to assist them in the progressive development of their free political institutions, according to the particular circumstances of each territory and its peoples and their varying stages of advancement;

(c) to further international peace and security;

(d) to promote constructive measures of development, to encourage research, and to cooperate with one another and, when and where appropriate, their specialized international bodies with view to the practical achievement of the social economic, and scientific purposes set forth in this Article; and

(e) to transmit regularly to the Secretary-General for information purposes, subject to such limitation as security and constitutional considerations may require, statistical and other information of a technical nature relating to economic, social, and educational conditions in the territories for which they are respectively responsible other than those territories to which Chapters XII and XIII apply.

Legal reforms often include what lawyers call a 'grand-father clause', a proviso that reforms apply henceforth to everyone – *except* the reformers. But Article 73 has no grandfather clause. Hence the explosive potential of Article 73 cannot be overstated. It challenges, in express terms, historical claims by states to control peoples who are distinct from the ruling group; it insists that even existing states must contemporaneously justify their rule by the will of the people.

Although there have been ample opportunities to limit the thrust of this provision, it is significant that the tendency among international decision-makers has been to expand rather than to contract it. The International Court of Justice, in the *Namibia* case, indicated, as we saw earlier, that this provision is to be given an extensive interpretation in keeping with the basic principles of the contemporary international system.

The western Somali territory under Ethiopian administration would appear to fall into the category designated in Article 73 of the United Nations Charter as 'territories whose people have not yet attained a full measure of self-government'; and so member states of the United Nations administering them have special obligations to the inhabitants and to the international community.

The mere fact of a persistent popular uprising would lead one to believe that there is a feeling of deprivation of human rights in western Somaliland.[36] Indeed the record would suggest that the administrator has failed to ensure 'political, economic, social and educational advancement'; it has, for example, extensively used Amharic rather than Somali in schools and government offices in Western Somaliland; it has failed 'to develop self-government, to take due account of the political aspirations of the people and to assist them in the progressive development of their free political institutions' and it has failed to encourage self-determination. These failures to discharge the 'sacred trust' mentioned in Article 73 and affirmed by the International Court of Justice in the *Namibia* case would appear to be material violations of the agreements under which Ethiopia undertook administration and by which it must justify its contemporary authority.

In the post-Charter period, the mere fact that an alien state seizes control over a territory and purports, by its internal law, to integrate it is no longer sufficient to consolidate or perfect an international title. The principle of the right of self-determination of peoples and, in particular, General Assembly Resolutions 1514 (XV) and 1541 (XV)[37] now require that an erstwhile integrator fulfill prescribed conditions. Principle VI of the Annex to Resolution 1541 (XV)[38] states:

A Non-Self-Governing Territory can be said to have reached a full measure of self-government by:
(a) Emergence as a sovereign independent State;
(b) Free association with an independent State; or
(c) Integration with an independent State.

The implementation of any one of these three options requires free, voluntary and informed choice. The proportionately higher demand for meeting international standards in integration of culturally, racially, or linguistically distinct peoples which Principle IX sets is quite understandable. Unless the Metropolitian itself is extremely democratic and liberal, these distinctions will rapidly become impediments to the full participation of the integrated peoples and will, hence, involve a type of post-hoc denial of the right of self-determination. The Declaration on Friendly Relations between States provides in relevant part:

The territory of a colony or other Non-Self-Governing Territory has, under the Charter, a status separate and distinct from the territory of the State administering it; and such separate and distinct status under the Charter shall exist until the people of the colony or Non-Self-Governing Territory have exercised their right of self-determination in accordance with the Charter, and particularly its purposes and principles.[39]

Because the procedures of Principle VI have not been complied with, attempts by Ethiopia to incorporate parts of western Somaliland are null and void. Hence the title to the territory of western Somaliland must be deemed pendent until an appropriate exercise of self-determination takes place.

4. Conflicts Between International and Regional Law

A regional organization cannot supersede a fundamental policy of the UN and insist that, though that policy may apply everywhere else in the world, it will not apply to member-states of that region. The issue is pertinent here because of AHG/Res 171, the Organization of African Unity's resolution of 1964 on boundaries. But it may be useful to consider the background of that resolution before we conclude that there is a conflict between regional and international law.

From the time of the All-African Peoples' Conference in Accra in 1958, the problem of 'artificial frontiers drawn by imperialist powers to divide the people of Africa' has been a continuing concern of African political leaders.[40] While the Charter of the OAU properly expresses concern for the principle of territorial integrity, it affirms 'the inalienable right of all people to control their own destiny', and incorporates by express reference the United Nations Charter. Thus, it superordinates the right of self-determination as does the Charter. An effort to do otherwise would be in vain, for Article 103 of the Charter states that in conflicts between the Charter and the obligations of other international agreements, the Charter prevails.

In 1964, the Assembly of Heads of States and Governments of the OAU, passed a resolution, under an agenda item entitled 'Study of Ways and Means which may help to avoid *new* border disputes between African countries'. It said:[41]

The Assembly of Heads of State and Government meeting in its First Ordinary Session in Cairo, UAR, from 17 to 21 July 1964:
Considering that border problems constitute a grave and permanent factor of dissention,
Conscious of the existence of extra-African manoeuvres aimed at dividing African States,
Considering further that the borders of African States, on the day of their independence, constitute a tangible reality,
Recalling the establishment in the course of the Second Ordinary Session of the Council of the Committee of Eleven charged with studying further measures for strengthening African Unity,
Recognizing the imperious necessity of settling, by peaceful means and within a strictly African framework, all disputes between African States,
Recalling further that all Member States have pledged, under Article VI of the Charter of African Unity, to respect scrupulously all principles laid down in paragraph 3 of Article III of the Charter of the Organization of African Unity,
    1.   Solemnly reaffirms the strict respect by all Member States of the Organization for the principles laid down in paragraph 3 of Article III of the Charter of the Organization of African Unity;
    2.   Solemnly declares that all Member States pledge themselves to respect the borders existing on their achievement of national independence.[42]

AHG/Res 171 was obviously animated by a valid concern: boundary disputes can stimulate conflict and provide opportunities for extra-continental intervention. The principle of self-determination, as I mentioned earlier, has an explosive potential which was deplored even at the time Wilson undertook to transform it into a principle of international law. But the principle itself is premised on the idea that the only stable state of affairs will be one with wide popular support, ie one in which self-determination has been achieved. Most important, the principle has become a fundamental norm of international law. Hence even if a regional grouping wanted to suspend its application, it could not. Moreover, it is difficult to see how someone can abjure the right of self-determination for someone else. Do I have the right to announce that I am hereby suspending *your* right of self-determination?

AHG/Res 171 can properly be understood as affirming on the regional level the strong policy in favour of the presumptive validity of boundaries where they exist and the requirement that disputes about them be solved peacefully, without the introduction of extra-continental force. But the western Somali case is not a boundry problem. There are no legal boundaries and extra-continental forces have already been introduced by one party to the conflict. AHG/Res 171 cannot be understood as abridging the right of self-determination.

If there is a legal right to self-determination in Western Somaliland, it is pertinent to consider briefly the alternative ways in which this right could be exercised. Before turning to the range of institutions and political devices by which self-determination might be achieved, I will suggest certain 'design principles' which should inform the choice of particular means.

1. The principle of socio-political stability:
   To be a durable and continuously effective instrument, self-determination should establish communities with sufficient internal stability and vigour to stand against outside force and to prevent the introduction of extra regional forces.

2. The principle of ecological integrity:
   Territorial structures created to protect the integrity of groups will serve no purpose if they lead to the deterioration or destruction of the ecology of that territory. In the Horn, the annual movement of pastoral Somalis from coastal savanna to inland steppe is absolutely indispensable both for the survival of the nomadic Somalis as well as the maintenance of the ecology. This principle would therefore require the creation of porous boundaries, if boundaries at all, between the areas of Western and coastal Somalia. The ecological principle does not preclude intergration or association with Ethiopia but it does weigh against it.

3. The principle of the rationalisation of boundaries:
   Boundaries should be designed to be instrumental to the achievement of major social goals. In particular, they should facilitate rather than

impede social contact between group members, a point of particular significance to the Somalis. Because their population is quite homogenous, a simple boundary would include most of them. Pockets of other nationalities in such a territorial settlement could be handled with guarantees, nationality options or reciprocal resettlements. One would note the general undesirability of creating a land-locked state when other alternatives are available.

4. Identification of the relevant group:

    Most of the members of historic Somaliland are members of a common ethnic and language-dialect group and are members of the same religious persuasion. Hence an argument for a plebiscite which would include all Somalis (Republic and Ogadeni) has a certain cogency. But to overlook the strong historical distinctions between Ogadeni and coastal Somalis and create an inclusive plebiscite necessarily dominated by the numerically larger Republic population all but assures a result calling for integration of the western areas into the Republic. I would suggest that the relevant group for consultation include only those Somalis who inhabit, involuntarily left, or regularly migrate to Western Somaliland. Procedurally, creation of this limited consultation group would avoid charges of annexation by plebiscite. It must also be considered whether other groups within the theatre of conflict, such as Oromo and Hararis, should be part of a single inclusive plebiscite or be permitted to have separate plebiscites accommodations might be reached by negotiation, prior to a plebiscite, on constitutional structures that gave territorial or sectoral jurisdictions to different areas, groups etc. There are substantive policy reasons for avoiding fragmentation. In addition to creating non-viable socio-economic constellations, they invite meddling by outside powers. International law expresses guarded preferences for the avoidance of territorial division but accepts them when order and justice are more likely to be served.

With these general principles in mind, it may be useful to look at a number of models of self-determination. We will group them in terms of independence, association or integration.

Western Somalia could opt for independence both from Ethiopia and from Somalia. As an independent state it could, of course, establish a variety of types of union with surrounding areas: customs unions, currency unions, common markets, military alliances and so on. Here, however, we encounter what might be called the problems of differential association: insofar as the new state associates with one of two other contending states, it may act as a destabiliziing factor. A complex network of links with both parties, which tended to balance out the power the component associations give, might be developed. An inclusive structure obviating differences between old antagonists seems desirable; in the right circumstances, as Jean Monnett showed, it can work. A common market could be formed including all of the states, though the recent history of East African would make the probability of such a development seem to be quite remote.

As an independent state, Western Somalia would be eligible for-membership in both regional and international organizations. Independence need not necessarily lead to a system of regional confrontation or militarization, with both Ethiopia and Somalia seeking to incorporate the new state in its own latent war community. Models such as post-war Austria indicate that if there is political consensus, it is possible to create a militarily neutral state, deemed sufficiently innocuous under the genetic limitations of its creation to be acceptable to a variety of contending powers.

A major problem with the independence alternative would be that it would tend to cement boundaries in precisely those areas in which maximum porosity would be desirable. This too could be obviated by treaty, but the history of the region suggests that such compacts promise the most limited success.

A second option consistent with the general principles of self-determination would be association. An associated state is a state which is generally recognized as 'independent' and as a separate international legal personality capable of discharging most of the functions of statehood. However, it is factually subordinated for some and, in some cases, for virtually all international and domestic competences to another state. An associated state may be a member of the United Nations and of regional and functional organizations if their general membership and operative elite so desire. Its 'independence' is not necessarily less than that of ostensibly independent and non-associated states, but it is deemed sufficiently independent to warrant the title 'state'. The function of international recognizing an associate as a sovereign state is to legitimize a functional subordination whose validity might otherwise be challenged by norms of decolonization and self-determination.

In considering the associated statehood option for Western Somalia, a critical question will be to which of the major states in the area will the new state choose to associate itself. It is rather difficult to conceive of a voluntary asociation on the part of the residents of Western Somalia with Ethiopia. Even assuming that there were some indigenous interest, language and religious distinctions would create tremendous hurdles for a legitimate association as spelled out in General Assembly Resolution 1541 (XV). On the other hand, an associated state relationship with the Somali

Republic is quite conceivable.

A species of association might involve more than the mere addition of an associate and could include reconstitution of the principal. It is possible to imagine an arrangement in which the Somali Republic would reconstitute itself as a federation, allowing a certain degree of autonomy to provincial or state components within its current territory. Western Somalia would then become a new state or province within such a federal arrangement, sharing certain powers with the federal government and reserving other powers for itself. The most successful model for this type of internal reconstruction is to be found in the 1972 Addis Ababa agreement which concluded the long and bitter Sudanese civil war. Under this agreement, Northern Sudan, the effective Metropolitan of a large and only partially subordinated region, reconstituted itself and allows a degree of autonomy and separate political organization to the southern region. Although the southern region is not an associated state in the international sense of the term, it partakes, from a functional standpoint, in a number of the actions of associate statehood as conceived in self-determination theory.

The third possibility under self-determination theory is integration. Here the self-determining unit voluntarily decides to incorporate itself totally either within the metropolitan state that formally exercised jurisdiction over it or with another state. The procedural requirements for a lawful integration, as envisaged in Resolution 1541 (XV), are stringent, for the invitation to abuse by a metropolitan power already exercising effective control in the territory is most seductive. The line between integration and annexation can be very fine indeed. Nonetheless integration is deemed a licit possibility. Self-determinations such as the Hawiian and Alaskan adherence to the American federal union or the incorporation of the British Cameroons with the former French Cameroon provide current examples of lawful integrations. Moroccan appropriation of the Western Sahara region appears to be an unlawful integration.

It is difficult to imagine Western Somalia voluntarily integrating itself into Ethiopia. Indeed, in the light of Imperial Ethiopia's violation of commitments given to the United Nations in the Eritrean association arrangement which David Pool discusses in the following chapter, one would be quite reluctant to contemplate an integration without substantial and continuing international protection of the Metropolitan's guarantee to the Western Somali component. However, an integration with the Somali Republic is quite feasible, given the cultural, linguistic and religious affinities. The critical factor would be an appropriate degree of inter- national supervision to confirm that integration of the people of the territory into the existing state of Somalia was in fact a voluntary exercise of self-determination.

There are other institutional arrangements which might be adapted to implement the Western Somali self-determination. They may be expressed in variations on the three principle modalities of self-determination as determined by the United Nations General Assembly. The determination critical for the lawfulness of any scheme is popular support. Thus, the peace designer will face two preliminary issues: identification of the self-determining unit in Western Somalia and its internal structure and second, determination of the relationship between that unit or composite entity and the existing political communities of the region. The problem is not technical. If there is a shared political will to resolve this festering conflict, a territorial arrangement consistent with minimum order and human dignity can be devised.

Notes

1. Public Records Office (London), Foreign Office 1/32 Rodd to Salisbury, No 15, 4 May, 1897, quoted in full in Somali Information Services, *The Somali Peninsula* (86 (1962).
2. For convenient compilation of the texts of the agreements, see id at 79–128.
3. Hertslet, *The Map of Africa by Treaty*, 423–29 (3rd ed).
4. See generally I. M. Lewis, *The Modern History of Somaliland from Nation to State* 63–91 (1965).
5. T. Farer, *War Clouds over the Horn of Africa*, (6–4 (1976); J. Drysdale, *The Somali Dispute*, 65 (1964).
6. Hansard, 4 June, 1946, cols 1840–41.
7. Lewis, *op cit* at 83.
8. I. Kaplan, et al, *Area Handbook for Ethiopia*, 120, 301 (2nd ed 1971).
9. *Times* (London) 27 Oct, 1956.
9a. Silberman, *Frontiers of Somaliland* (Hammerskjold Library [no date]).
10. See General Assembly Resolutions 392 (V), 15 December, 1950; 854 (IX) 14 December, 1954; 947 (X), 15 December, 1955; 1608 (VI), 26 February, 1967; 1213 (XII), 14 December, 1957; 1345 (XIII), 13 December, 1958.
11. Drysdale, *op cit* at 29–30.
12. Hertslet, *The Map of Africa by Treaty*, 1223 (3rd ed).
13. For texts, see *The Somali Peninsula*, *op cit* supra note 1.
14. *ibid* at 99.
15. Silberman, *op cit*
16. S. Touval, *Somali Nationalism: International Politics and the Drive for Unity in the Horn of Africa*, 156 (1963).
17. Hertslet, *op cit* at 423–29.
18. Lewis, *op cit* at 59.
19. *Ibid* at 61.
20. Legal Consequences for States of the Continued Presence of South Africa in Namibia [1971] ICJ Reports paragraph 91.
21. H. Hopkinson, Minister of State for Colonial Affairs, *Parliamentary Debates*, House of Commons, fifth series, vol 546, col 907 (17 November, 1955) quoted in Touval at 158.

22. [1975] ICJ Reports 12, 43.
23. Drysdale, *op cit* at 56.
23a. Cayuga Indians Claim, *Annual Digest*, 246 (1925–26).
24. 2 UNRIAA 829, 867.
25. Chen and Reisman, 'Who Owns Taiwan', 81 *Yale L. J.* 599, 624 (1972).
26. See Menelik's Circular Letter, cited in Footnote 1 supra.
27. See D. J. Latham-Brown, 'The Ethiopia-Somaliland Dispute', 5 *International and Comparative Law Quarterly*, 245 (1956).
28. For historical review of these authoritative texts, see Western Sahara case, *op cit* supra n 22.
29. GA Res 2200 A (XXI), Annex 21 UNGAOR Supp 16, at 49–60, UN Doc A/6316 (1966). Both Covenants came into effect in 1976.
30. GA Res 1514, 15 UNGAOR Supp 16, at 66, UN Doc A/4684 (1960).
31. GA Res 1541, 15 UNCAOR Supp 16 at 29, UN Doc A/4684 (1960).
32. GA Res 2625 (XXV), 24 October, 1970. UNGAOR 25th Sess, Supp No 28 (A/8028), p 121.
33. [1971] ICJ Reports, paragraph 52.
34. [1975] ICJ Reports 31–33.
35. See pages 1 and 5 supra.
36. [1971] ICJ Reports supra note 20.
37. Cited in notes 30 and 31 supra.
38. See pages 1 to 5 supra.
39. Cited in note 32 supra.
40. For the text of the Resolution, see C. Legum, *Pan-Africanism: A Short Political Guide*, 229 (1962).
41. For text of the Charter, see 58 AJIL 873 (1964). On the equivocality see B. Boutros-Ghali, The Addis Ababa Charter, 546 *Int'l Conciliation* 29–30 (1964); Touval, 'The Organization of African Unity and Africa Borders', 21 *International Organization*, 102 (1967).
42. AHG/Res 17(1). The Resolution was immediately challenged by the Somali Foreign Minister and subsequently categorically rejected by the Somali Republic (*The Somali Republic and the Organization of African Unity*, *op cit* at 20–22). Significantly, President Nyerere of Tanzania, author of the Resolution, explained in the discussion following the Resolution that the purpose of the Resolution was as a guide for the future: 'its adoption should not prejudice any discussion already in progress.' Id at 24; McEwan, International Boundaries of East Africa, 25 (1971). Even with such authentic clarifications, the Resolution contains implications and ambiguities utterly alien to the basic policies on which independent Africa had reared itself. Consider the temporal problem, the reach through time of the Resolution. The critical date, for crystallization of boundaries, is the 'achievement of national independence'.

ERITREAN NATIONALISM

David Pool

The political roots of the Eritrean struggle for independence from Ethiopia can be traced back to the formation of parties and organizations which sprang up during the period of British military administration which lasted from 1941 to 1952. Although there were localized rebellions during the preceding Italian colonial rule (1889–1941), there was no co-ordinated political movement or activity that could be identified as nationalist. Nevertheless, the evolution and vicissitudes of Eritrean nationalism – its ideological expression and organizational form – have been linked with patterns of external domination – Italian, British and Ethiopian – and with internal social and economic changes. The division between the nationalist parties of the 1940s, the establishment of the Eritrean Liberation Front (ELF) in 1961 and the emergence of the Eritrean Peoples Liberation Front in the early 1970s are founded on the differential transformation of a society divided between pastoralist and peasant.

To detail the interaction between nationalist movements and Eritrean society this essay will examine four processes: colonial Eritrea and its transformation; Eritrean nationalist politics in the 1940s; the establishment of the ELF; the crisis which brought about the formation of the EPLF and the consequences of these developments. The argument presented is that Italian colonial rule began a process of social, economic and political integration and thereby forged the basis of Eritrean nationalism but the expansion of colonial capital initiated different transitions on two pre-capitalist forms of production. Parts of the settled peasantry of the highlands and eastern coastal area were transformed into a proletariat, sub-proletariat and petty bourgeoisie and other parts linked directly and indirectly to the new urban markets and the export trade. Sections of the pastoralists of the west, north east and south became settled and some clans established themselves as traders in grain and livestock. The majority, however, remained untouched by the deep changes occurring in the highlands and east. It is this historically different transition and its effect on the nationalist parties and the fronts which lie at the root of the political divisions and varying forms of nationalism rather than a division between

Muslim and Christian or Tigrinya and Tigre-speaker, as has often been argued. At the same time, because social and political changes occurred with differential regional effects, and because there was a regional distribution of Muslim pastoralists on the one hand and Christian peasants on the other, political conflict has been conceived of as fundamentally sectarian or regional. To clarify the inter-relationship between social change, religion, region and language it is essential to present a brief account of the geography and regional distribution of the Eritrean communities.

Eritrea is a relatively small country with a varied terrain and climate: savannah and desert in the west, temperate highlands in the centre and a long desert coastal plain. This mainly arid coast, stretching for about a thousand kilometres along the Red Sea, gives Eritrea its strategic significance for, at the southern tip, the coastal strip extends to the straits of Bab al-Mandab. Located on this coast are the ports of Massawa and Assab without which Ethiopia would be landlocked.

The coastal area is dominated by the Plateau, the northern extension of the Ethiopian highlands, and comprises the provinces of Hamasin, Serai and Akalai Guzai. With altitudes of between 6,000 and 8,000 feet, the Plateau is cut by both deep and shallow fertile valleys. It stretches northwards to the Northern Highlands of Sahel province, more stark and arid than those of the centre. It is these highland areas which have provided sanctuary for bandits in the past and now provide excellent guerrilla country and terrain for base areas.

To the west are the Barka lowlands which stretch to the Sudan border. The seasonally flowing Barka river brings strips of fertile land to this area of scrub and semi-desert. In the south west is an agriculturally richer area lying between the Gash and Setit rivers, the latter, with the Mareb, forming the south western border with Ethiopia.

The variety of terrain is matched in variety by linguistic groups. In the highlands live the bulk of Eritrea's settled peasantry the majority of whom are adherents of Christianity. The Red Sea coast is inhabited by Afar (Danakil) speaking pastoralists to the south of Massawa and Tigre speaking pastoralists to the north. Both Tigre and Afar are adherents of Islam. The western lowlands are populated by nomads, semi-nomads and recently settled cultivators. All of these are Muslim and speak Tigre although there are pockets of Beja or mixed Beja–Tigre speakers. In the Gash–Setit delta are the settled Kunama and Baria peasant communities speaking their separate versions of Nilotic.

Although the bulk of the population is rural, Eritrea is quite highly urbanised with about 20 per cent of an estimated population of three million living in cities and towns.[1]

The major linguistic groups are:

1. Tigrinya

   Most of the Tigrinya-speakers live on the Plateau, are Christian and live in villages or towns. A significant proportion of the merchants in the highlands, the Jibarti, are Muslim and speak Tigrinya, as do Tigre speaking Muslims who have been long resident in the towns of the Plateau.

2. Tigre

   Most of the Tigre-speakers are Muslim and inhabit the north eastern coastal plains and western lowlands. Most are nomads and semi-nomads but the original inhabitants of Massawa and its village hinterland are also Tigre speakers. It is the language of the Bani Amir, the dominant confederation of the west and the Sahel tribes of the north and north west. The Mensa clan are, however, Christian.

3. Saho

   The Saho live on the eastern edge of the Plateau and the foothills of the coastal plain of Akalai Guzai province. The majority are Muslim and pastoralists but there are also pockets of settled peasants and adherents of Christianity.

4. Afar (Danakil)

   All Muslim and a majority nomadic; they inhabit the harsh Dankalia Red Sea coast. Some Afar have settled in the ports of Massawa and Assab.

5. Beja

   Spoken by Beja pastoralists in the north west, the majority of whom live in the Sudan.

6. Baza/Kunama

   Spoken by the Kunama who are settled village dwellers and adherents of traditional religion, Christianity and Islam. They live in the area between the Gash and Setit rivers.

7. Baria

   Spoken by the Baria of the eastern Gash in the western lowlands, they are settled agriculturalists and mainly Muslim but with some converts to Christianity.

8. Bilen

   Spoken by the people of Keren, an important market town, and its environs. They are equally divided between Christian and Muslim.

   Most of these linguistic groups have their distinct cultural forms particularly in their songs and dances. Some Eritreans also speak Arabic, particularly those from areas which have had contact with the Arabs of the Sudan and Arabian peninsula.

Linguistic Groups in Eritrea[2]

Tigrinya	524,000
Tigre	329,000
Saho	66,000
Bilen	38,000
Danakil (Afar)	33,000
Baria	15,000
Kunama	22,000
	1,031,000

The Uneven Transformation of Eritrean Society

Until 1890 Eritrea was a contested area. The Ottoman Empire, and later Egypt, its successor to the Ottoman positions on the coast, the Sudanese empires in the west and the Ethiopian empires to the south fought with each other for tribute. With the waxing of European power the contest was for territorial control, a battle which ended when Italy, with the encouragement of Britain, established its colony on the Red Sea and named it Eritrea.

The colony was divided into two main types of societies: settled peasants and pastoral nomads. The peasantry was concentrated in the highlands and semi-lowlands of the Keren region, the coastal area of Massawa and Harkiko and the southern part of the western region. It was formed of different nationalities and included Muslims and Christians although the latter predominated. The pastoral nomads, Muslim with varying knowledge of and interest in Islam, inhabited the western lowlands, the northern environs of Keren up to the Sudan border, and the Red Sea coast as far as the border with Djibouti.

The impact of colonial rule brought about two transitions: the creation of manufacturing industry and a service sector in the highlands and coastal area around Massawa, increasing trade between the pastoral nomads of the west and north east and a tendency toward settlement by some sections in predominantly pastoral areas. The level of urbanization in the west in 1940 is indicative of the relatively slow transition. The settlements that existed were large villages: Tessenei, a market town close to the Sudan border, had a population of 5,000: Agordat 4,000: Barentu 1,000. Of a western province population of about 334,000 in 1950, only 254,000 were pastoralists.[3] In the north, small towns like Afabat and Naqfa were then seasonal camps for pastoralists. In contrast, the estimated population of Asmara was 126,000 and Massawa 26,000. While the Plateau and coastal plains were drawn into the modern economic sector created by the Italians, only a limited process of settlement occured in the west and north, although a shift to casual labour did take place.

Differential dependence on the modern sector developed. The peasantry of the highlands and Massawa became increasingly urbanized and proletarianized. Villages became dependent on income from labour in the Italian-owned factories and on road and railway construction projects. At the same time the limited educational institutions were more available in the highland areas rather than in the pastoral west. Some change occurred during the period of British military administration (1941-52) when the proletarianized peasantry were forced to return to their villages with the end of the war boom, the run down of factories and the dismantling and auctioning of Italian war industry. The peasantry of the highlands and coastal areas thus contains an element of an earlier working class.

In the west, the main change was the settlement of some sections of the pastoralists and their involvement in migrant labour. It has been estimated that some 12,000 of the Habab and Bani Amir worked on the Tokar cotton plantation in Sudan.[4] The chiefly clans moved into the cattle trade and, in a system of indirect rule, acted as administrators.

Besides an intensification of the differences between societies of pastoral nomads and peasants, historically there had been a conflict between the two.[5] The Bani Amir had for years feuded with the villages on the western sectors of the highlands and with the settled Kunama, a peasant Nilotic group, of the south west. In the past, the fighting between the settled Kunama and Bani Amir had included raiding for slaves. On the eastern escarpment there had been a similar conflict between the pastoral Saho and the settled peasants of eastern Serai. Seasonal migration, the search for pasture, the historic background of the marauding nomad preying on the settled peasant, searching for spoils of cattle and property underlay the relationship.

The two transitional populations were frequently in competition for land and grazing. Population pressure in the highlands, increased by Italian alienation of land, forced highlanders to pasture their cattle on the lowlands and also resulted in migration to the cities for work. The double change intensified the traditional clash between sedentary and nomad, on the one hand, and, on the other, brought a closer inter-relationship between peasant and the new capitalist sector. For the nomads, failure of rains and pressure on grazing with its attendant loss of livestock brought either increasing settlement, migrant labour or the continuing clash between nomad and settled in the peripheries of the highlands.

This different pattern of social and economic change underpinned the division of the Eritrean liberation movement into two wings in the late

1960s. It was also at the root of the divisions between the Eritrean political parties in the 1940s and 1950s compounded at that time by differing conceptions of Eritrean independence.

Eritrean Nationalism and British Military Administration 1941-52

The British defeat of the Italian army in 1941 changed the nature of Eritrean politics. The British were to rule temporarily – until the Allied powers agreed on the disposition of the former Italian colonies. In the event of a disagreement, the decision would be left to the United Nations. While the Italian colonial administration brought about the integration and restructuring of an Eritrean national society, the British administration created the framework for the political expression of Eritrean nationalism. During the period from 1941 to 1950 there was a complex interaction of internal class and political conflicts fuelled by competing external influences. The guiding hand of Britain, the strategic interests of the United States, the claims of Italy and Ethiopia exerted an influence on a population which was 80 per cent illiterate and had been deprived of political participation during the fifty years of Italian rule. The new focus of political activity was the investigatory commissions of the Four Powers (1948) and the United Nations (1950) whose brief was to consult Eritrean opinion on the future of Eritrea. The British authorities allowed Eritrean groups to organize politically, the result of which was a bifurcated national movement shaped by the interplay of internal social change and external pressures. The major division was on the alternatives of union with Ethiopia or independence.

In 1949, those supporting an independent Eritrea coalesced into the Independence Bloc which became the Eritrean Democratic Front in 1951, after the UN decision to incorporate Eritrea into a federation with Ethiopia. It was formed of the Muslim League of Western Eritrea, the Independent Eritrea party and varyingly titled Italian settler parties.

The movement for independence had its origins in the 'serf emancipation movement' formed in 1942 to organize for liberation of the *tigre* from the rule of the *nabtab* and *shumagulle*, the aristocratic clans of the west and north. The movement was encouraged by the British and was a reaction to the blocked process of change during the Italian period. In brief, the pastoralists in the west and north (the Bani Amir and Habab being the most numerous) were divided into 'aristocrats' and 'serfs' with the dominant position of the former based on an historic claim of conquest over the indigenous peoples.[6] The aristocratic clan livied tax on their conquered subjects who payed a range of dues and provided services in return for protection. The sedentarization of *nabtab* and *tigre* in the vicinity of market towns or at seasonal encampments broke down the distinction between the two particularly where the *tigre* settled peasants developed wealth in produce, animals or through trade equal to the *nabtab*. In areas where settlement did occur the payment of dues and the provision of services were less onerous.

Although differences in wealth between *nabtab* and *tigre* began to change during the Italian periods, the Italian colonial administration perpetuated the political subjection of the serf through a pyramidal 'native' administration system. It was during British rule, however, that the 'rebellion of the serfs' took place and a restructuring of tribal organization which ended *nabtab* dominance. The former ruling clans considered that their position would be better assured through a political association between Eritrea and an Ethiopia ruled by an Emperor and aristocratic hierarchy. The mass of the emancipation movement, organized in the Muslim League, favoured independence. Thus in northern and western Eritrea, there was a division along class lines underpinning the divergent movements. Although the main bloc in the independence movement was the Muslim League, and the Islamic nomenclature did serve to emphasize religion, the core was the serf movement with the goal of national independence as an instrument for freeing themselves from semi-feudal domination. Also favouring independence were the Liberal Progressive Party comprising a group of highlanders with a prominent bloc from Akalai Guzai, the province bordering Ethiopia.

The forces which favoured union with Ethiopia originated in the Society for Love of Country, the leadership of which argued that only union with Ethiopia would ensure the end of colonial rule. Organized as the Unionist Party, it encouraged an understandable chauvinism against the remaining Italian settlers. It did also mobilize sentiment on an anti-Muslim basis, a trend initially directed against the Jibarti, the Tigrinya-speaking Muslims of the highlands predominant in trade and commerce, as a consequence of their disbarment from land ownership.

It was generally agreed by most contemporary observers that in the early 1940s the overwhelming majority of Eritreans favoured independence. Two processes significantly affected this position so that the Unionist solution to the problem of Eritrea received widening support. Firstly the organizations of Italian settlers and those of mixed Italian and Eritrean parentage, the Italo–Eritrean Association subsequently named the New Eritrea party, favoured an Italian trusteeship followed by independence and was thus a member of the independence movement. The Unionists' strong opposition to the Italian settlers and the return of Italy was an important factor in generating support among the urban and rural population of the Plateau, where the exploitative and racist nature of Italian colonial rule, particularly during the fascist period, had been most deeply felt. The economic and social transformation of the peasantry had gone along with expropriation of land, child labour and discriminatory racial laws establishing separate 'native quarters' and low wages in the factories. Nor did the British military administration change the advantageous social, economic and administrative positions which the Italians occupied. Indeed, land expropriation continued and commercial concessions were allocated in favour of the Italian community. Furthermore, in the early period of the occupation Italians were retained in key local positions in the gendarmerie and municipalities. Interim solutions like a British or Italian trusteeship were viewed as vehicles for the continuation of Italian power within Eritrea. Independence, likewise, was conceived as an Italian conspiracy.

A second and equally important factor was the role of Ethiopia in giving direction and assistance to the Unionist movement and the part played by the church hierarchy in influencing the Christian community. Kennedy Trevaskis, a British official, has depicted the role of the priesthood under the direction of the Ethiopian Orthodox Church:

> By 1942 every priest had become a propagandist in the Ethiopian cause, every village had become a centre of Ethiopian nationalism and popular religious festivals such as Maskal (the Feast of the Cross) had become occasions for open displays of Ethiopian patriotism. The cathedrals, the monasteries and village churches would be festooned with Ethiopian flags and the sermons and prayers would be delivered in unequivocal language.[8]

Religious propaganda went along with religious pressure. In 1949, before the arrival of the UN Commission, the church announced in the newspaper *Ethiopia* that those who supported independence would not be baptised, married or buried and would be given neither communion nor absolution. The effect of what was a declaration of excommunication on a traditionally religious society was considerable.

The Unionist party was also linked to Ethiopia through the Ethiopian liaison officer in Asmara, Colonel Nega Selassie. It used less spiritual influence to further its goals: assassinations, bombs and grenades were used against supporters of independence.[9]

In general, Eritrean 'opinion' as expressed by political leaders was divided. It was not so much divided on religious grounds as on other factors. Local rivalries played their part but Muslims and Christians were members of the Unionists although a combination of fear of the return of Italian rule and Ethiopian-sponsored religious and political coercion had a weightier influence on the latter. Those who favoured independence were equally heterogeneous and differently influenced. The majority of westerners and northerners feared a restoration of the powers of the ruling clans; the Italian and those of mixed Eritrean–Italian parentage saw an independent Eritrea as a means of ensuring their social and economic prestige and power; the intellectuals and trade unionists of the towns, largely Christian but uninfluenced by religion, opposed a union under the aegis of the autocratic Ethiopian empire.

The regional security interests of the western powers and the polarized political situation resulted in a compromise: autonomy for Eritrea within an Ethiopian–Eritrean Federation. The United States of America was influential in securing this solution because of its control in the United Nations in the immediate post-war period. Ethiopian guarantees of the use of a telecommunications complex near Asmara seem to have been crucial.[10]

Although the compromise solution was to prove unworkable, it was an addition to the proposed solutions to the Eritrean problem which have remained current to the present: independence, unconditional unity or some form of autonomous association with Ethiopia.

The Federation 1952–62 and the Establishment of the ELF[11]

It was on the basis of United Nations Resolution 390 (V) A, of December 1950, that Eritrea was federated with Ethiopia. The first part of the resolution read that

1. Eritrea shall constitute an autonomous unit federated with Ethiopia under the sovereignty of the Ethiopian crown.
2. The Eritrean government shall possess legislative, executive and judicial powers in the field of domestic affairs.

The federation lasted until 1962 when the autonomy arrangement was dissolved and Eritrea was declared a province of Ethiopia. Between 1952 and 1961, the year when the ELF was founded, a combination of Ethiopian repression and poor co-ordination between nationalist groups considerably weakened the Eritrean nationalist movement. At the same time, Ethiopian repression and the concerted subversion of Eritrean autonomy alienated both those who had accepted the compromise and many of those who believed in the viability of the union. Political parties and trade unions, recognized in the Federal constitution, were dissolved. Newspapers were suspended. Eritreans were brought before Ethiopian courts, the jurisdiction of which were extended by imperial decree to Eritrea. In 1956 Tigrinya, one of the main national languages, was replaced by Amharic which was declared the only language for government and business documents, educational institutions and the law. Opposition to such developments ˙crystallized in 1958 when a general strike was declared following a series of demonstrations in Asmara, Massawa and Keren.

The power of the police and the army was considerably enhanced, and the nationalist movement formed clandestine organizations which provided the bridge between the nationalist activity of the 1940s and the armed struggle of the 1960s.

The Eritrean Liberation Movement (ELM) was formed in 1958 and had its origin in networks of exiled workers, students and small traders. Another loosely connected organization which emerged from the towns of the Plateau was the *Mahaber Showat* (Association of Seven) based on cells of seven members. These movements were poorly co-ordinated and badly led and generally accepted the tactic of peaceful struggle. Nevertheless, they provided the focus for opposition to Ethiopian policies and formed the nucleus for the subsequent secret organizations linked to the liberation fronts. The experience of clandestine political activity under a vigilant Ethiopian security system was to prove invaluable in the later decades.

The lack of success of the nationalist movement of the 1950s and particularly the disenchantment with peaceful means were the major factors in the establishment of the ELF in 1961. Contributory was the Ethiopian shift towards the dissolution of the federation and the annexation of Eritrea and the inability of Eritrean politicians to engage the concern of the United Nations. Furthermore, an attempted coup in Ethiopia by young officers in 1960 suggested that the imperial dynasty was not so omnipotent.[12]

The ELF was formed by a group of political exiles in Cairo led by Idris Muhammad Adam, a nationalist and former speaker of the Eritrean Assembly, Ibrahim Sultan, former secretary-general of the Muslim League, and Woldab Wolde Mariam, former head of the General Union of Eritrean Workers. Its expansion into Eritrea was a result of Idris Muhammad Adam's kinship connection to Hamid Idris Awate, a nationalist with a history of banditry and resistance to the British. It is not clear whether the first shots were fired as a result of Idris Muhammad's political direction or whether the armed struggle began independently of the exiles in Cairo and became linked to them subsequently. Whatever the sequence of events, both Idris and Hamid were from the Bani Amir and related and this connection was crucial in shaping the relationship between the external leadership of political exiles and students abroad and the fighters within Eritrea, the core of whom were from Bani Amir clans.

Initially, the ELF comprised only a handful of fighters and its military activities reflected its size and social base: sporadic attacks on isolated army and police posts. With the growth of armed resistance came increased Ethiopian concern reflected in a strengthening of the army in Eritrea. This growing Ethiopian presence, however, brought an increase in the number of armed bands and clandestine organizations in the towns. In 1965 the burgeoning ELF was reorganized by the external leadership into four zones under relatively autonomous regional commanders. The basis of this new zonal organization was the tribal or ethnic groups. A sectarian tinge was added to the zonal organization when a fifth zone was carved out for the central highlands in 1966, a Christian commander appointed and Christians redistributed to it from other zones. Although there was a central military training camp, fighters were distributed on the basis of region, religion and tribe.

Opposition to the zonal form of organization began in 1967 when a heterogeneous group of dissidents raised the demand for 'Unity of the Forces', aimed to correct the contradiction between a national movement with national goals and a military structure which recognized and perpetuated the narrowest of social divisions. The demand grew as much out of military necessity as out of political principle. The regional commands were given *carte blanche* to generate their own sources of finance and to conduct military operations. There was no overarching internal political leadership with the result that not only was there an absence of military co-ordination but even competition and rivalry between the different units. Furthermore, the lack of co-ordination facilitated the Ethiopian 'pacification programme' of 1967 when a large-scale Ethiopian offensive was planned against the ELF. Modelled in part on United States' military tactics in Vietnam, the Ethiopian army and security services established fortified villages and population-free zones. The offensive was organized on a zonal basis capitalizing on the weak links between the military commanders.

The introduction of zonal organization was a more advanced form of struggle: the ELF had expanded from the peripheral west to the industrial and population centres; it was national in scope and recruitment; and it had increased its military capacity bringing a large-scale Ethiopian counter-offensive. But, its structure was anti-national: it heightened social and cultural divisions rather than minimizing or transforming them. The ELF embedded and reflected a traditional consciousness in its political and military structures. Now national in military scope, the reorganized front was simply the early armed bands writ large. The call for unification of the zones reflected a new political and military consciousness and marked the beginning of an internal crisis which lasted from 1966 to 1970 resulting in the formation of the EPLF. Key slogans were: 'Unity of Forces', 'Leadership in the Field' and 'The Problem of the Peasantry'. The issues, then, included not only military strategy but also the internal structure of the front, the relationship between the fighters and the leadership and the relationship between the front and the peasantry. The coalescing of such a broad range of fundamental issues was a mark both of the depth of the crisis and of the failure of the ELF to transform as it expanded.

'Democracy for the Fighters' and 'Leadership in the Field' concerned political organization. This was partly a reaction against the external leadership, partly a reaction against the tight relationship between the external leadership and the military command of western Eritrea (controlling supply lines from Sudan), and partly a call for greater participation for the rank and file fighters in shaping a national political strategy for the front. The demand for leadership in the field was not simply the traditional conflict between besuited cocktail-sipping diplomats and those who bear the hardships and shed their blood in guerrilla warfare, but a reaction against the external propaganda of the Supreme Council.[13] Eritrea was portrayed as a predominantly Arab and Muslim society and the Eritrean liberation struggle as a fight for Islam and Arabism. Such propaganda served to raise finance and political support in Arab capitals but did little to portray the reality of the struggle or of Eritrean history and society. Furthermore, it only served to entrench hostility between Christians and Muslims within the ELF – hostility which had already begun to take a savage turn in the mid-1960s. In the Asmara region, the problem of the relationship between the fighters and peasants involved not only issues of peasant and pastoralist, of Muslim and Christian, but brought into question the total political and military strategy of the ELF.

The expansion of the ELF into the highlands in the 1960s introduced there an element of coercion which had already been a characteristic of the ELF's politics in the west. The early armed bands of Bani Amir and the zonal organization of the Barka regions had continued to prey on the settled Kunama, rustling cattle and attacking villages. It was a perpetuation of the traditional rivalry of the Bani Amir and their settled neighbours under the auspices of the front. Because of the early dominance of the Bani Amir in the ELF, few Kunama joined and the problem was not confronted.

The beginning of military activities in the highlands went along with pressure on the population to supply food, water, intelligence and other assistance to the Front. There had also been instances of cattle rustling by the Saho group from villages on the eastern escarpment and by the western zonal unit from the valleys which stretched westwards into the highlands. A further problem resulting from the military expansion of the ELF was increased Ethiopian army reprisals against villages co-operating with the ELF and, in classical fashion, the peasants were pinched between the two. The Front was not strong enough to provide military protection and the possibility of clandestine co-operation between it and peasants was constrained by the coercive practice of some of the ELF commanders. Many villages were either neutralized or alienated and ceased providing assistance. Because the villages around Asmara were crucial for clandestine night-time attacks into Asmara, the issue became central for the dissidents and particularly for fighters within the Hamasin group. The problem of the Asmara villages had a religious tinge insofar as the villages around Asmara were Christian.

These, then, were the major dimensions of the internal crisis of 1966–70. The playing out of the crisis itself took on the dimensions of a Christian–Muslim struggle in that a significant proportion of the early dissidents in the first period were Christian Tigrinya-speaking highlanders. Initially, the conflict was managed within the military zones: the demand that if the Saho, Tigre and Bani Amir had their military zones, why not the Tigrinya-speakers. The political demands that have been mentioned were far broader in scope and demanded a wholesale change of the internal nature and external relations of the front, its tactics and strategy. The pressure of change did not come from Christian Tigrinya-speakers alone: of the three groups which formed the EPLF in 1970 only one was wholly Tigrinya-speaking and of Christian highland origin. Yet from the mid-1960s onward, there had been an increasing number of recruits from the urban centres and the villages of the highlands and Massawa–Harkiko areas, of students, peasants and workers. These demands reflected not simply their higher level of political consciousness but the impact of a movement based on a backward social core expanding into a more highly developed region.

The process of the crisis was prolonged and bloody and from 1966 onward the ELF leadership characterized demands for change as sectarian. Opposition was identified with the Christian highlanders. Tensions, personal and political, exploded – Christians were assassinated and many deserted. It has been estimated that between 1966 and 1969 about 400 to 450 were either killed, surrendered to the Ethiopian authorities, or fled to the Sudan.

A pamphlet distributed widely in the Eritrean field shortly after the formation of the EPLF was an attempt to counteract the sectarian depiction of the dissidents. A key section entitled 'We Are Freedom Fighters And Not Prophets of Christianity' stated their position:

> It is an incontestable fact that besides a few who do not espouse any religion, the Eritrean population is about equally divided between Christianity and Islam. Instead of promoting our national cause, the leaders of 'Jebha' (ELF) declare that the population is 80 per cent Muslim and the remaining 20 per cent Christian. We also very well know that they rally in the name of Islam rather than in the name of the Eritrean people.
>
> Our conviction is that the Eritrean people were and still are

oppressed . . . How many Christians or Muslims exist in Eritrea is of no importance or concern to us. Let this be the worry of those whose interest is to spread the Bible or Koran . . . We do not recognize that oppression discriminates on the basis of religion.

Should there be any struggle in Eritrea whose aim is to liberate only those who are Muslims we will oppose it. We are also opposed to any effort made by the 'Jebha' to oppress or exploit Christians. We are unequivocally opposed to all forms of oppression. We will not close our eyes and remain silent when we see Christians being oppressed for fear that we may be labelled as the defenders of Christians. We will actively oppose it not because we are advocates of any religion but because it is oppression. We are freedom fighters who will not forget our revolutionary responsibility for fear of what might be said about us.[14]

This pamphlet is quoted at some length because it is relatively contemporaneous with the split and, although now outdated, gives a flavour of the conflict. It is illustrative of the way in which sectarianism was utilized by the ELF leadership to quell demands for transformation and also of the intertwining of two factors: the expansion of the ELF and the crisis generated by that expansion. Unlike FRELIMO, for example, where internal crises were temporally spaced, all the crises came together and the reaction of ELF leadership was not simply that of tactical responses but of physical liquidation and the mobilization of sentiments which found an echo in the breasts of its core group: the pastoral nomads and their recently settled brothers whose traditional practices were to rustle the cattle of the settled and move into their grazing areas when the grasses were insufficient and who were, only incidentally, Muslim. These practices did not cease with the expansion into the highest concentration of the Eritrean peasantry – indeed they continued. Because the ELF did not or could not cast off the burden of an armed struggle which was linked to banditry and looting, the accretion of a new core led to a crisis the resolution of which was a split and the formation of the EPLF.

The pamphlet cited previously stated the harsh choice eloquently:

Conditions being such, should one opt to face butchery in the hands of the 'Jebha' simply because one was born a Christian or should one surrender to the enemy, the Haile Selassie government? Which option is better? Dying at the hands of religious fanatics or giving one's hand to the enemy? Both are abominable; both are poisonous pills to swallow: both mean death. Moreover, to make neither choice is tantamount to sitting on the edge of a sharp blade. But rather than choose either of the two alternatives, it is better to sit on the edge of a sharp blade.

The Eritrean Peoples Liberation Front[15]

Those who chose to sit on the edge of the blade formed the EPLF, although originally called the Popular Liberation Forces.[16] The internal bloodletting brought together three different groups: the Obel group named after the river in southern Eritrea where the group had formed, the Popular Liberation Forces (PLF) which was composed of Eritreans who escaped to Sudan, crossed to South Yemen and landed on the Eritrean Dankalia coast and a group of largely Tigrinya-speakers who established themselves in the highlands.

The new strategy of the EPLF was directed toward incorporating the peasantry, the urban workers and the intelligentsia more fully into the nationalist struggle particularly since the hegemony of the ELF derived from the failure of the nationalist movement in the urban areas. When the strikes and demonstrations which occurred in Keren, Asmara and Massawa were crushed and the clandestine movement which emerged turned to peaceful struggle, the field had been left open to the nationalists of the west, the core of whom were linked to the Bani Amir. Although the ELF did gain working class support, it came from expatriate Eritrean workers and in the form of financial contributions from work in Saudi Arabia and Sudan. Mediated through the ELF leadership in Cairo, the Supreme Council, whose origin lay in the political organizations of the 1940s, this Eritrean diaspora had no influence. The expansion of the ELF into the highlands had proved of limited success and had shaped the dimensions of the internal crisis and the struggle to resolve it shaped the EPLF.

Central to the EPLF's strategy were the politicization of the peasantry and land reform and political education for fighters and members of the EPLF mass organizations.

All recruits to the front and its associated organizations were required to participate in political education. For the mass organizations it was combined with classes in literacy and for the fighters with military training. The dramatic expansion of the EPLF between 1975 and 1977, particularly with the liberation of towns, made political education somewhat repetitive and formal, lacking innovative style or creative method. At the same time, it gave a basic grounding in the tools of class analysis and the analysis of the Eritrean struggle in both class and nationalist terms. For this end classic shorter texts of Marx, Lenin and Mao were translated into Tigrinya. In the villages and towns emphasis was placed on basic literacy skills. Although the size of the classes often made it difficult to make much progress, for the women attendance at such classes, discussing politics and learning the alphabet were dramtic changes in their daily lives.

Political education within the Front was much more concentrated and the formality of teaching was reduced by the cameraderie of shared life in the rear base areas. It was combined with military training, lasted six months and was compulsory. No matter the level of formal education or technical skill, peasant and PhD did both political and military training. In the early stages of the growth of the front, priority was given to training in paramedics and veterinary skills. 'Barefoot doctors' and armed propaganda squads would enter villages at night, discuss their goals and village problems, give literacy classes and provide simple medical assistance. The whole purpose was to counter the consequences of ELF's practices and forge a more direct relationship with the peasantry, through the establishment of EPLF cells within the village. Propaganda and organization work was also pursued in the Ethiopian controlled towns through the EPLF's cells. Since many of the workers of Asmara lived in village suburbs and commuted to work, the organization of factory workers took place in the villages.

Interaction between military and political work, expanded both active support and membership. It played a significant part in the growth of the front, one index was the magnitude of activities in the rear base area. More recruits and supporters required a greater infrastructure. Raids into the towns were organized through the secret cells specifically to capture material to develop the activities of the front. Cells in factories co-operated with secret cells in the towns and the front to capture textiles for the workshop making uniforms, agricultural implements for distribution among the peasantry, typewriters to expand the propaganda work of the information department. Political mobilization was an intrinsic element of military sucess.

The Front also followed an active policy of breaking down the rooted distinctions between Muslim and Christian, rural and urban, worker and intellectual and man and woman. Songs and dances from the different regions became part of the cultural activities of the front. A strong emphasis was placed on the virtues of the spartan life of the village, necessarily reinforced by the harsh life in Sahel, the base area, to which those of urban background found adaptation very difficult. There was an emphasis on the need for all to participate in work. On a mundane level, this meant that the central committee member like the rawest recruit had his share of daily duties like making the fire and preparing food for his squad.

Women came to play an important role in the Front, possibly a reflection of the importance of women in the peasant economy, certainly a reflection of the 30 per cent proportion of women in the organization as a whole. Although no women were elected to the central committee at the 1977 congress, women have high positions as political organizers and are not confined to support roles. Around 13 per cent of front line fighters are women. As has been mentioned, women's political and literacy education was stressed in the liberated areas but so too women benefitted from land reform measures: if divorced, women received an equal proportion of land. In the rear base area women were trained as mechanics alongside men and in the villages young peasant girls were members of the people's militia units. These changes might seem minimal in western terms but in the context of Eritrean society where the majority of women follow lives of domestic drudgery within a male-dominated society, they were dramatic.[17]

The EPLF emerged as a qualitatively different liberation movement from the 'mother organization,' the ELF. Although many of the changes came about as a result of influences arising after 1971, the capacity to forge a different movement was directly linked to the social base of the ELF and its splintering as it expanded into the urban and peasant agricultural areas without any adaptation of its strategy. The crux of the problem for the ELF was that its original social base determined a military strategy which functioned well within a pastoral society with peasant societies at its periphery and as enclaves. Yet a military strategy of armed struggle divorced from a political strategy was fundamentally reactionary in a peasant society based on subsistence agriculture. Feeding a family is hard; feeding a band of fighters is a catastrophe. It was under the weight of these kinds of pressures that EPLF forged a strategy in which the military and political were symbiotic.

If the emphasis here has been on the EPLF rather than the ELF it is because the EPLF has come to act as the model for the ELF. Many of the changes introduced by the EPLF were subsequently followed by the ELF in its liberated areas. Furthermore, the organizational structure, the political and military training and discipline and the organizational efficiency brought the EPLF a marked military advantage. With the Ethiopian regime weakened by internal problems, in 1977 the EPLF captured Naqfa, Afabat, Keren, Decamhare, took most of Massawa and put Asmara under seige. An index of the military capacity of the EPLF, its planning and ability to concentrate forces, was the capture of Keren and Decamhare in the same week. The ELF had its military successes but Agordat and Tessenei in the outlying west and with smaller Ethiopian garrisons were long fought battles, in part a consequence of poor planning and a general strategy of dispersing small forces too widely over Eritrea.

The different military capacity of the fronts was evident in the results of the Ethiopian offensive of 1978 when the ELF was severely defeated. It was not only the greater fire power of the Soviet-armed Ethiopian army but also the ELF's inability to co-ordinate effectively with the EPLF and the Tigre Peoples Liberation Front (TPLF). Cadres from both fronts were surprised at the ELF's failure to send agreed numbers of fighters at appointed times. Certainly the internal political divisions within the ELF during 1977 had an effect on ELF military capabilities but linked to this factor was the continuing decentralized political and military structure. In contrast, the EPLF established a highly co-ordinated pyramidal arrangement between military zones which made possible rapid shifts from large concentrations of forces to dispersed guerrilla formations. The ease with which the EPLF could move between the two was still evident after the 1978 Ethiopian offensive when the EPLF was able to concetrate forces for the defence of the base areas, return to guerrilla formations in the highlands and to re-occupy Decamhare for several hours in 1979.

A further point of contrast between the two fronts is the political component of liberation strategy. The EPLF has pushed ahead with land reform aligning with the poor and middle peasantry and the ELF has taken the line that such changes should take place after liberation. There were quite marked differences between policies followed in the liberated towns during 1977. The ELF, for example, continued Ethiopian taxes on livestock, poultry and animal produce brought to market towns like Mendefere (Addi Uggri) while the EPLF restructured the whole market system in towns like Keren and Decamhare.

Despite these sharp differences of political and military strategy, the Fronts are at one on the issue of national independence and on the long term goal of unity. But these differences between the two fronts and the residue of bitterness and hostility stemming from the establishment of the EPLF and the subsequent civil war between 1972-74/75 make unity a long term prospect. The greater military success of the EPLF, the desertion of the ELF fighters for the EPLF in 1977 has, naturally, made the ELF leadership fearful of being 'swallowed'.

Compounding the differences between the two Fronts has been the problem of confronting the involvement of the Soviet Union on the side of Ethiopia since 1977. Both fronts have been under pressure to accomodate themselves to the Ethiopian regime by supporters and former supporters like South Yemen. The communist states have also tried to mediate between Ethiopia and the liberation fronts. Attempts at mediation which occurred in 1977-78 and 1980 have also been used to drive a wedge between the two fronts, a prime Ethiopian tactic. These attempts at mediation seem to have been an important influence on amplifying the Eritrean position on any negotiations with Ethiopia. In November 1980, the EPLF issued a declaration favouring a referendum of the Eritrean people on three points: full independence, federal association with Ethiopia, or regional autonomy. Despite continuing fighting between the ELF and the EPLF, the former have accepted the formula of a referendum. Although the Fronts have shifted from their earlier position of unconditional independence, despite twenty years of fighting the Ethiopian government remains fixed on unconditional unification, using military means as a long term strategy and mediation as a tactic to divide the Eritreans. Yet despite the different historical, social and political origins of the Fronts, the legacy of the civil war and the recent armed conflict, there is no evidence to suggest that while both fronts exist either would act unilaterally.

Notes

1. These figures have been dramatically changed during the long years of fighting with many thousands of Eritreans in refugee camps.
2. Based on British administration statistics for 1952, from K. Trevaskis,*Eritrea, A Colony in Transition* (Oxford, 1960), p 132.
3. The western province included all of western Eritrea and the area north and east of Keren.
4. J. S. Trimingham, *Islam in Ethiopia* (Oxford, 1952), p 157.
5. John Saul and Roger Woodis include pastoralists in the peasantry. See 'African Peasants' in T. Shanin (ed), *Peasants and Peasant Societies*. (London, Harmondsworth, 1971). This assumes away the importance of different transitions of varied pre-capitalist forms.
6. See S. F. Nadel, *Races and Tribes of Eritrea*, British Military Administration, Eritrea (Asmara, 1944) and his 'Notes on Beni Amir Society,' *Sudan Notes and Records*, Vol 26, 1945.
7. See Top Secret, J26, FO 371/63175, Public Record Office, London.
8. K.Trevaskis, op cit, p 60.
9. See K.Travaskis, ibid; *Report of the Four Power Commission*, Ch 7, Section 3; *Report of the United Nations Commission*, Memorandum submitted by the Delegations of Guatamala and Pakistan.
10. D. Pool, *Eritrea, Africa's Longest War* Anti-Slavery Society, Report No 3. (London, 1980) pp 41–45.
11. Different accounts of the crisis here appeared in National Democratic Programme (EPLF); *The National Democratic Revolution versus Ethiopian Expansionism*, EFL (Beirut, 1979); Osman Salih Sabbe, (ELF–PLF) *Juhudna min ajl al-Wakda* (Our Struggle for National Unity) (Beirut, 1978).
12. See R. Greenfield, *Ethiopia: A New Political History* (London, 1965).
13. Osman Salih Sabbe, a member of the Supreme Council, remained with the EPLF later forming the ELF–PLF, a small front not now recognized by the ELF and EPLF.
14. *Our Struggle and Its Goals*, Popular Liberation Forces, no author, probably issued in 1972.
15. They formed the PLF in 1972, taking the name of the Eritrean Peoples Liberation Front in 1977. Although the front changed in nature over this period, I shall call them the EPLF for convenience.
16. Most of the following account is based on interviews in Eritrea in autumn 1977 and *Revolution in Eritrea, Eyewitness Reports* (Brussels, 1979).
17. Trish Johnson, *Spare Rib* (London, April 1979).

CENTRALISM AND THE ETHIOPIAN PMAC

Patrick Gilkes

In December, 1974, Ethiopia's ruling Provisional Military Administrative Council, the PMAC or the Dergue, issued its 'Declaration of Socialism', taking Ethiopia into a Marxist–Leninist framework, at least in theory. As might be expected, this document, which provided the first real indication that Ethiopia's revolution of 1974 might be a socialist one, was not a particularly profound document. The 120 or so young officers and soldiers of the PMAC were largely ignorant of socialism; and, at the time, they relied upon left wing advisers from the student movement, many of them former exiles during Haile Selassie's reign, to provide both the theory and practice of socialism.

It was perhaps for this reason that the PMAC was in fact persuaded in 1975, into a far more radical approach to land reform than many of its members would have liked to see. A wholesale nationalisation of both rural and urban land was buttressed later in the same year by a series of measures providing a framework for mass organizations among the workers, the peasantry and in the towns. These set up industrial unions and an All-Ethiopian Trade Union (AETU), peasant associations at local, district, regional and finally national level – the All Ethiopia Peasant Association (AEPA), – and *kebele*, urban associations in the towns and cities. There was, it should be noted, little in all this that the civilian left-wing could object to, though the groups involved on the left could and did quarrel over the right to control implementation of these policies. In their struggles for power, they looked to and involved factions within the military council itself.

Much more important, however, was the eruption of long standing divisions over the nationality issue.[1] In 1974/5 two major sections of the civilian left were grouping themselves into parties – the All Ethiopia Socialist Movement, MEISON: and the Ethiopian Peoples Revolutionary Party, EPRP, – though neither were actually formed until later. They were divided on a number of issues but the two most important were: the nationality issue, and the question of cooperation with the military regime. On cooperation, MEISON was prepared to accept, at least for a time, that a military regime could be 'progressive' and was prepared to act with the PMAC. The EPRP refused, though it did try to use some of the individuals within the PMAC, and at one stage, in 1976, it indicated its preparedness to cooperate under certain well-defined conditions. It was after this offer had been rejected that the EPRP took the disastrous decision to turn to urban guerilla warfare in Addis Ababa, a decision which played into the hands of its opponents and led to its own destruction. The second area of disagreement between the two movements was over the issue that concerns us here, the nationality question. Both EPRP and MEISON agreed on the principle of the right of self-determination of nationalities up to and including secession. The EPRP however went a stage further, giving its support to the independence struggle of the Eritrean movements. For its part MEISON rejected the Eritrean claims to be a genuine liberation movement.

These two stands of opinion remained the basic viewpoints in the arguments over the nationality issue in Addis Ababa throughout the whole period between 1974 and 1980. There has been a tendency to claim that since April, 1976 when the regime published its socialist programme, the National Democratic Revolution Programme (NDRP), the whole discussion was over and done with, because the programme makes no mention of the right to secession. However, this is very far from being the case; the argument still remains a live issue.

The Official policy on nationalities
First perhaps one should look at what the PMAC's NDRP actually has to say. '. . . the right to self-determination of all nationalities will be recognized and fully respected. No nationality will dominate another one since the history, culture, language and religion of each nationality will have equal recognition in accordance with the spirit of socialism. The unity of Ethiopia's nationalities will be based on their common struggle against feudalism, imperialism, bureaucratic capitalism and all reactionary forces. This united struggle is based on the desire to construct a new life and a new society based on equality, brotherhood and mutual respect. Nationalities on border areas and those scattered over various regions have been subjected to special subjugation for a long time. Special attention will be made to raise the political, economic and cultural life of these nationalities. All necessary steps to equalize these nationalities with the other nationalities of Ethiopia will be undertaken. Given Ethiopia's exsisting situation, the problems of nationalities can be resolved if each nationality is accorded full right to self-government. This means that each nationality will have regional autonomy to decide on matters concerning its internal affairs. Within its environs, it has the right to determine the contents of its

political, economic and social life, use its own language and elect its own leaders and administrators to head its internal organs. This right of self-government of nationalities will be implemented in accordance with all democratic procedures and principles . . .'[2]

A month later the government published a nine point peace plan for the Eritrean region, the most contentious of the nationality problems and the longest drawn out. This was apparently seen as the first implementation of the NDRP and indeed the first example of the regime's socialist policies in action with reference to the nationality issue. Here are the relevant sections of the plan: '. . . to translate this into deeds, the Government will study each of the regions of the country, the history and interations of the nationalities inhabiting them, their geographic positions, economic life and their suitability for development and administration. After taking these into consideration, the Government will, at an appropriate time, present to the people the structure of the region that can exsist in the future. The entire Ethiopian people will then democratically discuss the issue at various levels and decide upon it themselves . . . (Section 2) . . . in order to apply in practice the right of self-determination of nationalities on a priority basis, the Provisional Military Government is prepared to discuss and exchange views with the progressive groups and organizations in Eritrea . . . (section 3) . . .'[3]

The plan then goes on to offer assistance for returning refugees, rehabilitation for those dislocated by the troubles, the release of prisoners, the lifting of the state of emergency and the setting up of a special commission to implement these suggestions.

The immediate reaction of the Eritrean liberation movements was to dismiss this programme as mere 'window dressing', and to argue that the PMAC remained totally committed to its first idea of 'Ethiopia Tikdem', Ethiopia First, its original motto which indeed summed up the PMAC's view of the need to hold on to Ethiopia's territorial integrity in the face of external threats. Equally it was argued that the PMAC was committed to maintaining the traditional rule of the Amhara nationality in the face of challenges by Eritreans, Somalis, Oromos and others. It was, for example, quite correctly pointed out that while the peace plan for Eritrea was being published, the military were also organizing another option – the so-called 'peasant march' intended to involve a massive, armed, peasant invasion of Eritrea to overwhelm the Eritrean guerillas. The effort never got off the ground to any serious degree and indeed was something of a disaster.[1] It was a typical military 'big stick' approach to try and persuade its opponents to accept the supposed 'carrot'.

Inevitably this episode encouraged those who claimed that the military had no real interest in any peaceful solution to the nationality issue as exemplified by the Eritrean question. At the same time, however, it concealed the fact that the PMAC's ideas about nationalities were both more elaborate and more sophisticated than was usually credited. Their ideas were not just concerned to maintain the exsisting boundaries. Such an over-simplistic view of the centralist case – all too common among foreign observers – failed to recognize the amount of serious and real discussion the whole nationality issue gave rise to in Addis Ababa and even in the press. As already noted, the positions taken up proved to be one major bone of contention within the civilian left, but this similarly affected the Dergue itself as well. Indeed, it is impossible to understand the in-fighting within the PMAC, or among the civilian left wing or quasi-left wing groups, unless account is taken of these discussions. It should be stressed that the PMAC itself was not a homogeneous body. While its ethnic make up reflected the traditional supremacy and position of the Amhara in the military, there was a considerable number of members from Eritrea and Tigre regions, as well as a number of Oromos and other nationalities.[5] As mentioned, it seems that the Eritrean peace plan was intended to be the regime's first effort to implement the NDRP, at least with reference to the nationality issue; and thus to be the first implementation of the key phrase of 'regional autonomy', which in the programme is apparently equated with the 'full right to self-government implemented with all democratic procedures'. But over and above this, virtually no details of the meaning attached to regional autonomy were given in the NDRP, in the Eritrean peace plan, or indeed subsequently. No details of any specific case have been spelt out, so it remains uncertain exactly how the PMAC sees regional autonomy. It does however appear that a strict interpretation of regional autonomy may be more limiting than the PMAC have in mind, or than was intended originally at any rate. Certainly the phrase was only added to the NDRP at the last minute in the final debates before publication. The original intention, apparently, was to leave the programme open-ended and undefined in this respect, in part because of the agreed complexity of the nationality issue as perceived from Addis Ababa and as seen by the PMAC itself.

One of the very few further official statements on the whole question comes from the Ethiopian Revolutionary Information Centre (ERIC) in 1979.[6] This emphasized that in one possible model for multi-national development, the USSR, there were four stages of regional autonomy that were all functional. These were: the union republic, the autonomous republic, the autonomous region, and the national area. The reality of these distinctions in the USSR is not relevant to the argument: what matters is that the ERIC saw regional autonomy as encompassing for example the Republic of Ukraine. ERIC also argued that there was only a quantitative, not a qualitative difference between regional autonomy and federation. This seems to push the concept of regional autonomy far further than the NDRP does, or indeed than any of the PMAC statements have done. Certainly it allows for a far greater range of options to be offered, for example to the Eritreans, than anything made public in the past.

One obvious question that arises here is the matter of what a 'nationality' actually is, or is seen to be. This again has not been spelt out in detail either by the PMAC, nor indeed by its opponents or any of the 'liberation fronts'. Time and again, government spokesmen have stressed the multiplicity of nationalities within Ethiopia's present borders. 86 or 85 is the usual number given, mostly seen as being in different stages of development. The PMAC itself, and such bodies as ERIC, have certainly tended to use Stalin's definition of a nation as when, in 1979, ERIC answered the question, What is a nation? with the answers:

'(1) It has a common territory; (2) it has a common language; (3) it has a common psychological make-up manifested in a common culture; (4) it is a historically constituted, stable community of people formed on the basis of an advanced economic life.' The reference here is clearly to Stalin's *Marxism and the National Colonial question*.[7]

As noted, however, the government in Addis Ababa has given no clear idea of who it believes might qualify as a nation under this definition, let alone qualify for regional autonomy or indeed secession. Despite the limitation of the phrase, regional autonomy only in the NDRP, the statements put out by ERIC do not totally dismiss the idea of secession, though they do limit it. The arguments here relate to the importance of anti-imperialist movements as opposed to nationalism. Again the references are, as one might expect, to Stalin and Lenin.

'The right of self-determination means only that the nation itself has the right to determine its destiny, that no one has the right to forcibly interfere in the life of the nation, to destroy its schools and other institutions, to violate its habits and customs, to repress its language or curtail its rights.'[8] ERIC glosses this quotation by adding that a nation has the right to secede and form its own state, and goes on to say that it is the obligation of any communist to accept that the right of self-determination includes the right to secession. However, this is promptly qualified by a quote from Lenin 'The right of nations to self-determination means only the right to independence in a political sense . . . consequently, this demand is by no means identical with the demand for secession, for partition, for the formation of small states.'[9]

There are indeed varied solutions to nationality problems at varying times. And the reason for this, ERIC argues, is because the primary contradiction is the one that exists among classes and this varies from case to case. Marxists, ERIC stresses, must support any movements that intensify the class struggle and tend to weaken imperialism. Once again the final word is given to Stalin. '... Cases occur when the national movements in certain oppressed countries come into conflict with the interests of the development of the proletarian movement. In such cases support is, of course, entirely out of the question. The question of the rights of nations is not an isolated self sufficient question; it is a part of the general problem of the proletarian revolution, subordinate to the whole and must be considered from the point of view of the whole.'[10]

The question therefore of what degree of autonomy should be allowed to what group or whether or not secession was permissible gave rise to considerable debate. The final position, summed up in the quotations above, reflected the generally held views of the left-wing civilian groups that supported the PMAC in 1976/77, most notably MEISON. It should be added that another such political group, ECHAAT (the movement of the oppressed peoples of Ethiopia), which has a strong Oromo bias, followed the same line at the time.[11] So, secession was theoretically justifiable, but only if conditions were ripe. The viewpoint was summed up by a member of the Political Office for Mass Organization Affairs POMOA, the government organized body of civilian leftists which was in charge of political education 1976-79.[12] '... We oppose secession from a progressive camp ... in Ethiopia there is no point in the nationalities seceding ... we are for regional autonomy. This has not yet been fully put into practice ... we need to identify the nationalities we have and the levels they are at. We need to have cadres from the different nationalities; we need to have a single centre, an institute of nationalities ...'[13] Or as another member of ERIC put it a little later, 'The Eritrean factions showed their anti-socialism in practice when they attacked our revolution.'[14]

The argument in fact was made quiet clear. Secession or planned secession, from a 'progressive' Ethiopia is by definition a reactionary move, not in the interests of the masses of the nationality concerned. The key point here is the use of 'progressive'.[15] The counter argument of the left-wing opposition of the EPRP was that since Ethiopia under the Dergue was not 'progressive', then secession was permissible.[16] The terms of the debate were largely seen as relevant to Eritrea, though of course there were activities among a number of other nationalities, and nationalist or quasi-nationalist organizations, operating by 1976 in Tigre region, among the Afars, the Oromos and the Somalis as well as EPRP organized groups among the Walomo and the Gurage.

The question of Eritrea.

The critical issue for the left wing in Addis Ababa however remained

Eritrea. Essentially the argument they put forward, and which was not surprisingly accepted by the PMAC with some enthusiasm, was that the Ethiopian government in 1974, and in subsequent years, underwent a fundamental change. It became a 'progressive' regime and displayed this by the urban and rural land reforms, and by the creation of the peasant and the *kebele*, urban, associations; and above all it launched a class struggle in Ethiopia. This was perhaps not too difficult an argument to give some credence to in 1975/76 at least, when most of the open opposition to the PMAC came from the dispossessed Amhara aristocarcy. So, the argument then went on, given all this the Eritrean movements showed which side of the divide they were on by ignoring these changes inside Ethiopia and ignoring the class struggle going on there. Worse, they continued to insist that the problem in Eritrea was a colonial one, and finally they consistently rejected all and any overtures. From the centralist viewpoint, there could be no doubt that the Eritrean movements could only be classified as reactionary, and their leadership as petty-bourgeois.

The PMAC's reactions to the Eritrean refusal to accept their overtures was typical of any military regime, whatever its credentials – to use force; though the PMAC itself has tended to argue that its operations have been defensive rather than offensive. It claimed that the Eritrean response to the PMAC peace offer of 1976 was renewed fighting; it argued that the military operations in Eritrea since 1976 and indeed before have been responsive only, and the Ethiopian advance into the region in 1978 was merely to recover what the guerillas had taken the previous year.

In fact the Dergue's perception of events in Eritrea seems to suggest that it feels betrayed by what it assumed was a progressive movement, the Eritrean Peoples Liberation Front, the EPLF. The EPLF after it broke away from the parent Eritrean Liberation Front, ELF, in the early 1970s, largely on religious grounds, did take up a more 'progressive' stance. That is it turned toward socialism; and, following the left wing successes in the Ethiopian revolution in 1974/75, the EPLF also implemented a programme of land reform, the creation of democratic local associations and of mass organizations in the areas it controlled. These moves encouraged the PMAC to see the EPLF as an organization with a similar viewpoint. And even earlier the PMAC also appeared to believe that as the EPLF had been so anti-Haile Selassie, it could be expected to co-operate with those who had overthrown him. Such a belief was shaken almost before it was thought of, by the events of late 1974. In December 1974 the Ethiopian government troops in Eritrea were pulled back into barracks to allow for talks between Eritrean civilian leaders in Asmara and the liberation movements. The liberation movements, both the ELF and the EPLF, took the opportunity to organize, and at the end of January 1975 launch, a surprise attack on

Asmara and they came very close to capturing the city. It should be noted in this connection that the PMAC had sent extra troops into Eritrea only a few weeks before this series of events. Subsequent events provided the PMAC with further justification for its interpretation of the actions of the EPLF, as those of a 'reactionary' organization. The PMAC held a series of meetings with the EPLF, and some with the ELF, in 1977/78, in which no progress was made towards a peaceful settlement in Eritrea. In the final meeting of the series with the EPLF, the PMAC was subsequently to argue that its worst fears of foreign involvement were confirmed when Issayas Aferworki, the assistant secretary general of the EPLF, known to be fluent in English, Amharic and Tigrinya, refused to speak in any of these languages and insisted on using Arabic.[17] The PMAC could also point to the donations to all the main Eritrean movements in 1977 of 2 million dollars apiece by the government of Kuwait;[18] and in the same year, to the visit of Issayas to Saudi Arabia where in his efforts to obtain support he played down the socialism of the EPLF, and his own political thinking, and publically claimed that he was no socialist and neither he nor the EPLF had ever been either socialist or Marxist. All this was grist to the PMAC's very real fears that they were the target of Arab encirclement, and worse of reactionary Arab encirclement, from Saudi Arabia, Kuwait and the Gulf States. The involvement of such countries as Iraq, Syria and from time to time, Libya, did not change the PMAC's accusations against the Eritreans.[19]

The PMAC despite its own record in this field also argued that other examples of reactionary trends in the Eritrean movements could be clearly seen in their treatment of dissidents, in particular with the liquidation of such groups as the 'menka' movement in the EPLF and the 'fallul' groups in the ELF in 1976/77. Both 'menka' and 'fallul' represented groups within the Eritrean movement as a whole which were prepared for compromise with the Ethiopian regime on the basis of ideology, or who were involved in attempts to change the attitudes of the respective leaderships. Many of the 'fallul' for example were Christians who left the ELF because they suffered from its Muslim bias; others were involved in efforts to make the leadership of the ELF 'more democratic'. Similarly in the EPRP, the 'menka' demanded more accountability from the EPLF leadership and accused Issayas and others of dictatorial tendencies. There has been a considerable amount of argument over how such dissidents were treated; it is however clear that the Eritrean leaderships have given short shrift to their opponents, and that any who have had the temerity to suggest that anything less than independence for Eritrea was possible, have been swiftly removed.[20]

The Eritrean nationalities.

Another key point in the centralist argument against the theoretical basis of the Eritrean claims to the right of secession was a critique of the Eritrean claims actually to be a nation. Addis Ababa in fact quite correctly points out that there are nine different nationalities in Eritrea including the Beja, Tigre, Bilen, Kunama, Baria, Saho, Afar and Tigrinya speakers; it also claims that the Eritrean movements do not represent all of them. Specifically the Ethiopian government points to two of these nationalities, the Kunama and the Afar, though the latter of course is only partly to be found inside Eritrea. Afars inhabit the eastern part of Eritrea, the eastern areas of Tigre, Wollo and Shoa regions and the northern part of Hararghe region as well as a large area of the neighbouring state of Djibouti.

Of these two ethnic groups, the Kunama are unique, because they are the only one of Eritrea's nationalities which have largely and consistently tended to support the Ethiopian administration. They themselves are quite clear as to the reasons for this.[21] As a Nilotic group, historically the Kunama have been the prey of the Tigre-speaking groups to the north and of the Beja to the west of them. Raids have not however, say the Kunama, been confined to the nomadic tribes; even the Christian Tigreans to the east have taken their toll as well. More immediately, the liberation movements have continued such operations, particularly the ELF, who even as lately as 1977/78 were trying to force the Kunama into fighting for them. They were numerous, and well authenticated cases of kidnap, and the Kunama suffered much in the way of thefts of food and stock. The Kunama claim that the EPLF showed little interest in helping them, and indeed carried out similar operations as well. The Kunama response to this was to support the Ethiopian forces and whole heartedly. Two long seiges of the Ethiopian garrison at Barentu in 1977 and 1978 were both only defeated because of Kunama assistance. In 1979 some 3,000 Kunama were fighting for the Ethiopian forces, and according to the Kunama themselves, both voluntarily and willingly. Half are operating in the Kunama's own area, the rest are elsewhere in Eritrea. The Kunama support for the Ethiopian administration was such that in late 1977, when the government's position in Eritrea was at its lowest ebb, serious consideration was being given to making the Kunama the first autonomous region, even though there was general agreement it wasn't really prepared for it. But it would have made a very useful political point. It might be noted here that it was only in late 1977 that there was any sign that the liberation fronts themselves realized that they had perhaps been at fault in their dealings with the Kunama; and this was virtually the first occasion that either the ELF or the EPLF seemed to accept the idea that Eritrea might itself have some kind of nationality problems.

Another ethnic group under active consideration for an autonomous region at the same time as the Kunama and for the same reason, was the Afar, where there is a political movement, the Afar National Liberation Movement (ANLM) which gives critical support to the PMAC and the Ethiopian administration on the basis of the 'class struggle' of the Afar nation.[22] The ANLM claims that after its formation in 1974 it appealed to both the ELF and the EPLF for support, but it did not in fact get it. One reason might have been the ANLM claims that both Massawa, the port of northern Eritrea, and the Dahlak Islands fall within an Afar region. The ANLM admits that in 1975 it supported Sultan Alimirrah at the time of his revolt, because they argued that he was a nationalist. He was of course the Sultan of Asaiita, from the traditional ruling clan, and appointed by Haile Selassie. However, Alimirrah's subsequent actions, and in particular the alliance he made with the conservative and acristocratic-led opposition movement, the Ethiopian Democratic Union (EDU) which was active in 1976/77, caused them to have second thoughts. The PMAC's National Democratic Revolution Programme (NDRP) of 1976 provided the ANLM with the basis for an alliance, out of which they claim to have obtained some important results: most of the local administrators in Afar areas are now Afars; an operative settlement programme was being carried out with 6,000 heads of family settled in 1979; a widespread and successful literacy campaign was launched in 1979, and so on. Most important perhaps, the Afars had their Gewane congress in April 1976 sponsored by the PMAC (the opening speech was given by a PMAC member).[23] Over 400 delegates attended from all the Afar clans, and representatives came from Djibouti, and from the Movement for the Liberation of Djibouti, a Marxist movement largely composed of exiled Afars. The congress was unanimous in calling for regional autonomy as soon as possible, and while little visible progress has been made towards this, the ANLM feel that a considerable amount of development has taken, and is taking place which will result in the creation of an Afar state.[24]

The PMAC would thus claim that in the case of these two nationalities, the Afars and the Kunama, there are two peoples who specifically cleave to the Ethiopian arguments over Eritrea for precisely the same reasons as the PMAC itself, having reached this position through their experiences of the 'class struggles' in these areas.

The argument from Addis Ababa equally discounts the Eritrean claims that the question of Eritrea is a colonial one, and that this is the root of the problem. Here the PMAC's theoretical argument runs: colonialism occurs when capitalism reaches the stage of imperialism. It cannot arise under a weak feudal regime. Under Italian and British rule, Eritrea was a colony, but in 1952 this colonialism ended. The subsequent rule of Haile Selassie was very oppressive but it was no more colonial than for the rest of Ethiopia. In addition Eritrea was not a source of cheap raw materials, cheap labour or a captive market under the Federation of 1952–62, nor later, as a colony would have been. Indeed rather the reverse; Eritrea had a higher per capita investment than any other part of the country. While the Eritrean Liberation movements fought against Haile Selassie, before his fall and the revolution in Ethiopia as a whole, then they were 'progressive'. But once they continued the fight after the Ethiopian revolution had taken place, then the Eritrean movements became 'anti-democratic, anti-socialist, agents of imperialism.'

Other nationalist movements

Given these arguments, and the basic premises involved (that the Ethiopian revolution was 'progressive' and so on), the PMAC's lumping together of such disparate movements as the EPRP, the EDU, the EPLF, the ELF and the Tigre Peoples Liberation Front (TPLF) as reactionary, does have a certain logic. Certainly the government in Addis Ababa would see the contacts and interconnections between various of these groups as providing confirmation. For example, the PMAC apparently see the EPLF as having been substantially responsible for the start of EPRP guerilla operations in Tigre region in 1975/76, in training and arming the EPRP – which indeed the EPLF did. It may be added that after the internal problems in the EPLF which led to the removal of the 'menka' groups, relations between the EPLF and the EPRP became progressively more strained. The EPRP refused to accept the Eritrean question as a colonial one, though it did support the Eritrean case for independence. By late 1977, after a series of meetings in Keren, the EPLF began to channel all its support to the TPLF, another movement devoted to Tigre region (as opposed to the EPRP's national aspirations) which had appeared in 1975/76. On a number of occasions the EPLF later sent units into Tigre to help the TPLF, to the point indeed where people in Addis Ababa began to argue that the TPLF had no existence of its own and was only EPLF forces operating further south. Such operations are no surprise. The Christian Tigrinya-speaking Tigray people straddle the border between the two regions, and provide the main support for both groups.

Publically at least their aims remain different. The EPLF insists on the independence of Eritrea; the TPLF are still ambivalent over the independence of Tigre region, though they certainly argue for the right of self-determination for the Tigrean people. There is of course a major contradiction here, and it is hard to see how, if the two organizations are genuinely independent of each other, they can avoid disagreements in the future, if the TPLF is serious in its demands. An alternative might well be an Eritrean claim to Tigre. The concept of a 'Greater Tigre' is one that has considerable appeal; it was used by the Italians during their period of rule, when Eritrea and Tigre were in fact ruled as a single province administered from the Eritrean capital, Asmara. Immediately after the Italian defeat in 1941 the British were playing around with the same idea, though nothing came of it.

It should be noted that the concept of redrawn of redefined internal boundaries implicit in this possibility has not been confined to discussions on Eritrea. The idea of such changes on a nationwide scale was taken up in a number of 'position papers' circulating in Addis Ababa in 1978/79.[25] A considerable number of options were being suggested, including for example the complete redrawing of the northern boundaries to create an Amhara region in much of Begemdir/Gondar, Gojjam and parts of Wollo and northern Shoa; a greater Tigre to include the whole of Tigre region and all the Tigrinya-speakers up to an including Asmara; a western region of Kunama; a northern region for the Beja, the Tigre and the Bilen; and an Afar region which would include Afars in Tigre and Wollo as well. Other position papers of this type harked back to the Italian administrative boundaries of the late 1930s, allowing for Oromo regions in the south or west, a Somali region in the south east, and a separate area around Addis Ababa. One thing virtually all these papers seem to have had in common was that their main arguments rested on ethnic bases; on the administrative side a wide variety of models was canvassed; Yugoslavia, the USSR, Nigeria and southern Sudan.

This is not the place to go into a detailed assessment of the validity of such movements as the TPLF, but it is clear that the PMAC and its left-wing Allies in Addis Ababa for a long time totally failed to appreciate that there might be any genuine national feelings among these movements operating in the north. Apart from Eritrea, obviously a special case at the time, the first revolts the PMAC had to face all had one thing in common; they were aristocratic led reactions to the changes of 1974–76 and in particular to the land reforms. Any appreciation there might have been for the TPLF as a genuine case of nationalism among the Tigrinya-speaking Tigrean people was seriously impeded by the activities of *Ras* Seyoum Mengesha, the former hereditary governor of the region, and his Tigre Liberation Front in 1975/76, and its operation in Begemder in 1977 as a part of the right-wing EDU. Similarly, as noted above, the first expression of Afar nationalism was headed by Sultan Alimirrah. The first elements of unrest in the southern provinces (apart from the Somali areas) among the Oromos, also appeared to be spearheaded by ex-landlords with EDU connections and contacts.

The question of perception is of course important in this connection.

And it might be stressed that the secrecy of the PMAC engendered similar ideas about that organization. It, like some of the movements referred to above, would not accept some of the comments made about it. For example the PMAC was widely seen as an Oromo organization in 1975/76; in 1974 many in Addis Ababa believed it to be an Eritrean group; since 1977, it has been widely regarded as an Amhara organization; many of the Amhara themselves saw it as peculiarly controlled by Amhara from Hararghe region. In part these differences in viewpoint can be explained by the PMAC's own actions. The land reform of 1975 was seen as pro-Oromo, as the Oromo tenants in the south were major beneficiaries. Equally these attitudes reflect the changing membership reactions to the military council itself which was gradually whittling down its numbers throughout this period from some 120 in July 1974 to around 80 in 1979.[26]

As in the north, so in the south. The PMAC made a connection between reactionary forces and what they were quick to call 'narrow nationalism', as in for example the TPLF or the Eritrean movements. In the south, the PMAC made the same equation. Here of course they had one different factor to back up their view of the situation – the Somali army invasion of Ethiopia in July 1977, which, I would argue, did irreparable damage to the concept of the Western Somalis as a nation in their own right struggling for self-determination.[27] Subsequent events suggest that the Western Somali Liberation Front (WSLF) – who were of course active outside the Ogaden region of south east Ethiopia long before this – also see this invasion as an error. The WSLF congress of early 1981 threw out the whole of its then central committee largely on the grounds that the group was too close to the government of President Siad Barre in Somalia. The invasion of 1977, plus the hugely exaggerated claims, made by the WSLF secretary general in 1977, to enormous areas of Oromo-inhabited land in the Chercher highlands and in northern Bale, presented a picture of Somali expansionism that the PMAC were quick to seize upon. Similar Somali backing for the Somali Abo Liberation Front (SALF) a Somali government supported front among the Oromos of the southern regions of Sidamo, Bale and Arussi, had the effect of splitting the Oromos opposed to the Ethiopian government, of affecting the validity of any Oromo movement and of seriously weakening any possible Oromo movement. It was not until 1980 that some talks were held between SALF and the Oromo Liberation Front, OLF, to try and solve such contradictions.[28]

Policy and practise
All this of course provided ammunition for the PMAC's characterization of Oromo nationalism, and by extension the OLF as 'narrow nationalist', and as reactionary. In fact the Dergue's view of Oromo nationalism has always

been even more limited than its views of other nationalities – despite the fact that two of the political groups that supported the PMAC in 1976/77 had substantial Oromo elements, MEISON and ECHAAT. Partly because of these differences, and partly because of the diversity of the Oromo, the PMAC has never given any indication that it sees the Oromos as a united group at all. It has, for example, had talks on two separate occasions with groups claiming to represent the Oromos in Bale and Hararghe, at different times. The various position papers that have circulated in Addis Ababa have also largely provided for several Oromo regions, rather than a single large one: that is in the west, in the south west, in Arussi, and in Hararghe. And these suggestions make no allowance for the Oromo pockets in Wollo and Shoa. There has been no indication of any recognition for the idea, as in Tigre, for an equivalent ethnic entity, 'Oromia'. It should be added that the OLF itself has only begun to make serious suggestions in this direction over the last couple of years, and the OLF is still far from having persuaded even all politically active Oromos that it is the answer.

It is of course certainly true that the PMAC's progress towards any activation of its theoretical concepts on the nationality issue has been painfully slow; indeed virtually non-existent. But this does not mean that the subject is being ignored. There are some other signs that interest in the idea of autonomous regions is not as dead as it is often thought to be. The Ministry of the Interior in Addis Ababa actually has a nationality department, set up in 1976. A surprising number of seminars have been held in a number of the regions, including Amhara areas; the Dergue has increased language broadcasting in for example Oromo and Tigrinya as well as Somali. The literacy campaign, one of the most successful of the government's programmes, has been carried out in five languages, Amharic, Tigrinya, Oromo, Arabic and Somali. Textbooks in all these languages have been prepared and distributed; and books in fifteen other languages are going to be used for the later stages of the literacy campaign, from late 1980 onwards. (In fact, according to the Ethiopian Herald by early 1981 texts in Kambetagna, Hadiyigna, Gedeogna, Tigre and Kunamigna were being distributed and used.)

The PMAC would argue that these facts add up to some progress; not much but something. No real progress, the PMAC say, can take place, however, until an Ethiopian Workers Party has been established, and has educated sufficient regional cadres for a 'progressive' party to establish itself firmly in the possible regions, and be in a position to deal with 'reactionary narrow nationalism'. In the meantime, the concept of regional autonomy, however it is to be interpreted, remains on the drawing board; and exactly what the theoretical end-product is to be is still a mystery – as mentioned above the possibilities include a Yugoslav or USSR model,

Nigeria or Southern Sudan, or perhaps no change at all. One thing that is certain, is that the basis for any alterations will be Ethiopa, within its present boundaries.

In the last analysis, acceptance of the PMAC's views of the nationality issue comes back to whether or not the PMAC and the present regime in Addis Ababa can be classified as 'progressive', or whether they have fallen into the hands of an ex-imperial Amhara bureaucracy, as their enemies allege; and whether their appreciation of the various nationalist movements as 'narrow nationalist' or 'opportunist' is correct. Whatever one's views on this, it is undeniable that the PMAC, by its own assessment the 'vanguard of the revolution' has raised the expectations of the nationalities within Ethiopia, but has, as yet, produced little concrete action to satisfy such expectations or aspirations. Indeed when opposition has appeared the PMAC has frequently turned rapidly to repression, the all too common response of a military regime. On the theoretical level, this does not necessarily vitiate the PMAC's approach to the nationalities question – but it may indeed make it impossible for the PMAC to achieve its plans.

Notes

1. The splits briefly referred to here originally arose among the student exiles in Europe and North America in the 1960s. Their divisions played little part in events in Ethiopia until they returned to the country in the latter part of 1974 or early 1975. Once in Ethiopia, where they were able to continue their feuding with guns, they managed to prove that immaturity was not merely a vice of the young. The tragedy was that their quarrels left no viable left wing party in existence, a factor that played a major part in allowing the military to establish themselves.
2. *The National Democratic Revolution Programme.* Addis Ababa, April 1976.
3. *The Declaration to Solve the Problem in Eritrea in a Peaceful Way*; Addis Ababa, 16 May, 1976.
4. Only 20,000 peasants were involved in this peasant's march, and virtually none crossed into Eritrea. One large group was attacked while still in Tigre and broken up. Another section was ambushed just inside Eritrea and suffered several hundred casualties. The majority then dispersed. The march proved to be far more useful to the Eritreans as propaganda than it did to the Ethiopian government militarily.
5. The last Eritrean member of the Dergue died in January 1977, assassinated by the Eritrean guerillas. Of the other non-Amhara nationalities, Tigrinya speakers (eg Lt Col Fisseha Desta, the assistant secretary-general of the PMAC) and Oromos (eg Colonel Teka Tulu, the Dergue head of security) remained signifant elements in 1980. Nevertheless the majority of the Dergue members after 1979 were Amhara, and a significant portion came from 'neftegna' families, Amhara settlers in the south and east, especially from the regions of Hararghe and Arussi.
6. The relationship of ERIC to the other ideological bodies operating at the time, such as the Political Office for Mass Organizational Affairs, POMOA, set up in 1976 to oversee political education in general, is a complicated one. There were in all five political

groups whose members were represented on POMOA and in 1977/78 the political infighting among these groups who all broadly speaking supported the PMAC and the military weakened the organization considerably. The other important ideological body, the Yekatit 66 school was similarly affected. ERIC had a preponderence of military cadres, not civilians, and it was well placed as the civilian groups faded out, to take a key role in 1978/79. Its importance however faded with the creation of the Commission to Organize a Workers Party in Ethiopia (COPWE), in September 1979.

7. Stalin: Marxism and the National Colonial Question; quoted in *Class Struggle and the Problem in Eritrea*, published by ERIC, Addis Ababa 1979, p 70.

8. Stalin: *Marxism and the National Colonial Question*, op cit p 74.

9. Lenin: *On the National and Colonial Questions*, op cit p 75.

10. Stalin: *Marxism and the National Colonel Question*, op cit p 88.

11. The Oromos are the largest single ethnic group in Ethiopia, but they are widespread in the west, south and east of the country with considerable cultural and even some linguistic differences, and do not form a politically united nationality.

12. The membership of POMOA fluctuated considerably in this period. At its largest the membership of the POMOA committee was 15, at smallest there were only 3.

13. Press conference, Addis Ababa, February 1978.

14. Personal conversation, September 1979.

15. 'Progressive' here is synonomous for 'good'. The PMAC, like the Eritrean movements and indeed all the other 'liberation fronts' now use 'progressive' in this way – all claim to have the purity of true Marxism–Leninism to support their stance. As a result 'progressive' has no real objective content as a meaningful indicator of left-wing involvement or ideology; it merely implies that the group so described agrees with one's own views.

16. The EPRP's point of view is to be found in the publications, *Democracia* and *Abyot*, the latter put out by its foreign relations committee in English and other European languages. Both were regularly published from July 1974 and 1976 respectively.

17. This version, given by the Ethiopians' delegates present, has been denied by the EPLF.

18. Kuwait gave all the three major groups this sum – the ELF, the EPLF, and the much smaller Eritrean Liberation Front/Popular Liberation Forces (ELF/PLF) newly created that year by the veteran nationalist, Osman Saleh Sabbe.

19. Somewhat ironically in this connection the PMAC were themselves obtaining arms from Israel until February 1978.

20. The occurrence of a number of massacres has been confirmed by defectors and deserters, not all of whom have joined the Ethiopian regime. It appears deep ill-feeling between the Eritrean factions encouraged some of these episodes. One such story was given to me by a survivor. A Christian battalion of the ELF deserted en masse to the EPLF in late 1977. The EPLF promptly put half of the members under arrest; the remainder were put into the frontline of the assult on the naval base at Massawa in December that year. Virtually all were killed in the attack. A couple of the few survivors claim firmly that the intention was to wipe them out because the EPLF leadership believed that former ELF fighters could not be trusted (Personal information). The use of the phrase 'class struggle' in this connection is aimed at Sultan Alimirrah and his family and supporters; the old clan hierarchies. Another target would be the Afar bourgeoisie in Djibouti as the ANLM has close links with the Marxist MLD, *Movement pour la liberation de Djibouti*. More important than Marxist ideology however is nationalism, which provides the main basis for the ANLM.

21. Much of the information in the following paragraph comes from conversations with Kunama political cadres and others in the town of Barentu in September 1979.

22. What follows is based on discussions with ANLM leaders in Addis Ababa in September 1979.

23. This arguably is the sole positive step that the PMAC has yet taken over regional autonomy.

24. The ultimate aim of the ANLM is an Afar state that will include all Afars, but the question of Djibouti, an independent country, poses a considerable problem – though Djibouti territory as a whole is essentially perceived as an Afar state, and Djibouti town and port regarded as being within an Afar inhabited area. In the long term the ANLM sees all the Afars being part of an Afar state which is perhaps federated to Ethiopia, or perhaps independent and based on an enlarged Djibouti.

25. These papers were drawn up by individuals, and groups, involved in POMOA, ERIC or in the Yekatit 66 school; and they were the fruit of a considerable debate.

26. The Dergue existed after 1979 but in attenuated form, with limited functions. The Dergue congress of 1980 was not attended by all members, and at least half the members were totally involved in formal government or military posts though still technically Dergue members. The 32 man central committee of the Dergue retained its cohesion (all being members of the central committee of the Commission to organize a Workers Party in Ethiopia (COPWE) set up at the end of 1979); in addition all the seven members of COPWE's executive committee were the core members of the Dergue's own standing committee. From 1979 on, Lt Colonel Mengistu's own position was enhanced considerably – it was he who handpicked all the members of COPWE's central committee in his capacity as Chairman of both COPWE and the PMAC. It should be added that even this did not provide Mengistu with the pinnacle of dictatorial power he is often credited with. His position in 1981 remained, as it had always been, dependant upon a careful balance of conflicting tendencies as well as on the realization of his own qualities as a leader.

27. This invasion has been consistently denied by the Somali authorities. However, there is plenty of photographic and eyewitness evidence to prove the attacks on Dire Dawa in September 1977, for example, were carried out by Somali army tanks and lorries, with the markings still clearly visible. (Personal observation)

28. Unity among the widely scattered Oromos is still a very theoretical concept despite a broad cultural and linguistic heritage in common. The Oromo may be the largest single ethnic group in Ethiopia but the area they inhabit is scattered throughtout the east, south and west of the country, with outlying groups further north in Tigre and Wollo. The OLF, founded in 1974, has made very little progress in pulling together the various Oromo groups. As of late 1980 its military operations were small and confined to small areas of western Hararghe and northern Bale. Elsewhere the OLF's political efforts had to vie with SALF, in Sidamo, Bale and Arssi; or with MEISON whose influence among the Oromos in Wollega in the west and around Jimma in the south west remained considerable.

APPENDIX I

16 January 1980

Mr Jeremy Swift
Chairman
Anti-Slavery Society
for the Protection of Human Rights
180 Brixton Road, London SW9 6AT

Dear Mr Swift

I refer to the discussions we had in regards to what is described as self-determination in the Horn Workshop which is being sponsored by the Anti-Slavery Society for the Protection of Human Rights.

I have made it clear to you that such 'workshop' would have deserved the name if it were to genuinely and scientifically dwell on the principles and objective realities governing self-determination.

However, after I discussed with you and the organiser, I regret to say that my findings and that of my government, have been confirmed beyond doubt, that what is described as a workshop has, in fact, no bearing whatsoever to scientific endeavour. Certain individuals enemical to the Ethiopian Revolution have connived to fan a false propaganda among academic circles and lend support to imperialist designs in the Horn of Africa. This futile exercise is also cleverly manipulated to boost particularly American imperialism which is at present engaged in search of military facilities in the littoral states of the Indian Ocean.

No wonder, therefore, why it is called workshop. The fact that one of the principal financiers is the Ford Foundation, and many of those invited are such men as Bereket Habte Selassie who is bent on taking views against Ethiopia's unity and revolution, as well as other outspoken reactionaries and members of the Somali expansionist regime, make it all the more evident that it is meant as a workshop of expansionism, reaction and imperialism.

I, therefore, once again, deem it necessary to protest against the perpetration of imperialist propaganda in the name of an organization which professes to stand for anti-slavery and human rights. If, and when, the project is launched, and your organization opts to become an instrument of imperialism, I must stress that my government cannot remain indifferent in the face of imperialist machinations and gross abuse and contempt of Scholastic practices.

Yours sincerely,
AYALEW WOLDE-GIORGIS
Ambassador

cc: Professor I. M. Lewis
    London School of Economics

APPENDIX II

23rd January, 1980

His Excellency
Ambassador Ayalew Wolde-Giorgis
Ethiopian Embassy
17 Princes Gate
LONDON SW7 1PZ

Your Excellency,
In my Chairman's absence in Africa, I accepted delivery of your registered letter addressed to him and dated 16 January 1980. In the absence of Mr Swift, therefore, I am replying on behalf of my Executive Committee.

Before replying to the substance of your letter I wish to comment on some points of detail. At your meeting with Mr Swift at this office on 11 January, at which I was present, you expressed surprise on seeing the names of two distinguished Ethiopian academics, Professor Wolde Mariam and Professor Negussie, listed among the proposed participants to be invited to attend the Seminar on Self Determination in the Horn of Africa, which the Anti-Slavery Society intends to hold. You expressed surprise when I said that, though some of the participants, including Professor Negussie, had been approached unofficially by Professor Lewis, this Society had not yet sent a single invitation to the Seminar. You kindly agreed to convey to your Government Mr Swift's offer to consider inviting more academics suggested by you and to ask Professor Pankhurst to be co-Chairman of the Seminar with Professor Lewis. I understand from Professor Lewis that at his meeting with you on 14 January, he offered to consider the inclusion of up to four academics (not politicians) acceptable to your Government and that you agreed to refer the question to Addis Ababa. Your Excellency's letter contains no reply to these offers.

I now come to the substance of your letter. As my Chairman said at our meeting, the aim of the Seminar we have planned to hold is to discuss objectively the principle of the right to self-determination with all its implications, in order usefully to discuss the applicability of this, which is one of the cardinal principles in the Charter of the United Nations, a region had to be chosen. No region would be uncontroversial. It was hoped, however, that, by taking trouble to ensure that all interests and shades of opinion were fairly represented in a gathering exclusively of academics, this aim might be attained. My Committee recognized that, in order to secure the participation in the Seminar of academics representing this broad spectrum of views and their free discussion of the papers presented, it would be necessary to assure them that only academics would be present and that there would be no publicity. It is intended subsequently to publish a report of the proceedings for sale in the academic world. We could hardly hope to see this in print in less than eighteen months. The Anti-Slavery society will be publishing it with the conventional disclaimer that the Committee does not necessarily agree with the views expressed (which, we expect, will differ widely). This, you will agree, disposes of any suspicion that the Anti-Slavery Society wishes to attract publicity for the Seminar – still less indulge in propaganda.

Your Excellency writes: 'The fact that one of the principal financiers is the Ford Foundation and . . . make it all the more evident that it is meant as a workshop of expanionism, reaction and imperialism.'

I repeat my Chairman's explicit assurance that neither during the discussions leading to the award of a grant by the Ford Foundation, nor at any other time, either in writing or orally, was any particular country, region or power bloc mentioned as a possible subject for study in any of the five projects to which the grant is contributed. Furthermore, this Society is bound by its Constitution and its charitable status not to engage in politics. It is however, committed by its consultative status with the United Nations Economic and Social Council to uphold and therefore to study objectively the principles enshrined in the Charter of the United Nations. The Anti-Slavery Society has, since it was founded in 1839, built, preserved, and taken care to ensure that it merits, a reputation for independence and objective reliability. This is acknowledged and respected by the international community.

If your Excellency will kindly refer to the copy I gave you of our house journal – the Anti-slavery Reporter – published in November 1979, you will find abundant and severe criticism of the United States of America. On pages 12–21 the criticism is implicit, since the world knows that a tyrannical regime in Guatemala has long received American aid. On pages 11–14 it is explicit in its condemnation of successive American administrations over a period of sixty years in their tutelage of the Dominican Republic. I will refrain from listing the many occasions when the Society had criticized and condemned the British and other governments, but as an example I enclose our report of 1972 on the Tribes of the Amazon Basin, to which are appended the comments of the Brazilian Government.

My Committee is therefore wondering if your Excellency has considered how your accusations of the Anti-Slavery Society's partiality and political motivation would bear scrutiny by the media in the light of the reports that we publish.

We agree with your Government's disapproval of any abuse or contempt of scholastic practice. Indeed, it is because of the Anti-Slavery Society's respect for academic independence – not to mention its own integrity – that it rejects interference in its decisions from whatever quarter.

In conclusion may I say on behalf of my committee how very much we would regret having to hold our Seminar without the participation of those Ethiopian academics associated with your Government and thus particularly well placed to present its views. These we would wish to hear, discuss and record together with those of the other participants.

Yours sincerely,
(signed)
Secretary.

Enc.

INDEX

The Eastern Horn of Africa

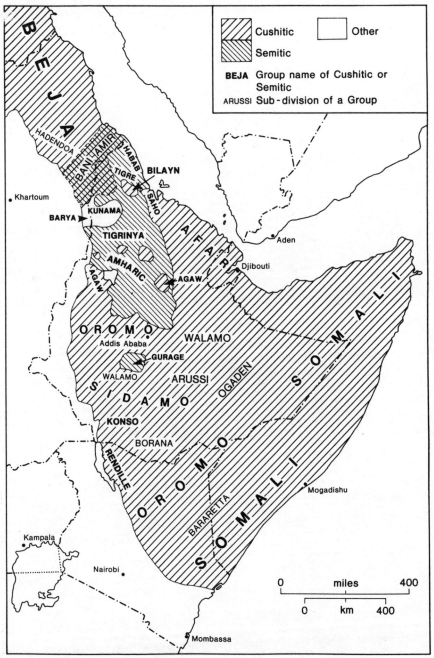

Languages and Peoples of the Horn of Africa